M000197444

MURTY CLASSICAL
LIBRARY OF INDIA

Sheldon Pollock, General Editor

KAMANDAKI
THE ESSENCE OF POLITICS

MCLI 28

LIBRARY OF
CONGRESS
SURPLUS
DUPLICATE

MURTY CLASSICAL LIBRARY OF INDIA

Sheldon Pollock, General Editor

Editorial Board
Francesca Orsini
Sheldon Pollock
Sunil Sharma
David Shulman

KAMANDAKI

कामन्दकि

THE ESSENCE
OF POLITICS

Edited and Translated by
JESSE ROSS KNUTSON

MURTY CLASSICAL LIBRARY OF INDIA
HARVARD UNIVERSITY PRESS
Cambridge, Massachusetts
London, England
2021

Copyright © 2021 by the President and Fellows of Harvard College
All rights reserved
Printed in the United States of America
First printing

SERIES DESIGN BY M9DESIGN

Library of Congress Cataloging-in-Publication Data

Names: Kāmandaki, author. |
Knutson, Jesse, editor, translator. |
Container of (expression): Kāmandaki. Kāmandaka. |
Container of (expression): Kāmandaki. Kāmandaka. English. 2021.
Title: The essence of politics / Kamandaki,
edited and translated by Jesse Ross Knutson.
Other titles: Murty classical library of India ; 28.
Description: Cambridge, Massachusetts :
Harvard University Press, 2021. |
Series: Murty classical library of India ; 28 |
Sanskrit; Devanagari script.
Includes bibliographical references and index.
Identifiers: LCCN 2020015326 |
ISBN 9780674975767 (cloth)
Subjects: LCSH: Political science--India--History. | State, The. |
India--Politics and government--To 997.
Classification: LCC JC50 .K2513 2021 |
DDC 320.01--dc23
LC record available at https://lccn.loc.gov/2020015326

CONTENTS

INTRODUCTION

The *Kāmandakīya Nītisāra,* or *The Essence of Politics* by Kamandaki, is a work of political theory from early medieval India that offers a unique window onto the sociopolitical and ethical life of the period. It "churns the vast ocean," as the author calls it, of prior theory, while recasting the fundamental forms of power: how to acquire, sustain, and augment a kingdom through an array of time-honored modes of military and socioeconomic organization. It did so in a manner that would prove definitive: while Kamandaki was faithful to the traditional edifice, he conducted a renovation at once structural and cosmetic. The result combines elegance with relevance, ultimately making it the model for subsequent political thought across South and Southeast Asia.[1]

Likely composed in late-Gupta or early post-Gupta times, and redacted and refined across centuries (c. fifth–eighth century C.E.), *The Essence* was an attractive alternative to its predecessor, the exhaustive *Arthaśāstra (Treatise on Power).* This earlier treatise was attributed to Kautilya (also referred to as Chanakya and Vishnugupta), traditionally considered the minister of Chandragupta Maurya (c. 325 B.C.E.), who, according to legend, annihilated the rival Nanda dynasty through devilish cunning. The *Arthaśāstra*—also compiled over several centuries, perhaps receiving its canonical, Brahmanical shape early in the Gupta period—is an encyclopedia of political economy and statecraft, a reference book by and for professionals.[2] *The Essence,* by contrast, foregrounded formal elegance and accessibility, thereby acquiring a degree of traction over its predecessor. It can be read quickly and on-the-go—a perfect introduction to the field for young princes, upstart warlords, or anyone else making moves, from the spy lurking in the shadows to the flashy court poet. Its popularity may have contributed to the centuries-long disappearance of the *Arthaśāstra* itself, the founding work of ancient Indian political theory.[3]

Classical Indian Political Theory
and The Essence of Politics

Political theory or statecraft was as well-defined as any form of systematic knowledge in premodern India, even if it was wide ranging and referred to by many terms: "kingship-science" (*rājavidyā*), "politics" or "government" (*nīti; naya; daṇḍanīti*), as well as the "dharma of kings" (*rājadharma*) in early works of legal theory (*dharma-śāstra*). Most comprehensively though it is called "the science of power," *arthaśāstra,* identifying the field itself with the all-embracing compendium of Kautilya.[4] The actual subject matter of politics oscillates from thrilling accounts of intrigue and luxurious living, to highly nuanced military-scientific and strategic debates, covering even the driest details of accounting and animal husbandry. It was no small feat to make it readable, let alone captivating, as Kamandaki often succeeded in doing.

The Essence thus presents a unique contribution to Sanskrit political theory on the axes of form and content alike. On the formal side, it is elegant and pithy, which made it attractive to commentators and readers over the centuries. On the side of content, it presents a host of subtle innovations and emphases that redefined the field of political science in early medieval India.

The long tradition of classical Indian Realpolitik is, for better or worse, in many ways still alive across contemporary South and Southeast Asia, and the *Nītisāra* thus provides an entry point into some of the most concrete and enduring forms of political culture. Many of its lessons on the interrelated topics of wealth, power, morality, self-cultivation—peace, war, and everything in between—may likewise prove perennial for today's readers, no matter which hemisphere they inhabit. Its teachings may even seem timeless, but perhaps, in certain respects, we are still living in Kamandaki's time. Some of the primary elements of what we think of as politics, along with the basic outline of the state form as we know it, may extend far beyond our own time and place. Kamandaki's *The Essence* still has much to teach about the world we inhabit.

It also has, of course, much to teach modern readers about its own world, as well as what political elites considered worth learning about in early medieval India. The book's readability may suggest that it was in fact read in a novel way, not just by professionals and scholars, but also semi-professionals, nonprofessionals, future professionals, even dabblers and wannabes. Kings and queens were of course professionals of a sort, but I suspect that in most cases their counselors (*mantrin*) and ministers (*amātya*) would have been the ones to actually pore over Kautilya's founding work on the subject. *The Essence,* on the other hand, is something members of the royal household could have been more likely to pick up and browse through themselves. The author emphasizes that his teaching is directly addressed to the king (1.8), and there is every reason to believe that rulers read it and put it into action, using it as a true "mirror for princes": a tool for understanding, interpreting, and fashioning themselves.[5]

Kamandaki was widely popular. Most Sanskrit scholars know *The Essence* from its abundant citations in medieval commentaries, whenever the technicalities of statecraft and military strategy required adjudication by a strong and succinct intellectual authority. *The Essence* remains, however—in inverse proportion to its traditional importance—unknown today to a wider audience, despite recent historical scholarship attesting to its centrality and formative status for premodern Indian thought and practice.[6]

In addition to its crucial relevance for understanding politics and political thought, *The Essence* is political-theoretical poetry—if we can imagine such a thing—fashioned, however loosely, on the model of the *mahākāvya*, the courtly "mega poem": replete with elegant figures of sound and sense (*alaṃkāra*), chapters called something like "canto" (*sarga*), and with stylish variations of meter at the close of each chapter. Its verses are meant to inform and instruct as much as to fix themselves in memory through a compelling artistic evocation.

Kamandaki's text embodies a poetics of power replete with striking metaphors and dazzling images. A king is in bad shape until "he places his foot upon his enemies' heads, their helmets sparkling with crest jewels." Likewise:

"He must drag away royal fortune by his arms powerful as elephant trunks, gilt with the rays of light pulsating from his sharp, glittering sword so casually unsheathed" (14.11, 14.14). Kamandaki's verbal art resonates with traditions of Sanskrit martial poetry in general, but more precisely with the public power-poetry found in inscriptions of the period across South and Southeast Asia.[7]

Political Life Lived and Examined in Early Medieval India

The Essence's innovations were hardly restricted to the level of form discussed above: they were both subtle and substantial. Yet its reverence and self-effacement vis à vis its predecessor have sometimes led scholars to assume precisely this: that only its form was novel; that it simply summed up the conclusions of the *Arthaśāstra* in an artful manner. Yet Kamandaki truly rebuilt the old school with a new, more ergonomic design.

The Essence makes a large-scale investment in a trickier art of politics, juggling multiple scales of violence, according to its convenience, and employing an array of counterintuitive methods for gaining leverage, conceding that at times even an enterprising king must bow down. This was a major contribution to a discipline whose basic coordinates were well established centuries earlier; it was a contribution attuned to an emergent early medieval (late sixth–early thirteenth century C.E.) reality, defined by heightened competition among more or less equivalent states.[8]

Kamandaki's signature technical innovation was in the discussion of *upāya*, "methods." It may seem like a modest supplement to the field's vocabulary, but such overt transformation of the paradigm was never undertaken lightly. In addition to the tradition's four classic *upāya* "methods"—*sāma* "conciliation," *dāna* "donation," *bheda* "sowing dissension," and *daṇḍa* "coercion/violence"—Kamandaki crafted three new ones: *māyā* "illusion," *upekṣā* "disregard," and finally, *indrajāla* "magic." These three little words speak volumes about the spirit of the *Nītisāra*. This is war at the level of representation, perception, and expectation. It would have gladdened the cold heart of a ninja as much as the contemporary theorist of informal war and "durable disorder."[9]

In his new formulations for a new age, Kamandaki may have made a virtue of necessity, but we must add that he also made a necessity of virtue: the depth of his interest in questions of personal character was just as novel as his realism. He takes the reader into a newly deep interior, as far as politics is concerned: personal life as a zero degree of the political. He traces, in provocative and often poetic detail, an intricate mutual determination of spiritual and material life.

In the age's atmosphere of subtle strategy and careful calculation, the ruler's personality—his entire psychological and intellectual makeup—became a newly keen object of interest. *The Essence* reads at times like self-help literature for the rich and powerful or the chronically ambitious. The text displays an intense focus on the personal cultivation of the king, the paramount persona, but also every member of the state apparatus, from the intimate counselors and the generals, on down to the servants and harem-guards.

Personal and moral qualities receive as much attention as

weapons and battle formations. For the king, the practice of what we can call a "political spirituality" is advocated. Beyond the basic commitment to dharma and the Brahmanical order, which are also of course stressed, Kamandaki makes intellectual and spiritual exercise the foundation of politics.

Kautilya had already emphasized self-mastery (*vinaya*) and conquest of one's senses (*indriyajaya*) as the first steps for an enterprising king.[10] The concept of the "king-sage" (*rājarṣi*) is a very ancient one, but the coalescence between the spiritual and the political was taking on a finer point in the Gupta period and immediately after, by which time kingliness and godliness were conflated to such a degree that an emperor could be referred to—not just in epic poetry, but in official documents—as "a god whose residence is the earth; human only insofar as he enacts the rules and rites of the world."[11]

The Essence is far more introspective than earlier political thought and presents spiritual self-control as the model for rule. This is exactly the conception of kingship we find conjured in classical Sanskrit poetry of roughly the same period. If Kamandaki reads as political poetry, so does much of the classical *kāvya* tradition. Somewhat in contrast to the generally more idealizing literary treatments, where political spirituality is presented in a finished and perfected form, however, *The Essence* stresses the difficulty of this practice and just how easy it is for anyone to be subdued by the passions: "A woman impassions even a sage's mind, as the sunset reddens the clear and radiant moon. Even great men are split apart by women—delighting and intoxicating their minds—as great mountains are split apart by water droplets" (1.54–55).

Self-cultivation writ large, but more specifically, the consistent study and practice of philosophy, can offer an antidote to these dangerous passions. Both the *Arthaśāstra* and *The Essence* begin with a discussion of self-discipline and move directly to a treatment of the branches of learning that inculcate such self-discipline, in addition to other possible benefits. The key element in this education is philosophy or "critical inquiry" (*ānvīkṣikī*). In contrast to the *Arthaśāstra's* terse understanding of "critical inquiry" as simply three of the most ancient branches of thought, "Samkhya, Yoga, and Lokayata," Kamandaki identifies it significantly as "the science of the self" (*ātmavijñāna*) and "knowledge of the self" (*ātmavidyā*, 2.11).[12] *The Essence* is about a philosopher king, but for Kamandaki the ordinary king must always be extraordinary: "Exalted kingship is by its very nature elevated above the mundane world..." (1.67).

Kamandaki's treatise crystallizes a new political subjectivity, which entails a new relationship to the self and the world, both imagined as objects of conquest. Is this a military metaphor overtaking the realm of spirituality, or a spiritual metaphor overtaking the realm of the political? In either case it represents a strong reinvestment in the possibilities of monarchical authority, which both served and was served by the poetics of harmony we find in the great classical Sanskrit poets of the fifth–eighth century, such as Kalidasa, Bhatti, Bharavi, Magha, and so on.

The relationship to traditions of classical poetry may have been symbiotic, with poets drawing on Kamandaki as an attractive reference guide to political science, and Kamandaki drawing on the poets for aestheticized visions of sociopolitical harmony. In any case, intertextuality is broadly apparent. The description of the king as "he who has spies for his eyes," and countless other like turns of phrase, evince a shared field of discourse and sensibility.[13]

Kamandaki's work is just as much political art as science. It abounds—like a work of pure poetry—in so many shades of nuance as to seem at times confusing and contradictory, or even opportunistic and ad hoc. When one examines and compares the contradictions carefully, however, they reveal a multilayered and overdetermined playing field, suggesting a profound engagement with empirical reality, and a willingness to sacrifice simplicity at the altar of the real.

Kamandaki writes, for example, that: "A war puts oneself, one's friends, wealth, kingdom, and glory in danger's balance. Who other than a fool would do it?" (9.75), yet also concludes at one point that war is literally everything. What he really means, however, is that everything is war, even peace: "The only reasonable tactic is war. Alliance and other tactics have their origin in it…" (11.41).

Another example of the devil being in the details—in the execution more than the plan—is the discussion of the relationship between economics and politics. The work emphasizes economic development throughout as the sine qua non of legitimate rule: "Protection depends on the king. The economy depends on protection. When the economy is ruined, people do not live even though they breathe" (1.12). Yet, understandably, the economic base is simultaneously cause and effect, both the outcome and the indispensable condition of rule. On the one hand the sociopolitical and moral order are derived from the economic in an unapologetically vulgar fashion: "The people love a king, even if his conduct is poor and he has no lineage, so long as he lavishes wealth. Riches count as lineage in this world; there is no better lineage than wealth" (5.62). Yet the order of determination is also easily reversed, and the imperative of maintaining wealth is not absolute, at least in theory: "If the king lavishes treasure for the sake of dharma even his destitution is beautiful, like the thin cool-rayed moon of autumn after the gods have drunk most of its nectar" (5.89).

The immaterial can become material, and the material, immaterial. Kamandaki is not afraid to be on both sides of an apparent contradiction in his pursuit of strategy's subtleties. He may be hedging his bets, but we can also read this tendency more sympathetically as the pragmatic before the programmatic: a material context–sensitivity that culminates in paraconsistent logic.

Political Art and Science in The Essence of Politics

As just alluded, Kamandaki's political method is most often oblique. It can be summarized as a protracted war of position, emphasizing subterfuge, disinformation, and plausible deniability, along with a newly minimalist approach to violence.[14] He advocates open warfare only when other methods have been completely exhausted, when victory is virtually certain as a result of meticulous and exhaustive preparation. He stresses the evasion of what contemporary strategists call "kinetic" conflict, even under direct attack by the enemy: he writes in 10.35 that a besieged king should adopt "the way of the bamboo, which bends and does not break," and never "the way of the snake, which hisses and bites when provoked."[15] Battles should only be fought at a time and place of one's own choosing, when and where overwhelming benefits will inevitably accrue. Almost always preferable are delicate compromises, alliances, and underhanded tactics.

Kamandaki's own approach as an author was likewise subtle, minimalist, and even underhanded: he made merely a handful of additions to the discipline's vocabulary. Yet the combined force of nuance and emphasis rearticulated the entire system to make it more relevant for its times. As alluded earlier, this must be seen against the backdrop of the centuries following the collapse of the Gupta empire (c. 550 C.E.), which witnessed the expansion and reorganization of state society, resulting in heightened competition among petty kingdoms. In this context there was often a lot more to lose than to gain from all-out war.[16] As Kamandaki never tires of observing: "In war, one's wife, oneself, friends, wealth, and everything can all come to naught in the blink of an eye ... a wise man should not be a warmonger" (9.74).

The Essence articulates the crux of politics on the eve of the early medieval period. Kamandaki recalibrated the technology of violence for a period of political pluralism. The older theory appears retrospective, and possibly even archaizing, in contrast: its zero-sum imagination speaks to earlier eras when major empires—such as the Maurya (c. 322–187 B.C.E.) or Gupta (c. 325–550 C.E.)—saw no real rival. The shift of scale in Kamandaki, from empire to regional polity, subtly reflects the transformation of the entire concept of the political.

It is in this same context that political life assumes a newly personal character, replacing what it had lost in physical extension with cognitive and interpersonal depth. Kamandaki's provocative emphasis on *vinaya* "self-mastery," discussed earlier, mirrors a pervasive emphasis on personal etiquette and moral characteristics in the Gupta period and after.[17] Kamandaki's concept of the political—what he often calls *naya* or *nīti,* literally, "directing" or "leading"—begins and ends with self-mastery and self-cultivation (1.21). This is a martial art in the most literal and comprehensive sense of the phrase. It is designed to guide one's step on all of life's myriad battlefields, but also to make the battle and its outcomes ultimately mean something: "The goal of power is happiness; when happiness is compromised, royal majesty becomes meaningless" (1.50).

The Essence is thus an owner's manual for the life lived with high stakes. Readers may be taught how to mobilize elephant-battalions for maximum destruction, but they also learn about different kinds of friendships and romantic relationships; how to read minds, how to impress people and win their trust; even how to maintain integrity and equanimity while living a ruthless and dangerous life.

The work thus acquires the universal relevance and applicability of a great work of literature—since all life is in some sense ruthless and dangerous—but we should keep in mind that the "life" Kamandaki examines here is always that of a political animal, and he usually has in mind the apex predator. The king's "life" is conceived first and foremost as a component of the kingdom. In the list of the seven mutually constituting state-elements (*prakṛti*)—the central cognitive map in Sanskrit political theory—the young prince studying the subject for the first time might not be surprised to learn that he literally comes first: "The kingdom is said to consist of seven mutually supporting limbs: ruler, minister, kingdom, fortification, treasury, army, and ally" (4.1). "*L'état c'est moi*" was taken very literally as a central teaching—Kamandaki writes that a king must: "examine the kingdom in both its internal and external aspects. The inner aspect is his own body. The outer aspect is known as his realm. The two depend on each other, and because of this relationship, they should really be thought of as one" (6.1–3).

The personal was political in a concrete sense, and it was also unwaveringly teleological. *The Essence* is—however psychological its concerns—a treatise on the state: how to build it, maintain it, or destroy it; and yet, precisely because this state was conceived as so truly absolute, it is just as much about the social system: the relationships and etiquette, even spirituality, implied by this project of building, maintaining, and conquering states.

The life of power has manifold scales, but their interconnection, rather than differentiation, seems to be the finer point for Kamandaki. Public and private are one and the same. Therefore *The Essence* comprises an etiquette book, a book of morals, a syllabus for intellectual and spiritual cultivation, even a list of tips on polyamorous sexuality. These are careful diagrams of both the inner and outer postures one must maintain to be enduringly loved and feared.

The work offers an analysis of the entire political,

economic, and social field, from the commanding heights of the army and treasury down to the minutiae of speech, gesture, food, and drink. Yet this grand whole only becomes more than the sum of its parts when there is a monopoly on violence, or at least a credible threat of violence. However dispassionately and calmly, the king must kill people, or at the very least, compellingly represent the power over life and death. His closest divine counterpart is after all the Vedic god of death: "he should bear the rod of coercion like Yama, the rod-bearing god of death" (2.36).

For Kamandaki a disjunction between the life of the soul and living by the sword is not even a recognizable option. In his concept of spiritual action, violence and tranquility— even peace and war (recall 11.41)—are one and the same: "When kings perform a righteous act of violence, they are like great sages. Thus when they slaughter bad people for the sake of dharma, they are not tainted by sin" (6.5).

The essence of politics for Kamandaki, then, is the unity of violence and spirituality. This is a spirituality that cannot be called merely religious. It both encompasses and transcends religion since "the king holds aloft both the mundane and heavenly worlds..." (2.36). In classical Sanskrit poetry, we find exactly this brand of material spirituality, expressed in the immediate continuity and contiguity of aesthetics and politics. The realms of art, spirituality, and warfare in early medieval India strove to stand in a relationship of virtual identity. Kamandaki's statement on this relationship— embodied in both the form and content of his work—is among the most consequential, combining the poet's touch with the lucid rigor of a great thinker.

The Vocabulary of Politics: Kamandaki's Cognitive Maps
Despite the brilliance of Kamandaki's treatment, it must also
be admitted that classical Indian political theory has some
very dry bones at its core. Its fundamental identity was maintained by several fixed sets of terms that compartmentalize
aspects of the knowledge-system. These raw materials were
inherited from an earlier tradition whose exactitude and
exhaustiveness were maintained by a series of mnemonic
verbal schemata. I conclude this introduction with a brief
outline and discussion of some of the most important terms.

Kamandaki records at length debates among a number
of teachers—their works are mostly now lost—about which
categories are truly distinct, which can possibly be subsumed
by others, and so on. On the one hand, providing these head-
ings seems to be an end in itself, but the discussion often
reveals that a lot is in fact at stake in deciding what to include
where. The lists thus provide a kind of conceptual punctua-
tion, a map of the field's priorities.

The most important of these is probably the kingdom
defined as the sum of seven *aṅga*, "limbs," also called *prakṛti*,
"state-elements" (chapter 4): *svāmin, amātya, rāṣṭra, durga,
kośa, bala, suhṛt,* respectively, "ruler," "minister," "realm,"
"fortification," "treasury," "army," and "ally." Such a kingdom is expanded and protected by a *vijigīṣu*, "expansionist
king": a king who seeks to become a transregional emperor
through war; this is the intended, ideal reader of Sanskrit
political science.

The "expansionist king" accomplishes his mission by
applying first the four canonical *upāya:* "methods" (chapter
18), *sāma, dāna, bheda, daṇḍa,* respectively "conciliation,"

"donation," "sowing dissension," and "coercion"—to which, as mentioned earlier, Kamandaki added three, namely, *māyā, upekṣā,* and *indrajāla:* "illusion," "disregard," and "magic." The fourth term in this list, *daṇḍa,* "the rod of coercion" is especially central, and challenging to translate because of its dense fusing of the concrete and abstract. Most concretely it refers to a "rod" or something like a cudgel. Somewhere in the middle of the semantic spectrum, it encompasses "punishment" of every kind, such as criminal justice and so on. At the other extreme, it refers to the royal power of legitimate violence in a comprehensive sense, encompassing the administration of war, assassinations, and the like. Chapter 14 says, "The king is, in essence, coercion," and the concept is clearly one of the closest to the core of the entire knowledge system (37). I have translated in a variety of ways, such as "rod of coercion," "coercive power," "punishment," and simply "the rod," depending on the context.

After the methods, the next most important set of terms is the six *guṇa,* "tactics," treated across several chapters: *sandhi,* "alliance" (chapter 9), *vigraha,* "war" (chapter 10), as well as *yāna, āsana, dvaidhībhāva,* and *saṃśraya,* "advance," "halt," "duplicity," and "taking refuge" (treated together in chapter 11). The system also assumes a triad of intrinsic *śakti,* "powers" (referenced throughout the work, e.g., as basic prerequisites for conquest at the beginning of chapter 16): *mantraśakti,* "strategy," *prabhuśakti,* "lordship," and *utsāhaśakti,* "determination." Each of the terms here had great importance individually, but the whole of each set was much more than the sum of its parts. As with the state-elements, their coordination is key. Yet Kamandaki never tires of repeating that the power of strategy is by far the most important, and that it is possible to triumph purely on the basis of strategy (12.7).

Despite this emphasis on pure strategy, the structure of the army is still important to note, for war-power, even when implicit, defines kingship (recall 14.37). The army is divided up in two ways, into both six and four. There are six types of troops (19.3): *maula, bhṛta, śreṇi, suhṛt, śatru, āṭavika,* "native troops," "mercenary troops," "troops from the guilds," "ally troops," "troops defected from the enemy," and "forest-people troops," respectively; but also four army-divisions (chapter 20): *padāti,* "foot-soldier," *aśva,* "cavalry," *ratha,* "chariot," and *gaja,* "elephant."

The fourfold division of the army evokes the pieces in the game of chess,[18] which may indeed have its ultimate origins in the subcontinent, while the concept of the *maṇḍala* (chapter 8), which I leave untranslated as "mandala," since it has entered the English lexicon (at least in some more or less related senses)—the concentric and contiguous circles into which all space was divided from a strategic point of view— evokes the chessboard and the general concept of a "move" in a board game. Geopolitics is here conceived geometrically with specific positions entitled to specific moves. In chapter 8, Kamandaki displays the circles and their inhabitants in front of and behind the king, conceived as the eternal center. Whatever the ultimate origins of chess, one can assert without any doubt that classical Indian political theory bears a profound connection. The mandala is the primordial board game, and rather than political metaphors emerging from association with such games (as we might assume), for instance, "the great game," classical Indian political schematics may have in fact been their original source.

The primacy of this geospatial imaginary in politico-military thought led in turn to a painstakingly technical, geometrical analysis of military action, culminating in the professional technique known as the *vyūha*, "battle array." *The Essence* concludes with a rapid-fire discussion of battle arrays, by far the driest topic in the book. Yet in Sanskrit literature, going back to the epics, these elaborate arrays have the gravity and glamor of elaborate Vedic rituals. Great generals, like Drona, deployed the most advanced arrays to the awe and terror of their enemies. Even amid these dry technical details, however, there remain some beautiful passages, reminding that aesthetic imperatives never fully subside. Whereas the drier and more technical passages show Kamandaki's fidelity to the discipline, the poetry shows his commitment to the sensibility of an ideal courtly audience and to the reader's pleasure. The composition as a whole crystallizes the continuity of politics, aesthetics, and spirituality in classical India.

Acknowledgments

I thank Sheldon Pollock, who provided vital moral support for this project when it was just an idea, guiding and inspiring me throughout in his incomparable way, and finally reading through everything with the deepest wisdom and care. He rescued me from so many embarrassing errors and wrong turns, while his characteristic Socratic questioning helped me see the true questions, whether or not I could find a satisfying answer. Working with him is humbling and exhilarating in equal measure, and his example is always a source of inspiration. I am honored to have been and to remain forever his student.

I thank my wife and comrade Nandini Chandra, without whom—as emotional and intellectual bulwark—no truly sustained work would be possible. Her laser-surgical sensitivity and uncompromising criticism are my guiding star: তোমারেই করিয়াছি জীবনের ধ্রুব তারা.

Next, I thank my dear friend and *gurukulabhrātṛ*, Whitney Cox, whose unfailingly sharp eyes and mind I have known and benefited from for so many years. His suggestions have been ingenious. His *divyacakṣus* is equaled only by his kindness of heart. I thank Dániel Balogh whose brilliant mind and vision were a true blessing: saving me from several disasters, while also offering countless ingenious suggestions.

I thank both Emily Silk and Heather Hughes from the MCLI team who each provided essential corrections and suggestions. Their consummate care for the task has been an indispensable support.

Finally, I thank Lee Siegel—whose gift for language always inspires—Arindam Chakrabarti, Jon Fernquest, Akash Kumar, James McHugh, Viren Murthy, Guriqbal (Bali) Sahota, Daud Ali, and so many others, have discussed the Nītisāra with me over the past several years, which has greatly enriched my experience of it. My Sanskrit class at the University of Hawai'i, Mānoa read through a substantial portion of the text in the Fall semester 2013—I must thank especially Sean Duggan and Richard Forster for their patience and enthusiasm.

Rajesh Mishra and Sanju Mishra of the Allahabad Museum and Library—a model for institutions of its kind in India—graciously helped me form an idea of the manuscript evidence available.

Any defects in the translation and edition of the text are my only truly singular contribution, for which I alone can take the credit.

NOTES

1   For its life in early medieval South Asia, see Ali 2004; also Ali 2007 for the *Nītisāra's* transmission of Gupta-period political and personal etiquette. Fernquest (2008) has traced the Pali reception of Kamandaki in medieval, and even modern, Burma. An unpublished Old Javanese work, *Kakawin Nītisāra*, testifies to the work's broad diffusion, at least in name, although the actual text has little to do with political theory as such (Thomas Hunter, personal communication, 2016). An Old Javanese version of the *Pañcatantra* story collection is likewise entitled the *Tantri Kamandaka* (Venkatasubbiah 1965). A recently discovered Old Malay legal work is likewise called the "Compilation of the Essence of Politics" *Nītisārasamuccaya,* though its relationship to classical Indian political theory hardly extends beyond its name (Kozok 2006).

2   See Kautilya 2013. Also see McClish's pathbreaking monograph on the compositional history of the *Arthaśāstra,* which argues in detail that the earliest layer, composed in the early centuries B.C.E., "represented an independent tradition of Indic statecraft . . . whose political philosophy was little influenced by *varṇadharma,*" while the final shape was provided by a thick layer of Brahmanism in the early centuries of the Common Era, a period "in which orthodox Brahmaṇical theology was exerting itself within statecraft in new ways" (McClish 2019: 5-6).

3   Though quotations in other works provided awareness of its existence, the actual text of the *Arthaśāstra* was lost in more recent centuries until R. Shamasastry rescued it via a single manuscript

discovered in Mysore in 1904, after which he both published (1909) and translated the work (1915) into English for the first time (see L. N. Rangarajan's introduction in Kautilya 1992: 21).

4   See Kautilya 2013.

5   Ali 2004: 33–34.

6   Singh 2010 offers a brilliant summation. Again, see Ali 2004.

7   On public *kāvya* as the paradigmatic monument of royal power see Pollock 2006; 1998.

8   On early medieval periodization see Chattopadhyaya 1994.

9   See McFate 2019.

10 "Mastery of the senses results from training in the knowledge systems and is to be accomplished by giving up anger, greed, pride, conceit, and excitement." (1.6 Topic 3a; Kautilya 2013: 70–71).

11 *Allahabad Pillar Inscription of Samudragupta* (line 28, pp. 8), *Corpus Inscriptionum Indicarum Vol. III.*

12 Manu seems to have been the first to gloss "critical inquiry" (*ānvīkṣikī*) as "knowledge of the self" (*ātmavidyā*) in a political-theoretical context, though he goes no further than the gloss. McClish has demonstrated that the seventh chapter of Manu's legal theory (*Manusmṛti*)—a short treatise on political theory (*rājadharma*) within the foundational work of *dharmaśāstra*—draws its coordinates from the *Arthaśāstra* (McClish 2014).

13 In Kamandaki's words:
    The lord of the earth who has spies for his eyes is ever awake, even when he sleeps. (13.30)
    And in those of the seventh/eighth-century poet Bharavi (2016):
    Oh king, rulers who have spies for their eyes should not be fooled by their servants devoted to their duties. (*Kirātārjunīya* 1.4)

14 See the appreciation in Singh 2010.

15 Cf. Kalidasa, *Raghuvaṃśa* 4.36 where the hero Raghu compels the kingdom of Suhma to adopt "the way of the bamboo" (*vaitasī vṛtti*). On which see also Kautilya, *Arthaśāstra* 12.1.1.

16 Chattopadhyaya 1994.

17 Ali 2007: 10.

18 The *padāti*, "foot-soldier," is the pawn; *aśva*, "cavalry," the knight; *ratha*, "chariot," the rook; and *gaja*, "elephant," the bishop.

NOTE ON THE TEXT
AND TRANSLATION

The text of the *Nītisāra* presented here is based on the standard edition of Ganapati Shastri,[1] which printed for the first time Shankararya's Sanskrit commentary, *Jaya-maṅgalā*.[2] I sometimes adopt readings from the other major edition, that by Rajendralala Mitra, which printed the anonymous Sanskrit commentary, *Upādhyāyanirapekṣā*.[3] Though I have not referenced it in the endnotes, the Ananda Ashram edition of 1958 has been a valuable resource: it was prepared by Rajeshwar Shastri Dravid and Ganapathi Shastri Hebbar, with the assistance of their students; it prints Shastri's text, with occasional emendations, conveniently juxtaposing both commentaries published in the earlier editions.

There is as yet no critical edition, and no systematic survey of the manuscripts has yet been reported. Based on the two foundational editions, however, and the manuscript evidence cited by each, the textual variation appears to be of relatively minor significance. This might suggest that the text was fairly standardized early enough in its life, either as a result of its wide circulation or perhaps even the stability of the thought system itself.

The printed editions are excellent resources and allow for a meaningful experience of the work as it was known in the early medieval period. The points where they disagree, and I am forced to choose between them, mostly pose questions of so-called "higher criticism": the pursuit of a text that makes basic sense semantically and stylistically. The choice between readings is usually fairly straightforward (when one or the other is obviously corrupt), or semantically minor. My edition offers something new simply in that it strives to constitute the text based on what is best in the two foundational editions. I offer a map of the meaningful differences between the two in the endnotes; supplementing, but by no means supplanting, the earlier editions.

The two previous English translations, by Manmatha Nath Dutt and Sisir Kumar Mitra, are valuable tools for the student and scholar.[4] They are extremely literal, more like modern commentaries along the lines of Vidyasagara's modern Sanskrit commentary.[5] The same is true of Formichi's Italian translation.[6] None of the previous translations was designed for readability. They are preliminary interpretations of the text, intended to introduce it for the first time to a scholarly audience, and we should keep in mind that the early translations were all made before the modern rediscovery of Kautilya's *Arthaśāstra* in 1908.[7] For these pioneering translators, Kamandaki's shorter digest was the most comprehensive primary source on Sanskrit political science available, and they had to learn the discipline entirely from Kamandaki's distillation of its essence, rather than the ultimate source: Kautilya's exhaustive *Arthaśāstra*.

As a translator, balancing the goals of fidelity and readability is a challenge, since *The Essence* is a technical work conducting its own delicate balancing act: maintaining elegance and evocation despite being a fundamentally didactic work on an often very dry topic. There are obviously numerous technical terms whose translation remains stubbornly awkward precisely because one must stay true to their status as technical terms, whose transparency is assumed (or else granted easily) in the original. I leave untranslated, for example, the term *maṇḍala*: territory conceived strategically; imagined as a big circle orbited by other territory-circles.[8] Within the mandala map, each of the allies and adversaries has its own quirky name: "rear adversary," "rear supporter," and so on. They are often only faintly descriptive, and almost just proper names. The names of the different types of alliances and military arrays are likewise often strange and seemingly arbitrary in the original. I have maintained their idiosyncrasy—which is after all part of this thought system's flavor—and simply translated as literally as possible. Elsewhere, though, I have tried hard to find a suitable English vocabulary for Kamandaki's thought, which involves a great deal of Kamandaki-style strategic compromise, no less than a strong alliance with you, my kind readers.

NOTES

1   Shastri 1912.

2   See Abbreviations for references used in the Notes to the Text.

3   Rajendralala Mitra 1982.

4   Dutt 1896. Sisir Kumar Mitra's translation is in Rajendralala Mitra 1982.

5   Vidyasagara 1875.

6   Formichi's translation was serialized from 1899–1904, then revised and republished in 1925.

7   Only Formichi's revision (1925) of his much earlier translation and S. K. Mitra (1982) had access to the *Arthaśāstra*.

8   On which see the Introduction and chapter 8.

THE ESSENCE
OF POLITICS

प्रथमः सर्गः

इन्द्रियजयप्रकरणम्

१ यस्य प्रभावाद्भुवनं शाश्वते पथि तिष्ठति ।
देवः स जयति श्रीमान्दण्डधारो महीपतिः ॥

२ वंशे विशालवंश्यानामृषीणामिव भूयसाम् ।१
अप्रतिग्राहकाणां यो बभूव भुवि विश्रुतः ॥

३ जातवेदा इवार्चिष्मान्वेदान्वेदविदां वरः ।
योऽधीतवान्सुचतुरश्चतुरोऽप्येकवेदवत् ॥

४ यस्याभिचारवज्रेण वज्रज्वलनतेजसः ।
पपातामूलतः श्रीमान्सुपर्वा नन्दपर्वतः ॥

५ एकाकी मन्त्रशक्त्या यः शक्त्या शक्तिधरोपमः ।
आजहार नृचन्द्राय चन्द्रगुप्ताय मेदिनीम् ॥

६ नीतिशास्त्रामृतं श्रीमानर्थशास्त्रमहोदधेः ।
य उद्दधे नमस्तस्मै विष्णुगुप्ताय वेधसे ॥

७ दर्शनात्तस्य सुदृशो विद्यानां पारदृश्वनः ।
राजविद्याप्रियतया सङ्क्लिप्तग्रन्थमर्थवत् ॥

८ उपार्जने पालने च भूमेर्भूमीश्वरं प्रति ।
यत्किञ्चिदुपदेक्ष्यामो राजविद्याविदां मतम् ॥

९ राजास्य जगतो हेतुर्वृद्धैर्वृद्धाभिसम्मतः ।
नयनानन्दजननः शशाङ्क इव तोयधेः ॥

१० यदि न स्यान्नरपतिः सम्यङ्नेता ततः प्रजा ।
अकर्णधारा जलधौ विप्लवेतेह नौरिव ॥२

2

CHAPTER 1

Conquering the Senses

Victory to the majestic king, god and wielder of the rod.[1] By his power the earth stays on its eternal path.

Vishnugupta was famed on earth, born in a line of sages of great lineage, who took the vow of abjuring all gifts.[2] Resplendent like the god of fire—an exceedingly clever man and supreme scholar of the Vedas—he learned all the four Vedas as if they were just one. His radiance was equal to Indra's lightning-bolt, and the lightning-bolt of his sorcery[3] uprooted the solid and majestic mountain of the Nanda dynasty.[4] In power he was like Karttikeya, the lance-bearing god.[5] By the power of his strategy,[6] he and he alone handed over the earth to Chandragupta, moon among men.[7] He mined the nectar of politics from the ocean of political science—I pay homage to the wise Vishnugupta.

The concise and meaningful text we expound here, out of love for the science of kingship, is based on studying the knowledge of that seer of vast vision, Vishnugupta. Our teachings represent the views of established scholars of kingship-science. They are addressed to the king and treat of establishing and protecting the kingdom.

The king is the cause of the earth's prosperity—this is the elders' consensus. He generates joy for the eyes, just as the moon excites the ocean. If there were no king as proper leader, the people would capsize like a ship in the ocean without a helmsman. A king who is righteous, devoted

११ धार्मिकं पालनपरं सम्यक्परपुरञ्जयम् ।
    राजानमभिमन्यन्ते प्रजापतिमिव प्रजाः ॥

१२ आयत्तं रक्षणं राज्ञि वार्ता रक्षणमाश्रिता ।
    वार्ताच्छेदे हि लोकोऽयं श्वसन्नपि न जीवति ॥

१३ पर्जन्य इव भूतानामाधारः पृथिवीपतिः ।
    विकलेऽपि हि पर्जन्ये जीव्यते न तु भूपतौ ॥

१४ प्रजां संरक्षति नृपः सा वर्धयति पार्थिवम् ।
    वर्धनाद्रक्षणं श्रेयस्तन्नाशोऽन्यत्सदप्यसत् ॥३

१५ न्यायप्रवृत्तो नृपतिरात्मानमथ च प्रजाम् ।
    त्रिवर्गेणोपसन्धत्ते निहन्ति ध्रुवमन्यथा ॥

१६ धर्माद्वैजवनो राजा चिराय बुभुजे महीम् ।
    अधर्माच्चैव नहुषः प्रतिपेदे रसातलम् ॥

१७ तस्माद्धर्मं पुरस्कृत्य यतेतार्थाय भूपतिः ।
    धर्मेण वर्धते राज्यं तस्य स्वादु फलं श्रियः ॥

१८ स्वाम्यमात्यश्च राष्ट्रं च दुर्गं कोशो बलं सुहृत् ।
    एतावदुच्यते राज्यं सत्त्वबुद्धिव्यपाश्रयम् ॥

१९ आलम्ब्य बलवत्सत्त्वं बुद्ध्यालोचितनिर्गमः ।
    सप्ताङ्गस्यास्य लाभाय यतेत सततोत्थितः ॥

२० न्यायेनार्जनमर्थस्य रक्षणं वर्धनं तथा ।
    सत्पात्रप्रतिपत्तिश्च राजवृत्तं चतुर्विधम् ॥

to protection, and a steadfast conqueror of enemy cities, is esteemed by the people as Prajapati, lord of the people.[8]

Protection depends on the king. The economy depends on protection. When the economy is ruined, people do not live even though they breathe.

The king, like the monsoon cloud, is the wellspring of creatures. Yet, if the monsoon is deficient, people can live, but not if the king is deficient. The king protects the subjects, and they in turn cause him to prosper. Protection is more important than economic prosperity, since when protection is lacking, prosperity is as good as nonexistent even when it exists. When the king conducts himself according to right, he endows himself and his subjects with the three aims of life: dharma, power, and pleasure.[9] When he acts otherwise, he surely destroys both himself and his subjects.   15

Through acting according to dharma, King Vaijavana enjoyed the earth for a long time, but from adherence to non-dharma Nahusha went straight to hell.[10] Therefore the king should put dharma first, and then work toward power. Through dharma the kingdom prospers, and royal riches are its sweet fruit.

The kingdom—founded on both fortitude and intellect—consists of these seven elements: ruler, minister, realm, fortification, treasury, army, and ally.

Drawing on powerful vigor, and using his intellect to examine outcomes, the king should always stay active to consolidate the seven parts of the kingdom. Royal practice is fourfold: rightful acquisition; protecting what is acquired; making prosper what has been acquired; donation of what is acquired to suitable recipients.   20

२१ नयविक्रमसम्पन्नः सूत्थानश्चिन्तयेच्छ्रियम् ।
नयस्य विनयो मूलं विनयः शास्त्रनिश्चयः ॥

२२ विनयो हीन्द्रियजयस्तद्युक्तः शास्त्रमृच्छति ।
तन्निष्ठस्य हि शास्त्रार्थाः प्रसीदन्ति ततः श्रियः ॥

२३ शास्त्रं प्रज्ञा धृतिर्दाक्ष्यं प्रागल्भ्यं धारयिष्णुता ।
उत्साहो वाग्मिता दार्ढ्यमापत्क्लेशसहिष्णुता ॥

२४ प्रभावः शुचिता मैत्री त्यागः सत्यं कृतज्ञता ।
कुलं शीलं दमश्चेति गुणाः सम्पत्तिहेतवः ॥

२५ आत्मानं प्रथमं राजा विनयेनोपपादयेत् ।
ततोऽमात्यांस्ततो भृत्यांस्ततः पुत्रांस्ततः प्रजाः ॥

२६ सदानुरक्तप्रकृतिः प्रजापालनतत्परः ।
विनीतात्मा हि नृपतिर्भूयसीं श्रियमश्नुते ॥

२७ प्रकीर्णे विषयारण्ये धावन्तं विप्रमाथिनम् ।
ज्ञानाङ्कुशेन कुर्वीत वश्यमिन्द्रियदन्तिनम् ॥

२८ आत्मा प्रयत्नादर्थेभ्यो मनः समधितिष्ठति ।
संयोगादात्ममनसोः प्रवृत्तिरुपजायते ॥

6

The ever-active king—imbued with both political acumen and martial power—should reflect on royal majesty. Self-mastery is the root of politics. It is founded on the conclusions of the *śāstras*.[11] Self-mastery consists of the conquest of the senses, and someone endowed with self-mastery is eligible to study the *śāstras*. The content of the *śāstras* and royal majesty both reveal themselves to one who is focused on self-mastery.

These nineteen qualities are the sources of success for a king: scholarship; intelligence; composure; skill; maturity; resilience; determination; eloquence; steadiness; the capacity to endure accidents and calamities; power; purity; kindness; generosity; truthfulness; gratitude; lineage; character; and restraint.

The king should first endow himself with self-mastery. Afterward, he should propagate it in his ministers, and then in his servants, sons, and subjects. A king who has cultivated self-mastery—who is intent on protecting his subjects, and whose subjects are always kept loyal—attains abundant royal majesty. With the goad of knowledge, he should bring the elephant of the senses—running amuck and rampaging in the forest of sensual enjoyment—under his control.

The self attaches to the mind and thereby assiduously engages with the objects of sensual enjoyment. Action arises through the union of self and mind. The mind triggers the senses out of greed for the meat of the sensual objects. With effort one should restrain the mind, for when it is conquered, the senses are conquered.

25

२९ विषयामिषलोभेन मनः प्रेरयतीन्द्रियम् ।
तन्निरुन्ध्यात्प्रयत्नेन जिते तस्मिञ्जितेन्द्रियः ॥

३० विज्ञानं हृदयं चित्तं मनोबुद्धिश्च तत्समम् ।
अनेनात्मा करोतीह प्रवर्तननिवर्तने ॥

३१ धर्माधर्मौ सुखं दुःखमिच्छाद्वेषौ तथैव च ।
प्रयत्नज्ञानसंस्कारा आत्मलिङ्गमुदाहृतम् ॥

३२ ज्ञानस्यायुगपद्भावो मनसो लिङ्गमुच्यते ।
नानार्थेषु च सङ्कल्पः कर्म चास्य प्रकीर्त्यते ॥

३३ श्रोत्रं त्वक्चक्षुषी जिह्वा नासिका चेति पञ्चमी ।
पायूपस्थं हस्तपादं वाक्चेतीन्द्रियसङ्ग्रहः ॥

३४ शब्दः स्पर्शश्च रूपं च रसो गन्धश्च पञ्चमः ।
उत्सर्गानन्दनादानगत्यालापाश्च तत्क्रियाः ॥

३५ आत्मा मनश्च तद्विद्धैरन्तःकरणमुच्यते ।
ताभ्यां तु सप्रयत्नाभ्यां सङ्कल्प उपजायते ॥

३६ आत्मा बुद्धीन्द्रियाण्यर्था बहिष्करणमुच्यते ।
सङ्कल्पाध्यवसायाभ्यां सिद्धिरस्य प्रकीर्तिता ॥

३७ उभे एते हि करणे प्रयत्नान्तरीयके ।४
तस्मात्प्रयत्नसंरोधाद्भावयेन्निर्मनस्कताम् ॥

३८ एवं करणसामर्थ्यात्संयम्यात्मानमात्मना ।
नयापनयविद्राजा कुर्वीत हितमात्मनः ॥

The following are all synonyms: "awareness," "heart," "consciousness," "mind," and "intellect." By means of a mental faculty identified along these lines, the self, inhabiting the body, practices both engagement and withdrawal. The signs of the self's existence (since a self is required as their substratum) are the following: dharma, non-dharma, pleasure, pain, desire, hatred, effort, knowledge, and latent tendencies spanning previous lives. The non-simultaneous, sequential nature of knowledge is the sign of the mind's existence.[12] The resolve it demonstrates toward various objects is known as its action.[13]

The conglomerate of the senses is as follows: ears, skin, eyes, tongue, and nose make five. Then there are the anus and genitals, the hands and feet, as well as the faculty of speech. Their respective spheres of action are as follows: sound, touch, form, taste, and smell make five. Then there is excretion, gratification, receiving, moving, and speaking. The self and the mind together are said by scholars to form the "inner instrument." When they work in unison, mental resolve is produced.[14]

The self, the knowledge-oriented senses, and their objects, taken together, are said to constitute the "outer instrument," whose success comes about through resolve and determination.[15] Effort is intrinsic to the two instruments, so by completely stopping effort one can transcend the mind.[16] In this way, using the power of the two instruments, and restraining the self by means of the self, the king—knowledgeable about correct and incorrect political paths—can work for his own benefit.

३९ एकस्यापि न यः शक्तो मनसः सन्निबर्हणे ।
महीं सागरपर्यन्तां कथं नु स विजेष्यते ॥

४० क्रियावसानविरसैर्विषयैरपहारिभिः ।
गच्छत्याक्षिप्तहृदयः करीव नृपतिर्ग्रहम् ॥

४१ सज्जमानो ह्वकार्येषु विषयान्धीकृतेक्षणः ।
आवहत्युग्रभयदां स्वयमेवापदं नृपः ॥५

४२ शब्दः स्पर्शश्च रूपं च रसो गन्धश्च पञ्चमः ।
एकैकमेषां भवति विनाशप्रतिपत्तये ॥

४३ शुचिः शष्पाङ्कुराहारो विदूरक्रमणक्षमः ।
लुब्धकादर्दितलोभेन मृगो मृगयते वधम् ॥

४४ गिरीन्द्रसदृशाकारो लीलयोन्मूलितद्रुमः ।
करिणीस्पर्शसम्मोहादालानं याति वारणः ॥६

४५ स्निग्धदीपशिखालोकविलोभितविलोचनः ।
मृत्युमृच्छत्यसन्देहात्पतङ्गः सहसा पतन् ॥

४६ दूरेऽपि हि भवन्दृष्टेरगाधे सलिले चरन् ।
मीनस्तु सामिषं लोहमास्वादयति मृत्यवे ॥

४७ गन्धलुब्धो मधुकरो दानासवपिपासया ।
अभ्येत्यसुखसञ्चारानाजकर्णझनझनान् ॥७

४८ एकैकशोऽपि निघ्नन्ति विषया विषसन्निभाः ।
क्षेमी तु स कथं नु स्याद्यः समं पञ्च सेवते ॥

४९ सेवेत विषयान्काले मुत्त्वा तत्परतां वशी ।
सुखं हि फलमर्थस्य तन्निरोधे वृथा श्रियः ॥

How can someone incapable of restraining his own mind conquer the earth bounded by the oceans? The king will be captured like a wild elephant if his heart is deluded by the distracting objects of sensual enjoyment, which become repugnant as soon as their work is done. When he becomes entangled in wrongful activities, his eyes blinded by the sense-objects, a king invites extremely dangerous catastrophe. 40

Sound, touch, form, taste, and scent are the five sense-objects. Each one of these on its own is enough to produce total destruction. The deer, for example, lives a pure life by feeding on sprouts of grass. He is capable of wandering vast distances, and yet, intoxicated by a hunter's song, he seeks out his own slaughter. Even the elephant—in form like the lord of mountains and able to uproot trees for sport—falls into captivity, mesmerized by the touch of the she-elephant. And the moth, its eyes enticed by the sight of the lamp's sweet flame, suddenly falls upon it and goes to certain death. Even though he is far out of sight, roaming in fathomless water, the fish tastes the meat attached to an iron hook to his own certain death. The bee thirsty for the liquor of ichor, and greedy for its scent, enters the flapping folds of the elephant's ear, so dreadful to traverse. Each one of the poison-like objects of sensual enjoyment is by itself capable of killing. How can anyone remain safe who serves all five? 45

The self-composed man can serve the objects of sensual enjoyment on occasion and then renounce his obsession with them. The goal of power is happiness; when happiness is compromised, royal majesty becomes meaningless. Those whose minds are subject to attachment constantly shed

५० निकामासक्तमनसां कान्तामुखविलोकने ।
गलन्ति गलिताश्रूणां यौवनेन सह श्रियः ॥

५१ धर्मादर्थोऽर्थतः कामः कामात्सुखफलोदयः ।
आत्मानं हन्ति तौ हत्वा युक्त्या यो न निषेवते ॥

५२ नामापि स्त्रीति संह्लादि विकरोत्येव मानसम् ।
किं पुनर्दर्शनात्तस्या विलासोल्लासितभ्रुवः ॥

५३ रहःप्रचारकुशला मृदुगद्गदभाषिणी ।
कं न नारी रमयति रक्तं रक्तान्तलोचना ॥

५४ मुनेरपि मनो ऽवश्यं सरागं कुरुते ऽङ्गना ।
प्रसन्नं कान्तिजननं सन्ध्येव शशिमण्डलम् ॥

५५ मनः प्रह्लादयन्तीभिर्मन्दं यान्तीभिरप्यलम् ।
महान्तोऽपि हि भिद्यन्ते स्त्रीभिरद्रिरिवाचलाः ॥

५६ मृगयाक्षास्तथा पानं गर्हितानि महीभुजाम् ।
दृष्टास्तेभ्योऽपि विपदः पाण्डुनैषधवृष्णिषु ॥

५७ कामः क्रोधस्तथा लोभो हर्षो मानो मदस्तथा ।
षड्वर्गमुत्सृजेदेनं तस्मिंस्त्यक्ते सुखी नृपः ॥

५८ दाण्डक्यो नृपतिः कामात्क्रोधाच्च जनमेजयः ।
लोभादैलस्तु राजर्षिर्वातापिर्हर्षतोऽसुरः ॥

५९ पौलस्त्यो राक्षसो मानान्मदाद्दम्भोद्भवो नृपः ।
प्रयाता निधनं ह्येते शत्रुषड्वर्गमाश्रिताः ॥

६० शत्रुषड्वर्गमुत्सृज्य जामदग्न्यो जितेन्द्रियः ।
अम्बरीषश्च नाभागो बुभुजाते चिरं महीम् ॥

streams of tears when they gaze upon the face of a beloved woman. Then they shed their royal majesty along with their youth. From dharma comes power; from power, pleasure; 50 and from pleasure, the fruit of happiness ripens. He who does not rationally serve these three aims ends up destroying them—and himself.

The mere word "woman" is intoxicating and enough to disturb the mind—how much more so her presence, eyebrows dancing with desire. Skilled in the arts of sexual intimacy, her voice tender and tremulous, her eyes reddened at the edges by drink, what passionate man would a woman not enchant? A woman impassions even a sage's mind, as the sunset reddens the clear and radiant moon. Even great men are split apart by women—delighting and intoxicating their minds—as great mountains are split apart by water droplets. 55

Hunting, gambling, and drinking are considered reprehensible for kings. Pandu, the Nishadha King Nala, and the Vrishnis each came to misfortune through these vices.[17] One should cast out the six enemies: desire, anger, greed, excitement, pride, and intemperance. When they have been abandoned, the king becomes happy. All these men were destroyed by resorting to the six enemies: King Dandaka by desire, Janamejaya by anger, the king-sage Aila by greed, the demon Vatapi by excitement, the rakshasa Paulastya by pride, and King Dambhodbhava by intemperance.[18] Casting out the six enemies, and conquering his senses, Jamadagnya, as well as Nabhaga's son Ambarisha, ruled the earth for a long time.[19]   60

विद्यावृद्धसंयोगप्रकरणम्

६१ वर्धयन्निह धर्मार्थौ सेवितौ सद्भिरादरात् ।
नितृहीतेन्द्रियः साधु कुर्वीत गुरुसेवनम् ॥

६२ शास्त्राय गुरुसंयोगः शास्त्रं विनयवृद्धये ।
विद्याविनीतो नृपतिर्न कृच्छ्रेष्ववसीदति ॥

६३ वृद्धोपसेवी नृपतिः सतां भवति सम्मतः ।
प्रेर्यमाणोऽप्यसद्वृत्तैर्नाकार्येषु प्रवर्तते ॥

६४ आददानः प्रतिदिनं कलाः सम्यङ्गृहीपतिः ।
शुक्लपक्षे प्रविचरञ्छशाङ्क इव वर्धते ॥

६५ जितेन्द्रियस्य नृपतेर्नीतिमार्गानुसारिणः ।
भवन्ति ज्वलिता लक्ष्म्यः कीर्तयश्च नभःस्पृशः ॥

६६ इति स्म राजा विनयं नयान्वितो निषेवमाणो नरदेवसेवितम् ।[८]
पदं समाक्रामति भास्वरं श्रियः शिरो महारत्नगिरेरिवोन्नतम् ॥

६७ इयं हि लोकव्यतिरेकवर्तिनी स्वभावतः पार्थिवता समुद्धता ।[९]
बलात्तदेनां विनयेन योजयेन्नयस्य वृद्धौ विनयः पुरःसरः ॥

६८ परां विनीतः समुपैति सेव्यतां महीपतीनां विनयो विभूषणम् ।
प्रवृत्तदानो मृदुसञ्चरत्करः करीव भद्रो विनयेन शोभते ॥

Associating with Wise Men

In order to propagate both dharma and power—which good men serve with respect—a man with senses under control should unswervingly search out a guru. Association with a guru is for learning the *śāstra,* and the *śāstra* leads to increased self-mastery. A king who has attained self-mastery through knowledge never becomes despondent in adversity. A king who serves men old in wisdom is well respected by good men. Even when urged on by wicked people, he never undertakes wrongful actions.

Working properly each day to acquire new arts, the king grows like the moon during the bright half of the month, which waxes each day by a digit. The king who conquers his senses and follows the path of political science comes to possess radiant majesty and glory that touches the sky.   65

Thus the king, adhering to correct politics and pursuing the self-mastery practiced by those kings who are gods among men, attains the pinnacle of royal majesty as radiant as the exalted head of the great jewel mountain, Sumeru.[20] Exalted   66 kingship is by its very nature elevated above the mundane world, but one must forcefully imbue it with self-mastery. Self-mastery is the prerequisite for political success.   67

People serve with devotion a king endowed with self-mastery. The true adornment for lords of the earth is self-mastery. A king endowed with self-mastery, who is generous and exacts only reasonable taxes, becomes auspicious and beautiful like a tame elephant, with ichor flowing from its temples, and trunk gently undulating.   68

६९ गुरुस्तु विद्याधिगमाय सेव्यते श्रुता च विद्या मतये महात्मनाम् ।
श्रुतानुवर्तीनि मतानि वेधसामसंशयं साधु भवन्ति भूतये ॥

७० सुनिपुणमुपसेव्य सद्गुरुं शुचिरनुवृत्तिपरो विभूतये ।
भवति हि विनयोपबृंहितो नृपतिपदाय शमाय च क्षमः ॥१०

७१ अविनयरतमादराद्गते वशमवशं हि नयन्ति विद्विषः ।
श्रुतविनयनिधिं समाश्रितस्तनुरपि नैति पराभवं क्वचित् ॥११

16

One should serve a guru to attain knowledge. And knowledge once learned is beneficial to great men's minds. Sages' minds are formed by Vedic learning, and they are therefore without doubt very conducive to fortune.   69

A person with self-mastery, who with purity of heart and obedience serves a true and very intelligent guru for the sake of his welfare, then becomes ready both for the position of king and for spiritual serenity.   70

Enemies viciously seize control of a king who is apparently in control, but who in fact lacks self-mastery. Yet even a small man never suffers the slightest defeat if he has taken as his guru someone who is a treasure house of self-mastery and learning.   71

द्वितीयः सर्गः

विद्याविभागप्रकरणम्

१ आन्वीक्षिकीं त्रयीं वार्तां दण्डनीतिं च पार्थिवः ।
   तद्विद्यैस्तत्क्रियोपेतैश्चिन्तयेद्विनयान्वितः ॥

२ आन्वीक्षिकी त्रयी वार्ता दण्डनीतिश्च शाश्वती ।
   विद्याश्चतस्र एवैता योगक्षेमाय देहिनाम् ॥१॥

३ त्रयी वार्ता दण्डनीतिस्तिस्रो विद्या हि मानवाः ।
   त्रय्या एव विभागोऽयं येयमान्वीक्षिकी मता ॥

४ वार्ता च दण्डनीतिश्च द्वे विद्ये अवस्थिताः ।२
   लोकस्यार्थप्रधानत्वाच्छिष्याः सुरपुरोधसः ॥

५ एकैव दण्डनीतिस्तु विद्येत्यौशनसी स्थितिः ।
   तस्यां हि सर्वविद्यानामारम्भाः सम्प्रतिष्ठिताः ॥

६ विद्याश्चतस्र एवैता इति नो गुरुदर्शनम् ।
   पृथक्पृथक्प्रसिद्ध्यर्थं यासु लोको व्यवस्थितः ॥

७ आन्वीक्षिक्यात्मविज्ञानं धर्माधर्मौ त्रयीस्थितौ ।
   अर्थानर्थौ तु वार्तायां दण्डनीत्यां नयेतरौ ॥

८ आन्वीक्षिकीत्रयीवार्ताः सतीर्विद्याः प्रचक्षते ।
   सत्योऽपि हि न सत्यास्ता दण्डनीतेस्तु विप्लवे ॥

18

CHAPTER 2

Branches of Knowledge

A king endowed with self-mastery should give consideration to critical inquiry, the three Vedas, the economy, and governance, in the company of scholars learned in these subjects and proficient in their practices. These four—critical inquiry, the three Vedas, the economy, and ever-lasting governance—are the branches of knowledge conducive to the welfare of human beings.

According to the followers of Manu, the branches of knowledge are three: the three Vedas, the economy, and governance, critical inquiry being considered a division of the three Vedas. The students of the gods' priest, Brihaspati, hold that there are only two branches of knowledge: the economy and governance, because power dominates the world. The position of Ushanas is that there is only one branch of knowledge: governance, because all other branches of knowledge have been shown to have their origins in it. 5

Our guru's opinion is that there are four branches of knowledge. They act independently to fulfill their purpose and provide well-being to the people. Critical inquiry is the science of the self. Dharma and non-dharma are regulated by the three Vedas. Power and its opposite pertain to the economy. Good politics and bad politics are the matter of governance.

Critical inquiry, the three Vedas, and the economy are said to be the positive branches of knowledge. Even if they

९ दण्डनीतिर्यदा सम्यङ्चेतारमधितिष्ठति ।
तदा विद्याविदः शेषा विद्याः सम्यगुपासते ॥

१० वर्णाश्रैवाश्रमाश्चैव विद्यास्वासु प्रतिष्ठिताः ।
रक्षेत्ता रक्षणात्तासां तद्धर्मस्यांशभाङ्नृपः ॥

११ आन्वीक्षिक्यात्मविद्या स्यादीक्षणात्सुखदुःखयोः ।
ईक्षमाणस्तया तत्त्वं हर्षशोकौ व्युदस्यति ॥

१२ ऋग्यजुःसामनामानस्त्रयो वेदास्त्रयी स्मृता ।
उभौ लोकाववाप्नोति त्रय्यां तिष्ठन्यथाविधि ॥

१२ अङ्गानि वेदाश्चत्वारो मीमांसा न्यायविस्तरः ।
धर्मशास्त्रं पुराणं च त्रयीदं सर्वमुच्यते ॥

१४ पाशुपाल्यं कृषिः पण्यं वार्ता वार्तानुजीविनाम् ।[3]
सम्पन्नो वार्तया साधु नावृत्तेर्भयमृच्छति ॥[4]

१५ दमो दण्ड इति प्रोक्तस्तात्स्थ्याद्दण्डो महीपतिः ।
तस्य नीतिर्दण्डनीतिर्नयनान्नीतिरुच्यते ॥

१६ तयात्मानं च शेषाश्च विद्याः पायान्महीपतिः ।
विद्या लोकोपकारिण्यस्तत्पाता हि महीपतिः ॥

१७ विद्याभिराभिर्निपुणं चतुर्वर्गमुदारधीः ।
विद्यात्तदासां विद्यात्वं विद ज्ञाने निरुच्यते ॥

are present, they are virtually absent when governance is defective. When a leader possesses proper governance, then the scholars of the other branches can look after their own branches of knowledge properly. The individual branches of knowledge have established all the castes and life-stages. By examining and protecting the castes and life-stages, the king partakes of a portion of their individual dharma.   10

Critical inquiry is knowledge of the self, so called because it "inquires into" joy and sorrow. Examining the true reality through critical inquiry, one can abolish both joy and sorrow. The three collections known as the *Ṛg, Yajus,* and *Sāman* are the three Vedas; when someone adheres to the three Vedas, he obtains both heaven and earth.

The ancillary sciences; the four Vedas—including the *Atharva;* hermeneutics, logic, law, and ancient lore all taken collectively are known as the triple knowledge. Animal husbandry, agriculture, and trade are known as the economy among those who depend on economic development. A good man with good economy never encounters the danger of unemployment. The rod of coercion is pacification, and since the king abides by it, he is himself known as the rod. The politics of the rod is known as governance, and the term "politics" has the etymological meaning of "leading," since it provides leadership.[1]   15

By means of governance the king should protect himself and all the other branches of knowledge. The branches of knowledge help people, and therefore the lord of the earth is their protector. By means of the four branches of knowledge, the high-minded king should skillfully understand the four goals of life:[2] dharma, power, pleasure, and spiritual

वर्णाश्रमव्यवस्थाप्रकरणम्

१८ इज्याध्ययनदानानि यथाशास्त्रं सनातनः ।
ब्राह्मणक्षत्रियविशां सामान्यो धर्म उच्यते ॥

१९ याजनाध्यापने शुद्धे विशुद्धाच्च प्रतिग्रहः ।
वृत्तित्रयमिदं प्रोक्तं मुनिभिर्ज्येष्ठवर्णिनः ॥

२० शस्त्रेणाजीवनं राज्ञो भूतानां चाभिरक्षणम् ।
पाशुपाल्यं कृषिः पण्यं वैश्यस्याजीवनं स्मृतम् ॥

२१ शूद्रस्य धर्मः शुश्रूषा द्विजानामनुपूर्वशः ।
शुद्धा च वृत्तिस्तत्सेवा कारुचारणकर्म च ॥

२२ गुरौ वासोऽग्निशुश्रूषा स्वाध्यायो व्रतचारणम् ।
त्रिकालस्नायिता भैक्षं गुरौ प्राणान्तिकी स्थितिः ॥

२३ तदभावे गुरुसुते तथा सब्रह्मचारिणि ।
कामतो वाश्रमान्यत्वं स्वधर्मो ब्रह्मचारिणः ॥

२४ समेखलो जटी मुण्डो दण्डी वा गुरुसंश्रयः ।
आविद्याग्रहणाद्ग्रच्छेत्कामतो वाश्रमान्तरम् ॥

liberation. Such is the essential nature of what constitutes a branch of "knowledge," since etymologically the verb "to know" has the sense of "cognizing."[3]

Arrangements of Caste

The eternal dharma common to Brahmans, Kshatriyas, and Vaishyas is said to be sacrifice, study, and donation, in a manner consonant with the *śāstras*. The sages say that the three activities for the superior Brahman caste are: superintending sacrifices, teaching, and accepting gifts from those who are pure. The livelihood of a Kshatriya is traditionally held to be bearing arms and protecting beings; that of a Vaishya, animal husbandry, agriculture, and trade. A Shudra's dharma is obedience to the three twice-born castes in order of precedence. His proper livelihood consists of serving them, as well as craftwork, dance, and other kinds of performance.

20

The proper dharma for the stage of celibate study consists in living with a guru, maintaining the ritual fire, Vedic recitation, maintaining the vow of celibacy, bathing three times a day, collecting alms, and living with the guru until his death. If the guru has passed away, one may reside with his son, or with fellow celibate students. Otherwise, if one wishes, one may move on to the next stage and become a householder. While studying with a guru, the disciple should wear the sacred girdle, keep dreadlocks or else a shaved head, and carry a staff until he has acquired knowledge. Then, if he wishes, he may move on to the next life-stage and become a householder.

२५ अग्निहोत्रोपचरणं जीवनं च स्वकर्मभिः ।
धर्मदारेषु कल्येषु पर्ववर्जं रतिक्रिया ॥५

२६ देवपित्रतिथिभ्यश्च पूजा दीनानुकम्पनम् ।
श्रुतिस्मृत्यर्थसंस्थानं धर्मोऽयं गृहमेधिनः ॥

२७ जटित्वमग्निहोत्रित्वं भूशय्याजिनधारणम् ।
वनेवासः पयोमूलनीवारफलवृत्तिता ॥

२८ प्रतिग्रहनिवृत्तिश्च त्रिःस्नानं व्रतचारिता ।
देवातिथीनां पूजा च धर्मो वनवासिनः ॥

२९ सर्वारम्भपरित्यागो भैक्षाश्यं वृक्षमूलिता ।
निष्परिग्रहताद्रोहः समता सर्वजन्तुषु ॥

३० प्रियाप्रियापरिष्वङ्गः सुखदुःखाविकारिता ।
सबाह्याभ्यन्तरं शौचं वाग्यमो व्रतचारिता ॥६

३१ सर्वेन्द्रियसमाहारो धारणा ध्यानयुक्तता ।७
भावसंशुद्धिरित्येष परिव्राड्धर्म उच्यते ॥

३२ अहिंसा सूनृता वाणी सत्यं शौचं दया क्षमा ।
वर्णिनां लिङ्गिनां चैव सामान्यो धर्म उच्यते ॥

३३ स्वर्गानन्त्याय धर्मोऽयं सर्वेषां वर्णिलिङ्गिनाम् ।
तस्याभावे तु लोकोऽयं सङ्करात्राशामाप्नुयात् ॥

३४ सर्वस्यास्य यथान्यायं भूपतिः सम्प्रवर्तकः ।
तस्याभावे धर्मनाशस्तदभावे जगच्च्युतिः ॥

24

The proper dharma for householders consists of maintaining the sacred fire; maintaining a livelihood according to one's proper caste duties; having sex with one's lawful wives when they are healthy and not on festival days; worshiping gods, ancestors, and guests; charity to the indigent; and putting into practice the content of the Vedic revelation and remembered literature.[4]

The proper dharma for someone withdrawn to the forest consists of keeping dreadlocks; maintaining the sacred fire; sleeping on the ground; wearing an antelope hide; residing in the forest; consuming water, roots, and wild rice; abjuring gifts; bathing three times a day; maintaining his vow of celibacy, as well as worshiping gods and guests.

Finally, the dharma for the renouncer consists of giving up all activities; eating alms; sitting under a tree; abjuring gifts; nonaggression; equanimity toward all beings; avoiding both friend and foe; being unperturbed by either pleasure or pain; inner and outer purity; restraint in speech; carrying out vows; control over all the sense organs; mental concentration; dedication to meditation; and complete purity of being.

The common dharma for all castes consists of nonviolence, proper speech, truthfulness, purity, compassion, and tolerance. This dharma assures immediate entry into heaven for all castes. Without dharma the world would certainly face destruction from caste miscegenation. The king is the proper initiator of all the above rules of caste and life-stage. Without him, dharma would be lost, and without dharma, the world's destruction would be inevitable. Aware of the divisions of caste and life-stage, and devoted to the proper conduct of

३५ वर्णाश्रमाचारयुतो वर्णाश्रमविभागवित् ।
पाता वर्णाश्रमाणां च पार्थिवः सर्वलोकभाक् ॥ ८

दण्डमाहात्म्यप्रकरणम्

३६ इति यस्मादुभौ लोकौ धारयत्यात्मवान्नृपः ।
प्रजानां च ततः सम्यग्दण्डं दण्डीव धारयेत् ॥

३७ उद्वेजयति तीक्ष्णेन मृदुना परिभूयते ।
दण्डेन नृपतिस्तस्माद्युक्तदण्डः प्रशस्यते ॥

३८ त्रिवर्गं वर्धयत्याशु राज्ञो दण्डो यथाविधि ।
प्रणीतो ऽथासमञ्जस्याद्वनस्थानपि कोपयेत् ॥

३९ लोकशास्त्रानुगो नेयो दण्डो ऽनुद्वेजनः श्रिये ।
उद्वेजनादधर्मः स्यात्तस्माद्धंसो महीपतेः ॥

४० परस्परामिषतया जगतो भिन्नवर्त्मनः ।
दण्डाभावे परिध्वंसी मात्स्यो न्यायः प्रवर्तते ॥

४१ जगदेतन्निराक्रन्दं९ कामलोभादिभिर्बलात् ।
निमज्ज्यमानं निरये राज्ञा दण्डेन धार्यते ॥

४२ इदं प्रकृत्या विषयैर्वशीकृतं परस्परस्त्रीधनलोलुपं जगत् ।
सनातने वर्त्मनि साधुसेविते प्रतिष्ठते दण्डभयोपपीडितम् ॥

both, the king—who is protector of castes and life-stages—
attains all worlds heavenly and mundane.   35

The Greatness of the Rod of Coercion

Since the king holds aloft both the mundane and heavenly
worlds—both for himself and his subjects—he should bear
the rod of coercion like Yama, the rod-bearing god of death.
People avoid him if he is too harsh, while he is overpowered if
too mild. Therefore, they praise the king who is measured in
his application of coercion. When the king applies coercion
according to rule, he swiftly fosters the three aims of life,[5]
while the rod wrongfully applied angers even forest-dwelling
ascetics. The rod should not be threatening. It should be
applied for the sake of royal majesty, in accordance with the
śāstras, and giving due consideration to the people's feelings.
A threatening application of coercion leads to deviation from
dharma, and as a result of such deviation the king himself
will be destroyed. Without the rod, the destructive law of
the fishes[6] prevails, in which people go astray, greedy for
each other's flesh.   40

The king's rod supports this helpless world, sinking
precipitously into hell because of desire, greed, and other
vices.

The people of the world are by nature overcome by the
objects of sensual enjoyment, and greedy for each other's
women and wealth. They can set forth on the eternal established path, which good men necessarily follow, only when
they are afflicted by fear of the rod.   42

४३ नियतविषयवर्ती प्रायशो दण्डयोगाज्
जगति परवशोऽस्मिन् दुर्लभः साधुवृत्तः ।
कृशमथ विकलं वा व्याधितं वाधनं वा
पतिमपि कुलनारी दण्डभीत्याभ्युपैति ॥

४४ इति परिगणितार्थः शास्त्रमार्गानुसारी
नियमयति यतात्मा यः प्रजा दण्डनीत्या ।
अपुनरपगमाय प्राप्तमार्गप्रचाराः
सरित इव समुद्रं सम्पदस्तं विशन्ति ॥

In this helpless world people control their sensual urges only when the rod is applied to them. An innately virtuous man is hard to find. In the same way a woman of good family tends to her husband—even when he is weak, lame, diseased, or poor—only through the threat of the rod. 43

Riches stream toward the self-composed king who reflects on political science, follows the *śāstra's* path, and restrains the subjects through governance. They flow to him, never to depart, as streams flow into the ocean.

आचारव्यवस्थापनप्रकरणम्

१ दण्डं दण्डीव भूतेषु धारयन्धरणीपतिः१
प्रजाः समनुगृह्णीयात्प्रजापतिरिव स्वयम् ॥

२ वाक्सूनृता दया दानं दीनोपगतरक्षणम् ।
इति सङ्गः सतां साधु हितं सत्पुरुषव्रतम् ॥

३ आविष्ट इव दुःखेन तद्व्रतेन गरीयसा ।
समन्वितः करुणया परया दीनमुद्धरेत् ॥

४ न तेभ्योऽभ्यधिकाः सन्ति सन्तः सत्पुरुषव्रताः ।
दुःखपङ्कार्णवे मग्नं दीनमभ्युद्धरन्ति ये ॥

५ दयामास्थाय परमां धर्मादविचलन्नृपः ।
पीडितानामनाथानां कुर्यादश्रुप्रमार्जनम् ॥

६ आनृशंस्यं परो धर्मः सर्वप्राणभृतां मतः ।
तस्माद्राजानृशंस्येन पालयेत्कृपणं जनम् ॥

७ न हि स्वसुखमन्विच्छन्पीडयेत्कृपणं नृपः ।
कृपणः पीड्यमानो हि मन्युना हन्ति पार्थिवम् ॥

८ को हि नाम कुले जातः सुखलेशोपलोभितः ।
अल्पसाराणि भूतानि पीडयेदविचारयन् ॥

९ आधिव्याधिपरीताय अद्य श्वो वा विनाशिने ।
को हि नाम शरीराय धर्मापेतं समाचरेत् ॥

१० आहार्यैर्नीयमानं हि क्षणं दुःखेन हृद्यताम् ।
छायामात्रकमेवेदं पश्येदुदकबिन्दुवत् ॥

CHAPTER 3

Demarcating Good Conduct

The king should, like Yama the rod-bearing god of death, wield the rod over beings and, like lord Prajapati himself, gratify his subjects. The righteous and beneficial vow of good men consists of correct speech, compassion, charity, protection for the indigent and those seeking refuge, as well as association with good people.

One should uplift the indigent in a spirit of supreme compassion, as if overcome by heavy sorrow for them. There is no one greater than good men who follow the vow of good men and lift up poor people, sunk in the turbid ocean of sorrow. Practicing supreme compassion and unswerving dharma, the king should wipe away the tears of the helpless and afflicted.   5

Since benevolence is the supreme dharma for all who draw breath, the king should protect poor people in a spirit of benevolence. One should never hurt a poor person in the pursuit of pleasure. A poor person who is tormented will burn up the king with his anger. What man born in a decent family could be enticed by a trace of pleasure to heedlessly hurt poor people? Since the body is rent with mental and physical maladies, and destined for demise either today or tomorrow, who could act in a way that deviates from dharma simply for the pleasures of the body? One should regard the body—made attractive for just a moment through the painstaking application of various cosmetics—as a mere

११ महावाताहतिभ्रान्तमेघमालातिपेलवैः।
कथं नाम महात्मानो ह्रियन्ते विषयारिभिः॥

१२ जलान्तश्चन्द्रचपलं जीवितं खलु देहिनाम्।
तथाविधमिति ज्ञात्वा शश्वत्कल्याणमाचरेत्॥

१३ जगन्मृगतृषातुल्यं वीक्ष्येदं क्षणभङ्गुरम्।
सुजनैः सङ्गतिं कुर्याद्धर्माय च सुखाय च॥

१४ सेव्यमानस्तु सुजनैर्महानतिविराजते।२
सुधालिप्त इव श्रीमान्प्रासादश्चन्द्ररश्मिभिः॥

१५ हिमांशुमाली न तथा नोत्फुल्लकमलं सरः।
आनन्दयति चेतांसि यथा सज्जनचेष्टितम्॥

१६ ग्रीष्मसूर्यांशुसन्तप्तमुद्वेजनमनाश्रयम्।
मरुस्थलमिवोदग्रं त्यजेद्दुर्जनसंश्रयम्॥

१७ श्रुतशीलोपसम्पन्नमकस्मादेव दुर्जनः।३
अन्तः प्रविश्य दहति शुष्कवृक्षमिवानलः॥

१८ निःश्वासोद्दीर्णहुतभुग्धूमधूम्रीकृताननैः।
वरमाशीविषैः सङ्गं कुर्यान्न त्वेव दुर्जनैः॥

१९ दीयते स्वच्छहृदयैः पिण्डो येनैव पाणिना।४
मार्जार इव दुर्वृत्तस्तमेव हि विलुम्पति॥

२० असाध्यं साधुमन्त्राणां तीव्रं वाग्विषमुत्सृजत्।
द्विजिह्वं वदनं धत्ते दुष्टो दुर्जनपन्नगः॥

२१ क्रियते ऽभ्यर्हणीयाय सुजनाय यथाञ्जलिः।५
ततः साधुतरः कार्यो दुर्जनाय शिवार्थिना॥

simulacrum, like the moon's orb reflected in water. How is it 10
that great men are carried away by those enemies, the objects
of sensual enjoyment? They are as insubstantial as a row of
clouds scattered by a gust of strong wind.

Recognizing that the life of embodied beings is as unsteady
as the moon reflected in water, one should always do what
is good. Realizing that this world is comparable to a mirage
that vanishes in an instant, the king should keep company
with good people for the sake of both dharma and pleasure.
A great man shines greatly in the company of good people,
just as the top of a glorious white palace shines awash in the
moon's rays. Neither the moon garlanded with cool rays nor
a pond with lotuses in bloom delights people's hearts like the
conduct of a good man. 15

One should shun contact with wicked people, which is as
terrible and threatening as the shelterless desert scorched
by the rays of the summer sun. A wicked person will without
cause penetrate the heart and burn up a man of learning and
good conduct, as fire penetrates and burns a withered tree.
It would be better to mingle with snakes—whose breath is
fire and whose faces are ashy from its smoke—rather than
wicked people. A wicked person, like a cat, robs the very
hand the pure-hearted feed it with. A wicked, evil person has
a forked tongue, spitting out virulent speech-poison, which
cannot be counteracted even by powerful incantations.[1] Yet 20
to secure your own welfare it is even more prudent to cup
your hands in reverence and honor a wicked person than to
honor a good person worthy of respect.

One should speak ordinary language that is delightful to all
beings, with the intention of captivating all people, in order

२२ ह्लादिनीं सर्वसत्त्वानां सम्यग्गुनजिहीर्षया ।
भावयेत्परमां मैत्रीं विसृजेल्लौकिकीं गिरम् ॥

२३ नित्यं मनोऽपहारिण्या वाचा प्रह्लादयेज्जनम् ।
उद्वेजनीयो भवति क्रूरवागर्थदोऽपि सन् ॥

२४ हृदि विद्ध इवात्यर्थं यया सन्तप्यते जनः ।
पीडितोऽपि हि मेधावी न तां वाचमुदीरयेत् ॥

२५ तीव्राण्युद्वेगकारीणि विसृष्टान्यशमात्मकैः ।६
कृन्तन्ति देहिनां मर्म शस्त्राणीव वचांसि च ॥

२६ प्रियमेवाभिधातव्यं सत्सु नित्यं द्विषत्सु च ।
शिखीव केकामधुरः प्रियवाक्कस्य न प्रियः ॥

२७ अलङ्क्रियन्ते शिखिनः केकया मदरक्तया ।
वाचा विपश्चितोऽत्यर्थं माधुर्यगुणयुक्तया ॥

२८ मदरक्तस्य हंसस्य कोकिलस्य शिखण्डिनः ।
हरन्ति न तथा वाचो यथा साधु विपश्चितः ॥

२९ गुणानुरागी स्थितिमाञ्छ्रद्दधानो दयान्वितः ।
धनं धर्माय विसृजेत्प्रियां वाचमुदीरयन् ॥

३० ये प्रियाणि च भाषन्ते प्रयच्छन्ति च सत्कृतिम् ।
श्रीमन्तो वन्द्यचरणा देवास्ते नरविग्रहाः ॥७

३१ शुचिरास्तिक्यपूतात्मा पूजयेद्देवताः सदा ।
देवतावद्गुरुजनमात्मवच्च सुहृज्जनम् ॥

३२ प्रणिपातेन हि गुरून्सतोऽनूचानचेष्टितैः ।
कुर्वीताभिमुखान्भूत्यै देवान्सुकृतकर्मणा ॥

३३ सद्भावेन हरेन्मित्रं सम्भ्रमेण च बान्धवान् ।८
स्त्रीभृत्यान्प्रेमदानाभ्यां दाक्षिण्येनेतराञ्जनान् ॥

to produce supreme amity. One should always fill the world with joy through captivating speech. A person whose speech is cruel threatens all beings, even if he is generous with his wealth. A wise man, even when he has been hurt, should never utter speech that makes people suffer and feel as if they have been stabbed deep in the heart. Harsh, disturbing insults hurled by unquiet souls slash people in the vitals like knives. One should always use pleasing language with good people and enemies alike. To whom is a man of pleasing speech not pleasing, like the peacock with its sweet cry? 25

Peacocks are adorned by their lovely cry passionate with lust, and wise men are well adorned by speech full of sweetness. The cries of geese, cuckoos, or peacocks passionate with lust are nowhere near as captivating as the speech of wise men. Someone who loves virtue, who is trustworthy, faithful, and compassionate, should bestow wealth for the sake of dharma, but he should also speak pleasing words. Those who speak pleasing words and show respect are gods in human form, glorious ones whose feet should be worshiped. 30

Someone who is pure—whose inner being is purified by orthodox belief[2]—should always worship the gods. He should worship the guru as a god, and worship his friend as his very self. One should worship parents and teachers[3] with prostration, and men of learning with expressions of Vedic learning; and, for the sake of one's personal welfare, one should win the gods' favor by rituals properly performed.

One should win over friends by trustworthiness, kinsmen by zealous devotion, women by love, servants by gifts, and everyone else by courtesy. The conduct of good men consists

३४ अनिन्दा परकृत्येषु स्वधर्मपरिपालनम् ।
कृपणेषु दयालुत्वं सर्वत्र मधुरा गिरः ॥

३५ प्राणैरप्युपकारित्वं मित्रायाव्यभिचारिणे ।
गृहागते परिष्वङ्गः शक्त्या दानं सहिष्णुता ॥

३६ स्वसमृद्धिष्वनुत्सेकः परवृद्धिष्वमत्सरः ।
नान्योपतापि वचनं मौनव्रतचरिष्णुता ॥

३७ बन्धुभिर्बद्धसंयोगः सुजने चतुरश्रता ।९
तच्चित्तानुविधायित्वमिति वृत्तं महात्मनाम् ॥

३८ सनातने वर्त्मनि साधु तिष्ठतामयं हि पन्था गृहमेधिनां मतः ।
अनेन गच्छन्नियतं महात्मनामिमं च लोकं परमं च विन्दति ॥

३९ इति पथि विनिवेशितात्मनो रिपुरपि गच्छति साधु
        मित्रताम् ।
तदवनिपतिमत्सराद्वृते विनयगुणेन जगद्वशं नयेत् ॥

४० क्व च नरपतिगर्वः सङ्ग्रहः क्व प्रजानां मधुरवचनयोगाल्लोकम-
        भ्याददीत ।१०
मधुरवचनपाशैरायतालानितः सन्पदमपि हि न लोकः
        संस्थितेर्भेदमेति ॥११

of practicing one's own dharma without blame for others' deeds; compassion for the poor; perennially sweet speech; helping a constant friend even at the cost of one's own life; devotion to guests in one's home; charity and forbearance to the best of one's abilities; not being arrogant about one's own good fortune, and not resenting the good fortune of others; refraining from speech that is hurtful to others, and holding one's tongue when necessary; maintaining a close bond with relatives; square dealings with friends, and always satisfying their wishes. 35

This is the accepted way for men living in the world who are well-situated on the eternal path. Keeping constantly to this way of the great, one wins both this world and the supreme one beyond. 38

Even an enemy quickly becomes a friend for a king who follows the above-mentioned path. Rejecting the usual haughtiness of kings, he can bring the people under his sway. 39

How vast the gulf between the pride of kings and the winning over of subjects! Through the habit of sweet speech the king should delight the people. When they are tied up and bound fast in the snares of sweet speech, the people will not veer from the path of order even one step toward dissension. 40

प्रकृतिसम्पत्प्रकरणम्

१ स्वाम्यमात्यश्च राष्ट्रं च दुर्गं कोशो बलं सुहृत् ।
परस्परोपकारीदं सप्ताङ्गं राज्यमुच्यते ॥

२ एकाङ्गेनापि विकलमेतत्साधु न वर्तते ।
तस्य सामग्र्यमन्विच्छन्कुर्वीताशु परीक्षणम् ॥१

३ आत्मानमेव प्रथममिच्छेद्गुणसमन्वितम् ।
कुर्वीत गुणसम्पन्नस्ततः शेषपरीक्षणम् ॥

४ साधु भूतलदेवत्वं दुर्धार्यमकृतात्मभिः ।
आत्मसंस्कारसम्पन्नो राजा भवितुमर्हति ॥

५ लोकाधाराः श्रियो राज्ञां दुरापा दुष्परिग्रहाः ।
तिष्ठन्त्याप इवाधारे चिरमात्मनि संस्कृते ॥

६ कुलं सत्त्वं वयः शीलं दाक्षिण्यं क्षिप्रकारिता ।
अविसंवादिता सत्यं वृद्धसेवा कृतज्ञता ॥

७ दैवसम्पन्नता बुद्धिरक्षुद्रपरिवारता ।
शक्यसामन्तता चैव तथा च दृढभक्तिता ॥

८ दीर्घदर्शित्वमुत्साहः शुचिता स्थूललक्षता ।
विनीतता धार्मिकता गुणाः साध्वाभिगामिकाः ॥

९ गुणैरेतैरुपेतः सन्सुव्यक्तमभिगम्यते ।
तथा तु कुर्वीत यथा गच्छेल्लोकाभिगम्यताम् ॥

CHAPTER 4

The State-Elements

The kingdom is said to consist of seven mutually supporting limbs: ruler, minister, kingdom, fortification, treasury, army, and ally. When the kingdom is deficient in even one limb it does not function well. To ensure the kingdom's integrity, the king must immediately examine these elements. First and foremost he should strive to ensure that he himself is endowed with virtue. Once he is so endowed, he can conduct an examination of everything else.

The glorious status of being god-on-earth cannot be borne by anyone whose nature is unperfected. Only a king endowed with self-perfection is worthy of being king. A king's royal majesty, which sustains the people, is difficult to obtain and difficult to maintain. It can be long preserved only in a self that is perfected, just as drinking water—difficult to harvest and store properly—only stays fresh in a well-fired receptacle. 5

The virtues that make a good king worth approaching are noble birth, strength, youth, character, courtesy, decisiveness, consistency, truthfulness, service to elders, gratitude, good fortune, intellect, choosing a retinue of virtuous men, having powerful feudatories, firm devotion, farsightedness, determination, purity, generosity, self-mastery, and righteousness. People certainly take recourse to a king endowed with these virtues, and he should behave in such a way that people find him very approachable.

१० प्रख्यातवंशमक्रूरं लोकसङ्ग्राहिणं शुचिम् ।
    कुर्वीतात्महिताकाङ्क्षी परिवारं महीपतिः ॥

११ दुष्टोऽपि भोग्यतामेति परिवारगुणैर्नृपः ।
    न दुष्टपरिवारस्तु व्यालाक्रान्त इव द्रुमः ॥

१२ निरुन्धानाः सतां मार्गं भक्षयन्ति महीपतिम् ।
    दुष्टात्मानस्तु सचिवास्तस्मात्सुसचिवो भवेत् ॥

१३ विभूतीः परमाः प्राप्य सतां सम्भोग्यतामियात् ।
    यासु सन्तो न तिष्ठन्ति ता वृथैव विभूतयः ॥

१४ वाग्मी प्रगल्भः स्मृतिमानुदग्रो बलवान्वशी ।
    नेता दण्डस्य निपुणः कृतविद्यः सुविग्रहः ॥२

१५ पराभियोगप्रसहः सर्वदृष्टप्रतिक्रियः ।
    परच्छिद्रान्ववेक्षी च सन्धिविग्रहतत्त्ववित् ॥

१६ गूढमन्त्रप्रचारश्च देशकालविभागवित् ।
    आदाता सम्यगर्थानां विनियोक्ता च पात्रवित् ॥

१७ क्रोधलोभभयद्रोहस्तम्भचापलवर्जितः ।
    परोपतापपैशुन्यमात्सर्येर्ष्यानृतातिगः ॥

१८ वृद्धोपदेशसम्पन्नः श्लक्ष्णो मधुरदर्शनः ।३
    गुणानुरागी मितवागात्मसम्पत्प्रकीर्तिता ॥४

१९ इत्यादिगुणसम्पन्ने लोकयात्राविदि स्थिरे ।५
    निर्वृतः पितरीवास्ते यत्र लोकः स पार्थिवः ॥

२० आत्मसम्पद्गुणैः सम्यक्संयुक्तं युक्तकारिणम् ।
    महेन्द्रमिव राजानं प्राप्य लोको विवर्धते ॥

40

The king, in his own best interests, should establish a retinue made up of men of renowned lineage, who are not cruel, but rather, obliging to the people. Even a bad king becomes agreeable thanks to the virtues of his retinue. But if his retinue is bad, he is like a tree infested with snakes. Ministers with wicked souls block good men's access to the king, and they devour him. Therefore one must have good ministers. After acquiring the most magnificent riches, a king should seek to please good men. Riches have been acquired in vain when good men have no access to them.

The endowments of the self are as follows: being eloquent and mature; being knowledgeable, mighty, strong, self-composed; skillful in deploying the rod of punishment; learned; having a beautiful physique; being resilient when attacked; understanding all countermeasures; discerning others' weaknesses; knowing the essence of peace and war; concealing one's plans and maneuvers; knowing the distinctions of time and place; properly acquiring wealth, and gifting wealth to the appropriate recipients; being free from anger, greed, fear, rancor, inertia, and inconstancy; renouncing harm to others, as well as calumny, enmity, jealousy, and evil; receiving the counsel of wise elders; being gentle; having a charming countenance; being devoted to virtues, and measured in speech. When he is endowed with these and other qualities, firm, and fully aware of what holds the world on its course, the people feel satisfied with him as if with their own father. Only then is he a king.[1]

When the king acts properly and draws fully on the virtues that are the endowments of the self, the people prosper, as if they had the great god Indra himself as their ruler.

41

२१ शुश्रूषा श्रवणं चैव ग्रहणं धारणं तथा ।
ऊहापोहोऽर्थविज्ञानं तत्त्वज्ञानं च धीगुणाः ॥

२२ दाक्ष्यं शौघ्र्यं तथामर्षः शौर्यं चोत्साहलक्षणम् ।
गुणैरेतैरुपेतः सन्राजा भवितुमर्हति ॥

२३ त्यागः सत्यं च शौर्यं च त्रय एते महागुणाः ।
प्राप्नोति हि गुणान्सर्वानेतैर्युक्तो महीपतिः ॥

२४ कुलीनाः शुचयः शूराः श्रुतवन्तोऽनुरागिणः ।
दण्डनीतेः प्रयोक्तारः सचिवाः स्युर्महीपतेः ॥

२५ उपधाशोधिताः सम्यगीहमानाः फलोदयम् ।
ते ऽस्य सर्वं परीक्षेरन्सानुरागाः कृताकृतम् ॥

२६ उपेत्य धीयते यस्मादुपधेति ततः स्मृता ।
उपाय उपधा ज्ञेया तयामात्यान्परीक्षयेत् ॥

२७ स्ववग्रहो जानपदः कुलशीलबलान्वितः ।
वाग्मी प्रगल्भश्चक्षुष्मानुत्साही प्रतिपत्तिमान् ॥

२८ स्तम्भचापलहीनश्च मैत्रः क्लेशसहः शुचिः ।
सत्यसत्त्वधृतिस्थैर्यप्रभावारोग्यसंयुतः ॥

२९ कृतशिल्पश्च दक्षश्च प्रज्ञावान्धारणान्वितः ।
दृढभक्तिरकर्ता च वैराणां सचिवो भवेत् ॥

42

The virtues of the intellect are: willingness to listen; learning, comprehension, retention; positive and negative reasoning; understanding things; and knowing the truth. The signs of determination are: dexterity, swiftness, aggression, and heroism. A king endowed with these virtues is worthy of being king. The three great virtues are generosity, truth, and heroism. A king endowed with these three virtues attains all the others.

The king's ministers should be people of good lineage, pure, heroic, learned, devoted, and capable of governing. The ministers—who have been assessed through various tests, who fully strive after success, and who are devoted—should examine all the things the king should and should not do.   25

The word "test" is etymologically derived from the verb phrase "'placing near," since tests place ministers near the king.[2] Tests should be understood as a means whereby one may examine the ministers. A minister should be self-restrained; native to the region; endowed with lineage, character, and strength; eloquent, mature, insightful, determined, and resourceful. He should be free from inertia and inconstancy. He should be friendly, resilient in distress, pure, and endowed with truthfulness, fortitude, forbearance, stability, power, and health. He should be a master of the arts, dexterous, possessing a fine intellect and retentive mind—a man of firm devotion who does not provoke hostilities.

The endowments of counselors are said to be good memory, focus on the objective, capacity for deliberation, informed decisiveness, steadiness, and secrecy of strategy.

३० स्मृतिस्तत्परतार्थेषु वितर्को ज्ञाननिश्चयः ।
    दृढता मन्त्रगुप्तिश्च मन्त्रिसम्पत्प्रकीर्तिता ॥

३१ त्रय्यां च दण्डनीत्यां च कुशलः स्यात्पुरोहितः ।
    अथर्वविहितं नित्यं कुर्याच्छान्तिकपौष्टिकम् ॥

३२ साधु तेषाममात्यानां तद्विद्येभ्यश्च बुद्धिमान् ।
    चक्षुष्मत्तां च शिल्पं च परीक्षेत गुणद्वयम् ॥

३३ स्वजनेभ्यो विजानीयात्कुलं स्थानमवग्रहम् ।
    परिकर्मसु दाक्ष्यं च विज्ञानं धारयिष्णुताम् ॥६

३४ गुणत्रयं परीक्षेत प्रागल्भ्यं प्रतिभां तथा ।
    कथायोगेषु बुध्येत वाग्मित्वं सत्यवादिताम् ॥

३५ उत्साहं च प्रभावं च तथा क्लेशसहिष्णुताम् ।
    धृतिं चैवानुरागं च स्थैर्यं चापदि लक्षयेत् ॥

३६ भक्तिं मैत्रीं च शौचं च जानीयाद्व्यवहारतः ।
    संवासिभ्यो बलं सत्त्वमारोग्यं शीलमेव च ॥

३७ अस्तब्धतामचापल्यं वैराणां चाप्यकर्तृताम् ।
    प्रत्यक्षतो विजानीयाद्द्रुतां क्षुद्रतामपि ॥

३८ कर्माऽनुमेयाः सर्वत्र परोक्षगुणवृत्तयः ।
    तस्मात्परोक्षवृत्तीनां फलैः कर्म विभावयेत् ॥

३९ सज्जमानमकार्येषु निरुन्ध्युर्मन्त्रिणो नृपम् ।
    गुरूणामपि चैतेषां शृणुयात्नृपतिर्वचः ॥

The king's household priest should be versed in the three   30
Vedas as well as governance, and he should perform the
apotropaic and benedictory rites enjoined in the Atharva
Veda. A prudent king should thoroughly examine the ministers' two key virtues, namely their insightfulness and their
diligence, with the help of scholars erudite in each of their
respective fields. From their kinsmen, he should learn about
their family, social standing, and composure. He should
investigate these three traits: their skill in executing various projects, their scientific knowledge, and their organi-
zational skills, as well as their maturity and innate genius.
In conversation he should ascertain both their eloquence
and truthfulness.

He should observe if they have determination, power,
capacity to endure hardships, steadiness, devotion, and
stability even when faced with disaster.   35

The king should learn about a man's devotion, friend-
liness, and purity from his behavior. He should learn
about his strength, fortitude, health, and character from
the people who live with him. He should discern with
his own eyes his freedom from inertia and inconstancy,
and that he does not habitually provoke hostilities. One
must also discern with one's own eyes whether he is noble
or base. One can completely infer his private character
and habits on the basis of his actions. Conversely one can
infer his future actions based on the outcomes of his private
character and habits.

The counselors should restrain the king when he becomes
entangled in wrongful activities. The king should listen
to their words as to those of gurus. When the lord of men

४० नरेश्वरे जगत्सर्वं निमीलति निमीलति ।
सूर्योदय इवाम्भोजं तत्प्रबोधे प्रबुध्यते ॥

४१ तद्बोधयेज्जगन्नाथं संबुध्येत यथा तथा ।
धीसत्त्वोद्योगसम्पन्नैस्तत्कार्यं तदुपाश्रितैः ॥

४२ नृपस्य ते हि सुहृदस्त एव गुरवो मताः ।
य एनमुत्पथगतं वारयन्त्यनिवारिताः ॥

४३ सज्जमानमकार्येषु सुहृदो वारयन्ति ये ।
सत्यं न ते हि सुहृदो गुरवो गुरवो हि ते ॥

४४ कृतविद्योऽपि बलिना व्यक्तं रागेण रज्यते ।
रागोपरक्तचित्तः सन्किं न कुर्यादसाम्प्रतम् ॥

४५ पश्यन्नपि भवत्यन्धः पुमात्रागावृतेक्षणः ।
सुहृद्वैद्याश्चिकित्सन्ति निर्मलैर्विनयाञ्जनैः ॥

४६ रागमानमदान्धस्य स्खलतः पृथिवीपते ।[७]
हस्तावलम्बो भवति सुहृत्सचिवचेष्टितम् ॥

४७ मदोद्धतस्य नृपतेः सङ्कीर्णस्येव दन्तिनः ।[८]
गच्छन्त्यन्यायवृत्तस्य नेतारः खलु वाच्यताम् ॥

४८ भूगुणैर्वर्धते राष्ट्रं तद्वृद्धिर्नृपवृद्धये ।
तस्मादुणवतीं भूमिं भूत्यै नृपतिरावसेत् ॥

४९ सस्याकरवती पण्यखनिद्रव्यसमन्विता ।
गोहिता भूरिसलिला पुण्यैर्जनपदैर्वृता ॥

46

is diminished, the whole world is diminished; when he flourishes, the whole world flourishes, like the lotus when the sun rises.   40

Counselors who are wise, courageous, and energetic, who are devoted to their king, should alert him so that he remains aware of his duties. For they are the king's friends—indeed, they should be thought of as gurus—who restrain him unrestrainedly when he is set upon the wrong path. Those friends who stop him when he is intent upon wrongful activities— truly they are not just friends, but gurus.

Even someone accomplished in learning can become tinged by a powerful passion and find himself overcome by passion. And then what inappropriate deed might he not commit? Even though he can see, a man is blind when his eyes are clouded by passion. But his doctor-friends can cure him by applying the eye-drops of self-mastery. When the   45 king is stumbling—blinded by passion, pride, and intoxication—the good conduct of his minister-friends becomes his support. And when a king acts unlawfully, as wild as an elephant in rut, his advisors are the ones who end up being censured for misconduct.

The kingdom prospers through the good qualities of its land, and the kingdom's prosperity conduces to the king's prosperity. Therefore, for the sake of wealth, the king should settle in a land with good traits.[3]

Land is commendable for yielding wealth when it has good crops and gold mines, as well as when it is flush with the riches of markets and diamond mines; when it is suitable for cattle; has abundant water; and when it is surrounded by other good countries; when it has pleasant forests full of

५० रम्या सकुञ्जरवना वारिस्थलपथान्विता ।
अदेवमातृका चेति शस्यते भूर्विभूतये ॥

५१ सशर्करा सपाषाणा साटवी नित्यतस्करा ।
रूक्षा सकण्टकवना सव्याला चेति भूर्भूः ॥

५२ स्वाजीव्यो भूगुणैर्युक्तः सानूपः पर्वताश्रयः ।
शूद्रकारुवणिक्प्रायो महारम्भकृषीवलः ॥

५३ सानुरागो रिपुद्वेषी पीडाकरसहः पृथुः ।
नानादेशैयैः समाकीर्णो धार्मिकः पशुमान्धनी ॥

५४ ईदृग्जनपदः शस्तो ऽमूर्खव्यसनिनायकः ।
तं वर्धयेत्प्रयत्नेन तस्मात्सर्वं प्रवर्धते ॥९

५५ पृथुसीममहाखातमुच्चप्राकारगोपुरम् ।
समावसेत्पुरं शैलं सरिन्मरुवनाश्रयम् ॥

५६ जलवद्धान्यधनवद्दुर्गं कालसहं महत् ।
दुर्गहीनो नरपतिर्वाताभ्रावयवैः समः ॥

५७ औदकं पार्वतं वार्क्षमैरिणं धान्वनं तथा ।
शस्तं प्रशस्तमतिभिर्दुर्गं दुर्गोपचिन्तकैः ॥

५८ जलान्नायुधयन्त्राढ्यं धीरयोधैरधिष्ठितम् ।
गुप्तिप्रधानमाचार्या दुर्गं समनुमेनिरे ॥

५९ सापसराणि दुर्गाणि भुवः सानूपजाङ्गलाः ।
निवासाय प्रशस्यन्ते भूभुजां भूतिमिच्छताम् ॥

elephants; when it has both wetlands and dry ground; and when it is not without an irrigation system. Land should not 50 be considered land at all when it is full of gravel and stones, overly forested, infested with thieves, unpleasant, full of thorny thickets, and inhabited by tigers. A land is commendable when it has a good governor who is not stupid or prone to vice; when it is fit to live in; endowed with quality soil; when it has a natural water supply, and when it is situated at the base of a mountain; when it is full of Shudra workers, artisans, and merchants; when its farmers are industrious; when the people are devoted, hate their enemies, and can endure calamities; when it is extensive, and full of people from different regions; when it is righteous, full of good animals, and wealthy. One should take pains to make such a land prosper. When it prospers, everything will prosper.

One should build a fortified town on a hill or a river, in a desert area or a forest region.[4] It should have extensive grounds, large moats, as well as high ramparts and gateways. To be great and durable a fort needs water, grain, and wealth. 55 A king without a fort is like bits of cloud blown apart by the wind. Scholars who analyze forts praise five types: the water fort, the mountain fort, the tree fort, the wasteland fort, and the desert fort. The great teachers define a fort as a hidden location—rich in water, food, weapons, and mechanical devices—that is guarded by steadfast warriors. Forts with secure escape routes, and territories with both dry lands and wetlands, are commendable habitations for kings who desire prosperity.

Scholars knowledgeable about treasuries agree on the following:[5] that a treasury is good when it has substantial

६० बह्वादानोऽल्पनिःस्रावः ख्यातः पूजितदैवतः ।
ईप्सितद्रव्यसम्पन्नो हृद्यः स्वात्रैरधिष्ठितः ॥

६१ मुक्ताकनकरत्नाढ्यः पितृपैतामहोचितः ।
धर्मार्जितो व्ययसहः कोशः कोशज्ञसम्मतः ॥

६२ धर्महेतोस्तथार्थाय भृत्यानां भरणाय च ।
आपदर्थं च संरक्ष्यः कोशः कोशवता सदा ॥

६३ पितृपैतामहो वश्यः संहतो दत्तवेतनः ।
विख्यातपौरुषो जन्यः कुशलः कुशलैर्वृतः ॥१०

६४ नानाप्रहरणोपेतो नानायुद्धविशारदः ।
नानायोधसमाकीर्णो नीराजितहयद्विपः ॥

६५ प्रवासायासदुःखेषु युद्धेषु च कृतश्रमः ।
अद्वैध्यः क्षत्रियप्रायो दण्डो दण्डविदां मतः ॥

६६ त्यागविज्ञानसत्त्वाढ्यं महापक्षं प्रियंवदम् ।
आयतिक्षममद्वैध्यं मित्रं कुर्वीत सत्कुलम् ॥११

समुत्पन्नेषु कृच्छ्रेषु दारुणेष्वप्यसंशयम् ।

६८ पितृपैतामहं नित्यमद्वैध्यं हृदयानुगम् ।
महल्लघुसमुत्थानं मित्रं कार्यार्थमिष्यते ॥१२

deposits and limited outlays; when it is famed for its riches, and when it is employed in the gods' worship; when it is well stocked with desirable forms of wealth like precious metals and jewels, and when it is guarded by congenial and trustworthy men; when it is rich in pearls, gold, and jewels—either inherited from ancestors or else rightfully acquired—and finally, when it can bear expenses. Someone in possession of a treasury must always keep it safe, since it is necessary for supporting the servants, and in case of any potential disaster. It is also necessary for the purposes of dharma and power. 60

Those knowledgeable about the rod of coercion consider that it consists of: an army that is coordinated and obedient, with a hereditary allegiance to the king and good morale; which receives its wages regularly, is composed of local natives, and whose valor is famed; which is skillful, and guarded by skillful soldiers. It should be made up mostly of Kshatriyas who are not duplicitous, who are battle-hardened and inured to the hardships of expedition and exertion. It should have its horses and elephants ritually lustrated, and it should be full of various types of warriors, endowed with various types of weapons, and skilled in various forms of warfare. 65

One should make an ally of someone of good family, endowed with generosity, learning, and fortitude; whose family network is large; who is well-spoken; who is capable of being an ally for the long term; and who is not duplicitous. The noble, pure-hearted ally should demonstrate his integrity without doubt even when horrible calamities arise. In forging an alliance, one should seek this sort of great,

६९ दूरादेवाभिगमनं स्पष्टार्था हृदयानुगा ।
वाक्सत्कृत्य प्रदानं च त्रिविधो मित्रसंग्रहः ॥

७० धर्मकामार्थसंयोगो मित्रात्तु त्रिविधं फलम् ।
यस्मादेतत्त्रयं नास्ति तत्सेवेत न पण्डितः ॥

७१ आदौ तन्व्यो बृहन्मध्या विस्तारिण्यः पदे पदे ।
यायिन्यो न निवर्तिन्यः सतां मैत्र्यः सरित्समाः ॥१३

७२ औरसं मैत्रसम्बद्धं तथा वंशक्रमागतम् ।१४
रक्षितं व्यसनेभ्यश्च मित्रं ज्ञेयं चतुर्विधम् ॥

७३ शुचिता त्यागिता शौर्यं समानसुखदुःखता ।
अनुरागश्च दाक्ष्यं च सत्यता च सुहृद्गुणाः ॥

७४ तदर्थेहानुरागश्च सङ्क्षिप्तं मित्रलक्षणम् ।
यस्मिन्नैतन्न तन्मित्रं तत्रात्मानं न निक्षिपेत् ॥

७५ इति स्म राज्यं सकलं समीरितं परा प्रतिष्ठास्य धनं ससाधनम् ।१५
गृहीतमेतन्निपुणेन मन्त्रिणा त्रिवर्गनिष्पत्तिमुपैति शाश्वतीम् ॥

७६ यथान्तरात्मा प्रकृतीरधिष्ठितश्वराचरं विश्वमिदं समश्नुते ।
तथा नरेन्द्रः प्रकृतीरधिष्ठितश्वराचरं विश्वमिदं समश्नुते ॥

constant ally of hereditary allegiance, who is not duplicitous, who complies with one's wishes, and who is quick to initiate action.

There are three ways of securing an ally: by rising to approach him when he is still at a distance; through speech that is heartfelt and of clear import; and by honoring him with gifts. The benefit of gaining an ally is likewise threefold: attainment of dharma, power, and pleasure—a wise man should not make an ally of someone who cannot offer these three.   70

The friendship of good people is like a river: small at the beginning, big in the middle, and growing with each step—it flows forth and never turns back.

An ally is known to be of four types: a family member; a relationship one has forged; someone from one's broader kin-network; and someone who has been rescued from danger. The virtues of a friend are seven: purity, generosity, heroism, equanimity in joy and sorrow, devotion, dexterity in action, and truthfulness. The fundamental sign of a friend is devotion to a common purpose. If this quality is absent in someone, then he is not a friend, and one should not get involved with him.

Thus we have delineated the entire kingdom. Its ultimate foundation is wealth and the military. If a skillful counselor oversees it, then one attains the eternal prosperity of the three aims of life: dharma, power, and pleasure. Just 75 as the inner self abides in the realm of nature and pervades the entire universe of animate and inanimate beings, so a king presides over all the state-elements and enjoys the entire universe with its animate and inanimate beings.   76

७७ प्रकृतिभिरिति सम्यगन्वितो जनपदमादरवांस्तु पालयेत्।१६
जनपदपरिपालनाच्चिरं व्रजति नृपः परमं श्रियः पदम्॥

७८ प्रकृतिगुणसमन्वितः सुधीर्व्रजति नृपः स्पृहणीयतां पराम्।
स च भवति रणेषु विद्विषां श्वसन इव प्रबलः पयोमुचाम्॥

Well-equipped with his state-elements, the king should protect the land with care. By protecting the land, he attains the supreme state of majesty forever. 77

The intelligent king, endowed with strong state-elements, is supremely enviable. In battles with his enemies, he is like a powerful wind to a cluster of clouds, scattering them and breaking them apart. 78

पञ्चमः सर्गः

स्वाम्यनुजीविवृत्तप्रकरणम्

१ वृत्तस्थं वृत्तसम्पन्नाः कल्पवृक्षोपमं नृपम् ।
   अभिगम्यगुणैर्युक्तं सेवेरन्ननुजीविनः ॥

२ द्रव्यप्रकृतिहीनोऽपि सेव्यः सेव्यगुणान्वितः ।
   भवत्याजीवनं तस्माच्छ्लाग्यं कालान्तरादपि ॥

३ अपि स्थाणुवदासीत शुष्यन्परिगतः क्षुधा ।
   न त्वेवानात्मसम्पन्नाद्वृत्तिमीहेत पण्डितः ॥

४ अनात्मवान्नयद्वेषी वर्धयन्नरिसम्पदः ।
   प्राप्यापि महदैश्वर्यं सह तेन विनश्यति ॥

५ लब्धावकाशो निपुण आत्मवत्यविकारवान् ।
   स्थाने स्थैर्यमवाप्नोति मन्त्री कर्मसु निश्चितः ॥१

६ आयत्यां च तदात्वे च यत्स्यादास्वादपेशलम् ।
   तत्क्लिश्यन्नपि कुर्वीत न लोकद्विष्टमाचरेत् ॥२

७ तिलाश्चम्पकसंश्लेषात्प्राप्नुवन्त्यधिवासनाम् ।
   रसोनभक्षास्तद्गन्धाः सर्वे साङ्क्रमिका गुणाः ॥३

८ अपां प्रवाहो गाङ्गोऽपि समुद्रं प्राप्य तद्रसः ।
   भवत्यपेयस्तद्विद्वान्नाश्रयेदशुभात्मकम् ॥४

56

CHAPTER 5

The Conduct of the King and His Retinue

Retainers devoted to their duties should approach and seek service with a king who is virtuous, devoted to his duties, and generous like a wish-granting tree.[1] A king may be served—even if he lacks wealth and the state-elements—if he is endowed with virtues making him worthy. For a respectable living can still come from him, even if it takes some time. A wise man would rather sit in isolation, afflicted with hunger, and wither like a tree stump, than seek his livelihood from a king devoid of virtues and self-mastery. A king who is not self-composed, and who is averse to sound policy, augments his enemy's prosperity. Even if he attains great lordship, he will eventually be destroyed along with it.

A skillful counselor who is unwavering in his service to a self-composed king, attains security in that position if he is decisive in his actions. Even if he suffers for it, he should do what is tasteful in both the present and the future: he should not do anything which people dislike. Sesame acquires great fragrance by rubbing up against champak flowers, and people who eat garlic smell like garlic—all qualities are contagious. Even when the river Ganges meets the sea, her water becomes undrinkable. Considering this a wise man should never associate with a base soul.

९ क्रिश्यन्नपि हि मेधावी शुद्धं जीवनमाचरेत् ।
   तेनेह श्लाघ्यतामेति लोकेभ्यश्च न हीयते ॥

१० अभिलक्ष्यं स्थिरं पुण्यं ख्यातं सिद्धैर्निषेवितम् ।५ ६
    सेवेत सिद्धिमन्विच्छञ्छ्लाघ्यं विन्ध्यमिवेश्वरम् ॥

११ दुरापमपि लोकेऽस्मिन्यद्यद्वस्त्वभिवाञ्छति ।
    तत्तदाप्नोति मेधावी तस्मात्कार्यः समुद्यमः ॥

१२ आरिराधयिषुः सम्यगनुजीवी महीपतिम् ।
    विद्याविनयशिल्पाद्यैरात्मानमुपपादयेत् ॥

१३ कुलविद्याश्रुतौदार्यशिल्पविक्रमधैर्यवान् ।
    वपुःसत्त्वबलारोग्यस्थैर्यशौचदयान्वितः ॥

१४ पैशुन्यद्रोहसम्भेदशाठ्यलौल्यानृतातिगः ।
    स्तम्भचापलहीनश्च सेवनं कर्तुमर्हति ॥

१५ दक्षता भद्रता दार्ढ्यं क्षान्तिः क्लेशसहिष्णुता ।
    सन्तोषः शीलमुत्साहो मण्डयन्त्यनुजीविनम् ॥

१६ अर्थशौचपरो नित्यं गुणैरेभिः समन्वितः ।
    भूतये भूतिसम्पन्नं साधु विश्वासयेन्नृपम् ॥

१७ प्रविष्टः सम्यगुचिते स्थाने तिष्ठन्सुवेषवान् ।
    यथाकालमुपासीत राजानं विनयान्वितः ॥

१८ परस्थानासनं क्रौर्यमौद्धत्यं मत्सरं त्यजेत् ।
    विगृह्य कथनं चापि न कुर्याज्ज्यायसा सह ॥

Even if he suffers for it, a wise man should lead a pure life; thereby he becomes praiseworthy and never falls from grace in the world's eyes. Someone who seeks success should serve a lord towering in his majesty, solid, pure, famous, and a refuge of sages—the very image of Mount Vindhya.   10

A wise man can get whatever he desires in this world, even if it is difficult to obtain. Therefore he should make an effort. A good retainer should long to win over the king, and he should cultivate learning, self-mastery, diligence, and the like.

Someone endowed with noble birth, intelligence, learning, magnanimity, diligence, valor, and steadiness is a man worthy of performing service. He should also have a good physique, fortitude, strength, health, stability, purity, and compassion. He should be free of calumny, dissension, disloyalty, trickery, dissipation, and should not give in to evil. Finally, he must be devoid of inertia and inconstancy.

Dexterity in action, amiability, tenacity, tranquility, resilience in distress, self-satisfaction, good character, and determination are the virtues that ornament a king's retainer.   15
A good retainer—whose total integrity in money matters has been proven, and who is ever endowed with the above-mentioned virtues—should strive to win the confidence of a rich king in order to obtain riches.

Granted formal entry, wearing fine attire, and standing in his proper place, a self-composed retainer should attend upon the king at the appropriate time. He must never stand or sit at another's place. He should renounce cruelty, arrogance, and jealousy. He should never argue with his seniors. He should reject deceit, deception, fraud, and

१९ विप्रलम्भं च मायां च दम्भं स्तेयं च वर्जयेत् ।
पुत्रेभ्यश्च नमस्कुर्याद्वृद्धेभ्यश्च भूपतेः ॥

२० न नर्मसचिवैः सार्धं किञ्चिदप्यप्रियं वदेत् ।
ते हि मर्मण्यभिघ्नन्ति प्रहासेनैव संसदि ॥

२१ भर्तुरन्वासने तिष्ठन्दृष्टिं नान्यत्र निक्षिपेत् ।[७]
ब्रूयान्न किञ्चिदन्योन्यं तिष्ठेच्चास्यं विलोकयन् ॥[८]

२२ कोऽत्रेत्यहमिति ब्रूयात्सम्यगाज्ञापयेति च ।
आज्ञां चावितथां कुर्याद्यथाशक्त्यविलम्बितम् ॥

२३ उच्चैःप्रकथनं कासं छ्रीवनं कुत्सितं तथा ।[९]
जृम्भणं गात्रभङ्गं च पर्वस्फोटं च वर्जयेत् ॥

२४ प्रविश्य चानुरागेण चित्तं चित्तज्ञसम्मतः ।
समर्थयंश्च तत्पक्षं साधु भाषेत भाषितम् ॥[१०]

२५ तन्नियोगेन वा ब्रूयादर्थं सुपरिनिश्चितम् ।
सुखप्रबन्धगोष्ठीषु विवादे वादिनां मतम् ॥[११]

२६ विजानन्नपि न ब्रूयाद्धर्तुः क्षिप्तोत्तरं वचः ।
प्रवीणोऽपि हि मेधावी वर्जयेदभिमानिताम् ॥

२७ यदप्युच्चैर्विजानीयात्रीचैस्तदपि कीर्तयेत् ।
कर्मणा तस्य वैशिष्ट्यं कथयेद्विनयान्वितः ॥

thievery. He should also make obeisance to the king's sons and close friends.

He should never say anything unpleasant to the king's pleasure companions, since in the court they can mortally wound you with their sarcasm. When attending upon his lord, the retainer should not cast his gaze in any other direction or say anything to anyone else. He should stand there looking at the king's face to anticipate whatever he might say. Whenever the lord says, "Who's there?" the retainer should reply, "It is I, command me as you please." He should carry out orders efficaciously and as promptly as his abilities permit. He should refrain from talking loudly, coughing, spitting, cursing, yawning, and cracking his knuckles or joints.

He should loyally seek to fathom his lord's heart, and have his understanding confirmed by other attendants who know his heart. When he speaks, he should speak well, supporting his lord's position. When asked by the lord to give his opinion, during one of his pleasure assemblies, he should say something thoroughly reasoned. If questioned on a matter of debate, he should say something which is given credence by his fellow interlocutors.

Even if he knows better, he should not reply in a haughty manner. And even if he is very experienced, he would be wise to show no arrogance. Even if his knowledge is grand, he should reveal it humbly. A self-composed man lets his actions reveal his talent.

When there is an emergency, or when the lord deviates from the accepted path in his deeds, or when there has been an unacceptable delay in an undertaking, the retainer, seek-

२८ आपद्युन्मार्गगमने कार्यकालात्ययेषु च ।
अपृष्टोऽपि हितान्वेषी ब्रूयात्कल्याणभाषितम् ॥

२९ प्रियं तथ्यं च पथ्यं च वदेद्धर्मार्थमेव च ।
अश्रद्धेयमसभ्यं च परोक्षं कटु चोत्सृजेत् ॥१२

३० परार्थं देशकालज्ञो देशे काले च साधयेत् ।
स्वार्थं च स्वार्थकुशलः कुशलेनार्थकारिणा ॥१३

३१ गुह्यकर्म च मन्त्रं च न भर्तुः सम्प्रकाशयेत् ।
विद्विष्टिं च विनाशं च मनसापि न चिन्तयेत् ॥१४

३२ स्त्रीभिस्तद्दर्शिभिः पापैर्वैरिदूतैर्निराकृतैः ।
एकार्थचर्यासङ्घातं संसर्गं च विवर्जयेत् ॥

३३ वेषभाषानुकरणं न कुर्यात्पृथिवीपतेः ।
सम्पन्नोऽपि हि मेधावी स्पर्धते न च तद्गुणैः ॥

३४ रागापरागौ जानीयाद्भर्तुः कुशलकर्मकृत् ।
इङ्गिताकारलिङ्गाभ्यामिङ्गिताकारतत्त्वावित् ॥

३५ दृष्ट्वा प्रसन्नो भवति वाक्यं गृह्णाति चादरात् ।
दिशत्यासनमभ्याशे कुशलं परिपृच्छति ॥

३६ विविक्तदर्शने स्थाने रहस्ये च न शङ्कते ।
तदर्थां तत्कृतां चोच्चैराकर्णयति संकथाम् ॥

३७ श्लाघते श्लाघनीयेषु श्लाघ्यमानं च नन्दति ।
कथान्तरेषु स्मरति प्रहृष्टः कीर्तयेद्गुणान् ॥

ing his lord's benefit, should give him sage advice, even when it is unsolicited. What he says should be pleasing, beneficial, true, and in the interests of dharma; eschewing anything implausible, uncourtly, bitter, or unsubstantiated. Being sensitive to time and place, he should promote other people's interests only at the proper time and place. Also clever about his own interests, he should promote them too, through the services of a skillful helper.   30

He should never reveal his lord's secret actions or plans. He should never even think of harboring malice toward him, let along injuring him. He should reject working together with, or even meeting with, the women of the harem, their supervisors, criminals, enemy emissaries, or those who have been banished. He should never imitate the king's clothing or speech: a wise man never competes with the king's virtues, even if he is so endowed. He should be skillful in grasping the king's pleasure and displeasure, inferring them from his gestures and facial expressions, being fully knowledgeable in both.

When the king is pleased with his retainer, he is happy to see him. He accepts what he says respectfully, offers him a seat close by, and asks after his well-being. He does not fear   35 meeting with him in private or on some secret matter, and listens intently to his own conversation as well as to conversations regarding him. He praises those of his deeds that are praiseworthy and is glad when others praise him. He calls him to mind in conversations on other topics and is delighted to glorify his virtues. He tolerates the retainer's salutary advice and does not approve when people reproach him. Rather he carries out what his retainer says and holds

३८ सहते पथ्यमुक्तः सन्न निन्दामनुमन्यते ।
करोति वाक्यं तत्प्रोक्तं तद्वचो बहु मन्यते ॥१५

३९ वृद्धौ प्रसन्नो भवति व्यसने परितप्यते ।
उपकारेषु माध्यस्थ्यं दर्शयत्यद्भुतेषु च ॥

४० तत्कृतं कर्म चान्येन कृतमित्यभिभाषते ।
विपक्षमुत्थापयति विनाशं चाप्युपेक्षते ॥

४१ कार्ये संवर्धयत्याशां फले च कुरुतेऽन्यथा ।
यद्वाक्यं मधुरं किञ्चित्तदप्यर्थेन निष्ठुरम् ॥

४२ आचरत्यात्मशंसासु परिवादं च केवलम् ।१६
अकोपोऽपि सकोपाभः प्रसन्नश्चापि निष्फलः ॥

४३ हसत्यकस्माद्व्रजति रूक्षं च समुदीक्षते ।१७
विज्ञाप्यमानो वृत्त्यर्थं सहसोत्थाय गच्छति ॥

४४ आघट्टयति मन्त्राणि ब्रुवन्हासं प्रपद्यते ।१८
सम्भावयति दोषेण वृत्तिच्छेदं करोति च ॥

४५ साधूक्तमपि तद्वाक्यं समर्थयति चान्यथा ।
अपर्वणि कथाभङ्गं करोति विरसीभवन् ॥

४६ उपास्यमानः शयने सुप्तलक्षेण तिष्ठति ।
यत्नेनाराध्यमानो ऽपि सुप्तवच्च विचेष्टते ॥१९

४७ इत्यादि ह्यनुरक्तस्य विरक्तस्य च लक्षणम् ।
रक्ताद्वृत्तिं समीहेत विरक्तं च परित्यजेत् ॥

४८ निर्गुणं ह्यापि भर्तारमापत्सु न परित्यजेत् ।
ततः परतरो नास्ति य आपत्सूपतिष्ठते ॥

४९ स्वस्थवृत्तेषु सत्त्वाढ्या नोपयान्त्यभिलक्ष्यताम् ।
विरोधे कर्मधुर्याणां तेषां नामातिरिच्यते ॥२०

his words in high esteem. He feels pleasure at his success and pain when he suffers.

When the lord is displeased, however, he shows indifference to previous favors, even extraordinary ones, and attributes the retainer's achievements to others. He quietly ignores his ruin and uplifts his rivals.[2] He fans 40 his hopes for reward, but dismisses his work's results and offers no reward. Whatever the king says, however sweet, has a cruel implication. Even when the retainer eulogizes him, the king only responds by reviling him. Even when the king is not angry, he feigns anger, and even when he is pleased, he offers no reward. He laughs for no reason and storms off, all the while glaring with malice. When asked to pay wages, he abruptly rises and leaves. He rebuts his counsel, cackles when he speaks, imputes faults, and cuts off his salary. He takes even his salutary speech the wrong way, gets annoyed, and cuts him off mid-sentence. When the king is 45 displeased he lies on his bed and pretends to be asleep. Even when people try hard to wake him, he still pretends to be asleep.

The foregoing are the signs of contented and discontented kings. One should try to work for a regularly contented king, and avoid the discontented.

One should never abandon a king in calamity even if he lacks all virtue. There is no one better than someone who stands by his king in calamity. In good times, those rich in fortitude receive no recognition. It is only in adversity that the names of those who hold true to their duties are remembered. An act of service to a great man is always praiseworthy and a matter for rejoicing. In time even a very

५० श्लाघ्या चानन्दनी चैव महतामुपकारिता ।
काले कल्याणमाधत्ते स्वल्पापि सुमहोदयम् ॥

५१ अकार्यात्प्रतिषेधश्च कार्ये चैवानुवर्तनम् ।
सङ्क्षेपादिति सद्वृत्तं बन्धुमित्रानुजीविनाम् ॥

५२ पानस्त्रीद्यूतगोष्ठीषु राजानमभितश्चराः ।
बोधयेयुः प्रमाद्यन्तमुपायैर्नालिकादिभिः ॥

५३ राजानं ये ह्युपेक्षन्ते सज्जमानं विकर्मसु ।
ते गच्छन्त्यकृतात्मानः सह तेन पराभवम् ॥

५४ जयाज्ञापय देवेति नाथ जीवेति चादरात् ।
आज्ञामस्य प्रतीच्छन्तो भृत्याः कुर्युरुपासनम् ॥

५५ भर्तुश्चित्तानुवर्तित्वं सद्वृत्तमनुजीविनाम् ।
रक्षांस्यपि हि गृह्यन्ते नित्यं छन्दानुवर्तिभिः ॥

५६ धीसत्त्वोद्योगयुक्तानां किं दुरापं महात्मनाम् ।
छन्दानुवर्तिनां लोके कः परः प्रियवादिनाम् ॥

५७ अलसस्याल्पतोषस्य निर्विद्यस्याकृतात्मनः ।²¹
प्रदानकाले भवति मातापि हि पराङ्मुखी ॥

५८ ये शूरा ये च विद्वांसो ये च सेवाविपश्चितः ।
तेषामेव विकासिन्यो भोग्या नृपतिसम्पदः ॥

५९ अप्रियोऽपि हि पथ्यः स्यादिति वृद्धानुशासनम् ।
वृद्धानुशासने तिष्ठन्नियतामुपगच्छति ॥

६० आजीव्यः सर्वभूतानां राजा पर्जन्यवद्भवेत् ।
निराजीव्यं त्यजन्त्येनं शुष्कं सर इवाण्डजाः ॥²²

small act of service can bring blessings and great rewards. In brief, proper conduct for the king's kinsmen, friends, and retainers consists of dissuading him from wrongful actions and encouraging him toward right ones. 50

His intimates should try to enlighten, through insinuation and similar methods, a king who is given over to parties with wine, women, and gambling. Unrefined souls who overly indulge a king prone to wrongful actions end up being defeated along with their lord.

His retainers should address him affectionately as "god" or "lord," with greetings such as "victory to the king" and "long life to the king." They should mind his orders and attend upon him. Obedience to the lord's will is the proper conduct for retainers, for even demons are won over by people eternally obedient to their will. What is difficult to attain for great men endowed with intellect, fortitude, and effort? Who is better in this world than people who speak pleasing words and obey one's will? When it is time to bestow rewards, even a mother turns her back on someone who is lazy, unambitious, ignorant, and unrefined. 55

Heroes, scholars, and men keen in their service alone enjoy the king's resplendent treasures. It is the elders' injunction that someone who is out of favor should still try to be of benefit to the king. Continually following the elders' injunction, he will eventually come into favor.

Like the rain cloud, the king is the wellspring of life for all beings on earth. The people abandon a king who is not a source of livelihood, just as birds abandon a dried-up lake. Lineage, conduct, learning, and heroism—none of these count. The people love a king, even if his conduct is poor 60

६१ कुलं वृत्तं श्रुतं शौर्यं सर्वमेतन्न गण्यते ।
दुर्वृत्ते ऽप्यकुलीने ऽपि जनो दातरि रज्यते ॥२३

६२ लक्ष्मीरेवान्वयो लोके न लक्ष्याः परतो ऽन्वयः ।
यस्मिन्कोशो बलं चैव तस्मिँल्लोको ऽनुगच्छति ॥२४

६३ उत्थिता एव पूज्यन्ते जना कार्यार्थिभिनरैः ।
शत्रुवत्पतितं को नु वन्दते मानवं पुनः ॥२५

६४ अर्थार्थी जीवलोको ऽयं ज्वलन्तमुपसर्पति ।
क्षीणक्षीरां निराजीव्यां वत्सस्त्यजति मातरम् ॥

६५ अहापयन्नृपः कालं भृत्यानामनुवर्तिनाम् ।
कर्मणामानुरूप्येण वृत्तिं समनुकल्पयेत् ॥

६६ काले स्थाने च पात्रे च न हि वृत्तिं विलोपयेत् ।
एतद्वृत्तिविलोपेन राजा भवति गर्हितः ॥

६७ अपात्रवर्षणं जातु न कुर्यात्सद्भिगर्हितम् ।
अपात्रवर्षणात्किं स्यादन्यत्कोशक्षयाद्दते ॥

६८ कुलं विद्यां श्रुतं शौर्यं सौशील्यं भूतपूर्वताम् ।
वयोऽवस्थां च संवीक्ष्य स्वाद्रियेत महामनाः ॥

६९ कुलीनान्नावमन्येत सम्यग्वृत्तान्मनस्विनः ।
त्यजन्त्येते हि भर्तारं घ्नन्ति वा मानहेतवः ॥२६

७० गुणैरुदारैः संयुक्तान्रोन्नयेन्मध्यमाधमान् ।
महत्तां प्राप्नुवन्तस्ते वर्धयन्ति नरेश्वरम् ॥

७१ उत्तमाभिजनोपेतान्न नीचैः सह वर्धयेत् ।
कृशोऽपि हि विवेकज्ञो याति संश्रयणीयताम् ॥

७२ निरालोके हि लोकेऽस्मिन्नासते तत्र पण्डिताः ।
जात्यस्य हि मणेर्यत्र काचेन समता मता ॥

and he has no lineage, so long as he lavishes wealth. Riches count as lineage in this world; there is no better lineage than wealth. The people love a king who has a treasury and an army. Men seeking reward for their works only honor the exalted. Who will praise a man who has fallen low like an enemy fallen in battle? People seeking wealth in this world only approach a radiant leader. Even a calf abandons its mother when her breast milk has dried up.

The king should offer remuneration without delay to his servants and retainers according to their duties. The remu- 65
neration he offers should be in no way deficient, and should be in accordance with time, place, and recipient. A king is reviled when his payment is deficient.

He should never lavish rewards on unworthy recipients, a practice good men revile. What will come about from lavishing riches on unworthy recipients, other than destruction of the treasury? The magnanimous king should honor a person only after examining his lineage, wisdom, learning, heroism, good character, seniority, age, and circumstances.

He should never disrespect wise men of good conduct and lineage because such people will abandon him, or else kill him out of wounded pride. The king should promote middle- and lower-level men in service who are endowed with noble virtues, because when they achieve great status, they will help the lord of men to prosper. Yet he should not 70
promote the lowly alongside those endowed with the highest nobility of stature. The people take to a king who appreciates distinctions, even if he has meager resources. Learned men refuse to abide in a world of darkness where precious jewels and glass are considered equal.

७३ विश्राम्यन्ति महात्मानो यत्र कल्पतराविव ।
स श्लाघ्यो भवति श्रीमान्सत्सम्भोगफलाः श्रियः ॥

७४ लक्ष्म्या लक्ष्मीवतां लोके विकासिन्यापि किं तया ।
बन्धुभिश्च सुहृद्भिश्च विसब्धं या न भुज्यते ॥

७५ आयद्वारेषु सर्वेषु कुर्यादाप्तान्परीक्षितान् ।
आददीत धनं तैस्तु भास्वानसूरैरिवोदकम् ॥

७६ अभ्यस्तकर्मणस्तज्ज्ञाञ्छुचीञ्छुद्धार्थसङ्गतान् ।
कुर्यादुद्योगसम्पन्नानध्यक्षान्सर्वकर्मसु ॥

७७ यो यद्वस्तु विजानाति तं तत्र विनियोजयेत् ।
अशेषविषयप्राप्ताविन्द्रियार्थेष्विवेन्द्रियम् ॥

७८ कोष्ठागारेऽभियुक्तः स्यात्तदायत्तं हि जीवितम् ।
नात्यायं च व्ययं कुर्यात्प्रत्यवेक्षेत चान्वहम् ॥

७९ कृषिर्वणिक्पथो दुर्गं सेतुः कुञ्जरबन्धनम् ।
खन्याकरो वनादानं शून्यानां च निवेशनम् ॥

८० अष्टवर्गमिमं साधु स्वस्थवृत्तं विवर्धयेत् ।
जीवनार्थमिहाजीव्यैः कारयेत्करणान्वितैः ॥

८१ यया ययेह वर्धेत वृत्त्या क्षीणोऽपि पार्थिवः ।
तस्यां तस्यां न संरोधं कुर्यात्पण्योपजीविनाम् ॥

८२ यथारक्षेच्च निपुणं सस्यं कण्टकिशाखया ।
फलाय लगुडः कार्यस्तद्वद्रोग्यमिदं जगत् ॥२७

70

They praise a majestic king in whose company great men rest at ease as if in the shade of a wish-granting tree. The fruit of royal majesty is truly meant to be enjoyed by the good. In this world the extensive riches of the wealthy are pointless unless fully enjoyed by friends, allies, and kinsmen. The king should appoint trusted and tested officials in financial offices, and then extract taxes by means of them the way the sun extracts water by its rays.   75

He should appoint energetic officials to each office, who are experienced in their jobs and knowledgeable about them, who are deemed pure, and who have the right objectives. He should appoint someone to a specific office who knows that specific field, just as in grasping the spectrum of sensory objects specific senses are required for specific objects.

He should be attentive to the state's granary, since life depends on it. He should neither waste nor exhaust the grain and should inspect the granary each and every day.

These are the eight spheres of life where the king must foster prosperity: agriculture; trade routes; fortifications; bridges; enclosures for the elephants; mines; cultivation of forest and jungle areas; and settling uninhabited areas. He should appoint officials with these eight specific under-takings designated as their livelihoods, men who will make them flourish and foster the common livelihood. However 80
the king becomes prosperous, he should do it in such a way—even if times are lean—that he never stifles the merchants.

Just as a farmer skillfully protects his crops by planting thorny bushes around them and wields a cudgel to protect his fruits from thieves and animals, so must the king main-tain and enjoy the earth. The subjects face danger from five

८३ आयुक्तकेभ्यश्चोरेभ्यः परेभ्यो राजवल्लभात् ।
पृथिवीपतिलोभाच्च प्रजानां पञ्चधा भयम् ॥

८४ पञ्चप्रकारमप्येतदपोह्य नृपतिर्भयम् ।
आददीत फलं काले त्रिवर्गपरिवृद्धये ॥

८५ यथा गौः पाल्यते काले दुह्यते च तथा प्रजा ।
सिच्यते चीयते चैव लता पुष्पप्रदा यथा ॥२८

८६ आस्रावयेदुपचितान्साधु दुष्टव्रणानिव ।
आयुक्तास्ते च वर्तेरन्नग्रामिव महीपतौ ॥

८७ स्वल्पमप्यपकुर्वन्ति ये पापाः पृथिवीपतौ ।
ते वह्नाविव दह्यन्ते पतङ्गा मूढचेतसः ॥

८८ संवर्धयेत्तथा कोशमात्मैस्तज्जैरधिष्ठितम् ।
काले चास्य व्ययं कुर्यात्त्रिवर्गप्रतिपत्तये ॥

८९ धर्मार्थं क्षीणकोशस्य कृशत्वमपि शोभते ।
सुरैः पीतावशेषस्य शरद्भिमरुचेरिव ॥

९० बृहस्पतेरविश्वास इति शास्त्रार्थनिश्चयः ।
अविश्वासी तथा च स्याद्यथा च व्यवहारवान् ॥२९

९१ विश्वासयेदविश्वस्तं विश्वस्तं नातिविश्वसेत् ।
यस्मिन्विश्वासमायाति विभूतेः पात्रमेव सः ॥

९२ प्रादुर्भवन्त्यर्थसमं यस्माच्चित्तान्यनुक्षणम् ।
तस्माद्योगीव सततं तानि पश्येत्समाहितः ॥३०

sources: state officials, thieves, enemies, the king's favorites, and the king's own greed. After curbing these five dangers, the king should extract wealth at the proper time in order to promote the three aims of life. Just as someone takes good care of a cow and then later milks it at the right time, or waters a plant and tends it so that it later gives flowers, so must the king behave toward his subjects.   85

The king should bleed corrupt officials like an abscess to remove them. The officials should regard the king like a fire capable of incinerating them. If the wicked officials commit the slightest misdeed in regard to the king, those deluded men will be incinerated like moths in a flame.

He should build up the treasury with knowledgeable officials presiding over it so that, at the appropriate time, he can spend money to promote the three aims of life. If the king lavishes treasure for the sake of dharma even his destitution is beautiful, like the thin cool-rayed moon of autumn after the gods have drunk most of its nectar.

Brihaspati concludes in his scholarly works that suspicion should be the primary attitude of the king: he should maintain this attitude of suspicion while conducting his affairs. He should inspire trust in those who lack trust, yet   90 not overly trust the trustworthy. A man whom the king can trust becomes a receptacle of his munificence. Since men's thoughts reveal their objectives at every moment, the king should constantly study them, with his mind concentrated like a yogi. For a king not averse to effort—who has good friends, and who is endowed with intellect—royal fortune becomes, like his shadow, an eternal consort.

When he is attended by retainers who are properly

९३ उद्योगादनिवृत्तस्य सुसहायस्य धीमतः ।
छायेवानुगता तस्य नित्यं श्रीः सहचारिणी ॥

९४ स्वनुगतपरितोषितानुजीवी मधुरवचाश्रितानुरक्तलोकः ।
सुनिपुणपरमाप्तसक्ततन्त्रो भवति चिरं नृपतिः प्रदीप्तरश्मिः ॥

rewarded, when he has won the loyalty of the people with his sweet words and good conduct, and when his government is in the hands of supremely trustworthy and highly skilled men, a king will long preserve the blazing radiance of glory. [93]

कण्टकशोधनप्रकरणम्

१ लोके वेदे च कुशलः कुशलैः परिवेष्टितः ।
आवृतश्चिन्तयेद्राज्यं सबाह्याभ्यन्तरं नृपः ॥

२ आभ्यन्तरं शरीरं स्वं बाह्यं राष्ट्रमुदाहृतम् ।
अन्योन्याधारसम्बन्धादेकमेवेदमिष्यते ॥

३ राज्याङ्गानां तु सर्वेषां राष्ट्राद्भवति सम्भवः ।
तस्मात्सर्वप्रयत्नेन राजा राष्ट्रं समुन्नयेत् ॥

४ लोकानुग्रहमन्विच्छञ्छरीरमनुपालयेत् ।
राज्ञः संरक्षणं धर्मः शरीरं धर्मसाधनम् ॥१

५ धर्म्यामारेभिरे हिंसामृषिकल्पा महीभुजः ।
तस्मादसाधून्धर्माय निघ्नन्दोषैर्न लिप्यते ॥२

६ धर्मसंरक्षणपरो धर्मेणार्थं विवर्धयेत् ।
ये ये प्रजाः प्रबाधेरन्तांस्ताञ्छिष्यान्महीपतिः ॥

७ यमार्याः क्रियमाणं हि शंसन्त्यागमवेदिनः ।
स धर्मो यं विगर्हन्ति तमधर्मं प्रचक्षते ॥

८ धर्माधर्मौ विजानन्हि शासनेऽभिरतः सताम् ।
प्रजा रक्षेन्नृपः साधु हन्याच्च परिपन्थिनः ॥

९ राज्योपघातं कुर्वीरन्ये पापा राजवल्लभाः ।
एकैकशः संहता वा तान्दूष्यान्परिचक्षते ॥

१० दूष्यानुपांशुदण्डेन हन्याद्राजाविलम्बितम् ।
प्रदूष्य वा प्रकाशं हि लोकविद्वेषमागतान् ॥३

CHAPTER 6

Removing Anti-State Elements

A king versed in the Veda as well as the affairs of the world, and attended by well-versed followers, should carefully examine the kingdom in both its internal and external aspects. The inner aspect is his own body. The outer aspect is known as his realm. The two depend on each other, and because of this relationship, they should really be thought of as one. All the other state-elements have their origin in the realm. Therefore the king should enhance the realm with all possible effort. The king should protect his own body for the gratification of the people. A king's dharma is protection, and his body is the means of dharma.

When kings perform a righteous act of violence they are like great sages.[1] When they slaughter bad people for the sake of dharma, they are not tainted by sin. The king, committed to securing dharma—fostering power by fostering dharma—should punish whoever harms the people. Any action is considered dharma that is commended by noble men who know Vedic lore; anything they condemn is said to be non-dharma.[2] Understanding dharma and non-dharma, and abiding by the judgment of good men, the king should protect the people well and kill their assailants. Those evil favorites of the king who thwart the kingdom, whether individually or as a group, are said to be wicked people. The king should promptly kill off wicked people by means of secret assassinations, or else he should charge them with

5

77

११ राजा रहसि दूष्यं हि दर्शनायोपमन्त्रयेत् ।
गूढशस्त्रा विशेयुस्तं पश्चादासंज्ञिता नराः ॥४

१२ विश्वस्ता हि विचिन्वीयुर्द्वाःस्थाः कक्ष्यान्तरागतान् ।
ते शस्त्रग्राहिणो ब्रूयुः प्रयुक्ताः स्म इति स्फुटम् ॥

१३ इत्यादि दूष्यान्सन्दूष्य प्रजानामभिवृद्धये ।
विनयज्छ्रियमुत्कर्षं राजा शल्यं समुद्धरेत् ॥

१४ यथा बीजाङ्कुरः सूक्ष्मः परिपुष्टोऽभिरक्षितः ।
काले फलाय भवति साधु तद्वदियं प्रजा ॥

१५ उद्वेजयति तीक्ष्णेन मृदुना परिभूयते ।
तस्माद्यथार्हतो दण्डं नयेत्पक्षमनाश्रितः ॥

78

crimes and kill them publicly after they have been exposed
as enemies of the people.   10

The king should summon a wicked person for an audience.
Then, when given the signal, some men should enter after
him carrying concealed weapons. Trusted guards should
gather them in an adjacent room, and then the men should
declare aloud, "We are in his employ."[3] In this way the king
should vilify wicked people for the sake of the people's
supreme prosperity. Thus the king should extract thorny
anti-state elements from the kingdom, to enhance his royal
majesty and eminence.[4]

The subjects are just like a tiny sprout that nourished and
tended in time brings forth great fruit. If the king is too harsh
people will shun him, while he will suffer defeat if he is too
mild. Therefore he should apply the rod impartially, as it is
deserved.   15

राजपुत्ररक्षणप्रकरणम्

१ प्रजात्मश्रेयसे राजा कुर्वीतात्मजरक्षणम् ।
लोलुभ्यमानास्तेऽर्थेषु हन्युरेनमरक्षिताः ॥

२ राजपुत्रा मदोन्मत्ता गजा इव निरङ्कुशाः ।
भ्रातरं वापि निघ्नन्ति पितरं वाभिमानिनः ॥

३ राजपुत्रैर्मदोन्मत्तैः प्रार्थ्यमानमितस्ततः ।
दुःखेन रक्ष्यते राज्यं व्याघ्राघ्रातमिवामिषम् ॥

४ रक्ष्यमाणा यदि च्छिद्रं कथंचित्प्राप्नुवन्ति ते ।
सिंहशावा इव घ्नन्ति रक्षितारमसंशयम् ॥

५ विनयोपग्रहान्भूत्यै कुर्वीत नृपतिः सुतान् ।
अविनीतकुमारं हि कुलमाशु विनश्यति ॥

६ विनीतमौरसं पुत्रं यौवराज्येऽभिषेचयेत् ।
दुष्टं गजमिवोद्धृत्तं कुर्वीत सुखबन्धनम् ॥

७ राजपुत्रः परित्यागं सुदुर्वृत्तोऽपि नार्हति ।
क्रियमाणः स पितरं परमाश्रित्य हन्ति हि ॥

८ व्यसने सज्जमानं हि क्लेशयेद्व्यसनाश्रयैः ।
तथा च क्लेशयेदेनं यथा स्यात्पितृगोचरः ॥

CHAPTER 7

Guarding Princes

In his own best interests and in the best interests of his subjects, the king should guard his sons. Unguarded, they can become rabidly covetous of his wealth and kill him. Princes can also be wild and crazy, as unresponsive to goading as wild elephants in heat. In their arrogance, they can kill their brother or even their father. The kingdom is just as difficult to protect from heedless princes coveting it left and right as a piece of meat when a tiger catches its scent. Even when carefully guarded, the princes can seize on any possible vulnerability and, like young lions, kill their guardian. The king should appoint servants to instill self-mastery in his sons, for when the princes lack self-mastery a family will swiftly be destroyed.

The king should consecrate as prince regent a son who possesses self-mastery. He should bind to himself a son prone to misconduct with the shackle of sensual pleasure, as one shackles an unruly elephant. A son, however much prone to misconduct, should not be abandoned, since if princes are oppressed, they will conspire with others to kill their father. What he should do is to oppress a prince addicted to vice with further temptations to vice so that he remains under his father's control.

5

81

आत्मरक्षितप्रकरणम्

९ याने शय्यासने भोज्ये पाने वस्त्रे विभूषणे ।
सर्वत्रैवाप्रमत्तः सन्वर्जेत विषदूषितम् ॥१

१० विषघ्नैरुदकैः स्नातो विषघ्नमणिभूषणः ।
परीक्षितं समश्रीयाजाङ्गुलीविद्विषग्वृतः ॥

११ भृङ्गराजः शुकश्चैव शारिका चेति पक्षिणः ।
क्रोशन्ति भृशमुद्विग्रा विषपन्नगदर्शनात् ॥

१२ चकोरस्य विरज्येते नयने विषदर्शनात् ।
सुव्यक्तं माद्यति क्रौञ्चो म्रियते मत्तकोकिलः ॥

१३ जीवञ्जीवस्य च ग्लानिर्जायते विषदर्शनात् ।
तेषामन्यतमेनापि समश्रीयात्परीक्षितम् ॥

१४ मयूरपृषतोत्सर्गान्न भवन्ति भुजङ्गमाः ।
तस्मान्मयूरपृषतौ भवने नित्यमुत्सृजेत् ॥

१५ भोज्यमन्नं परीक्षार्थं प्रदद्यात्पूर्वमग्रये ।
वयोभ्यश्च ततो दद्यात्तत्र लिङ्गानि लक्षयेत् ॥

१६ धूमार्चिर्नीलता वह्नेः शब्दस्फोटश्च जायते ।
अन्नेन विषदिग्धेन वयसां मरणं भवेत् ॥

१७ अक्लिन्नता सोदकत्वमाशुशैत्यं विवर्णता ।२
अन्नस्य विषदिग्धस्य तथा स्निग्धत्वमेव च ॥३

१८ व्यञ्जनस्याशु शुष्कत्वं क्रथने श्यामफेनता ।४
गन्धस्पर्शरसाश्चैव नश्यन्ति विषदूषणात् ॥

१९ छायातिरिक्ता हीना वा स्याद्रसे विषदूषिते ।५
दृश्यते राजिरूर्ध्वा च फेनमण्डलमेव च ॥

Self-Protection

The king should be constantly vigilant in regard to his travel, his sleeping arrangements, as well as his food, drink, clothing, and ornaments in order to avoid being poisoned. He should bathe in anti-venom water, wear anti-venom jewels, and only eat food that has been carefully tested in the presence of toxicologists and doctors.   10

The fork-tailed shrike, parrot, and myna birds all shriek in intense terror when they see a poisonous snake.[1] The chukar partridge's eyes lose their color when they see poison; the curlew goes mad; and the cuckoo dies. The pheasant wastes away when it sees poison. Therefore the king should only eat food that has been tested through exposure to one of these animals. There are no snakes where the droppings of peacocks and the one-horned deer are found. Therefore the king should always let peacocks and one-horned deer roam in his palace. In order to test the rice which he is about to eat, he should first throw a little bit into the fire, and then offer some to the crows and observe their reactions. When   15 the rice has been poisoned, smoke will rise from the fire, the flame will turn blue, and it will crackle loudly. The crows will die.

Poisoned rice does not become soft from cooking or it stays watery. It cools off rapidly, has the wrong color, and remains unctuous. Poisoned curry dries up quickly, has blackish foam when it boils; it loses its smell, texture, and taste. When fluids are poisoned they are either too bright in color or else less bright than normal; they show a vertical streak and a halo of foam.

२० रसस्य नीला पयसश्च ताम्रा मद्यस्य तोयस्य च कोकिलाभा ।
श्यामा च दध्नो विषदूषितस्य मध्ये भवत्यूर्ध्वगता च रेखा ॥६

२१ आर्द्रस्य सर्वस्य भवेत्तु सद्यः प्रम्लानभावो विषदूषितस्य ।
उत्पक्कता क्वाथविनीलता च प्रश्यामता चेति वदन्ति तज्ज्ञाः ॥

२२ शुष्कस्य सर्वस्य विषोपदेहाद्विशीर्णता चाशुविवर्णता च ।
खरं मृदु स्यान्मृदुनः खरत्वं तदन्तिके चाल्पकजन्तुघातः ॥७

२३ प्रावारास्तरणानां च श्याममण्डलकीर्णता ।
तन्तूनां पक्ष्मणां लोम्नां स्याद्धृंशश्च विषाश्रयात् ॥

१४ लोहानां च मणीनां च मलपङ्कोपदिग्धता ।
प्रभावस्नेहगुरुतावर्णस्पर्शवधस्तथा ॥

२५ संशुष्कश्यामवक्रत्वं वाग्भङ्गो जृम्भणं मुहुः ।८
स्खलनं वेपथुः स्वेदो ह्यावेशो दिग्विलोकनम् ॥९

२६ स्वकर्मणि स्वभूमौ स्यादनवस्थानमेव च ।
लिङ्गान्येतानि निपुणं लक्षयेद्विषदायिनाम् ॥

२७ औषधानि च सर्वाणि पानं पानीयमेव च ।
तत्कल्पकैः समास्वाद्य प्राश्नीयाद्व्रोजनानि च ॥

२८ प्रसाधनादि यत्किंचित्तत्सर्वं परिचारकाः ।
उपनिन्युनरेन्द्राय सुपरीक्षितमुद्रितम् ॥

२९ परस्मादागतं यच्च तत्तत्सर्वं परीक्षयेत् ।
स्वेभ्यः परेभ्यश्च तदा रक्ष्यो राजा हि रक्षिता ॥

३० यानवाहनमारोहेज्ज्ञातं ज्ञातोपपादितम् ।
अविज्ञातेन हि पथा सङ्कटेन च न व्रजेत् ॥

Poisoned juices turn blue; milk turns reddish; alcoholic drinks and water turn the color of the cuckoo; yogurt turns black and shows a vertical line in the middle.   20

Toxicologists say that fresh fruits and vegetables look suddenly discolored, and they seem overripe, blackish, and bluish when boiled.   21

Dried foods crumble and have a rotten appearance when laced with poison. Hard foods become soft, and soft foods become hard. Small insects die from contact with them.   22 Blankets and rugs get covered with black circles; while threads, feathers, and furs disintegrate from contact with poison. Metals and jewels seem smeared with ordure or dirt, and they lose their magical power, their smoothness, weight, color, and pleasant touch. The signs of people who administer poison, which a clever person will notice, are as follows: darkness of complexion, garbled speech, repeated yawning, stumbling, quivering, sweating, trance, staring vacantly, as   25 well as inability to focus on one's work or stay in one place.

The king should only consume medicines, drinks, water, and food after having them tasted by their preparers. The servants should bring clothing or ornaments before the king and present them to him only after they have been thoroughly inspected and sealed. Any gift that comes from others should be thoroughly inspected, for the king—the true protector—must be protected at all times from friends and enemies alike. The king should only ride in chariots or on animals that have been examined and cared for by well-known attendants. He should never travel by an unfamiliar or dangerous route.   30

३१ वीक्षितादुष्टकर्माणमाप्तं वंशक्रमागतम् ।
संविभक्तं च कुर्वीत जनमासन्नवर्तिनम् ॥

३२ अधार्मिकांश्च क्रूरांश्च दृष्टदोषान्निराकृतान् ।
परेभ्योऽभ्यागतांश्चैव दूरादेतान्समाचरेत् ॥१०

३३ महावातसमुद्भूतामपरीक्षितनाविकाम् ।११
अन्यनौप्रतिबद्धां वा नोपेयान्नावमातुराम् ॥

३४ परितापिषु वासरेषु पश्यंस्तटलेखास्थितमाप्तसैन्यचक्रम् ।१२
सुविशोधितमीननक्रजालं व्यवगाहेत जलं सुहृत्समेतः ॥

३५ गहनानि विवर्जयन्विशुद्धं बहिरुद्यानवनं समभ्युपेतः ।१३
विहरन्मधुरं वयोऽनुरूपं न च माद्येद्विषयोपभोगरागात् ॥१४

३६ सुविनीतसुवेगपृष्ठयानः सुखगम्यामुचितां च लक्ष्यसिद्ध्यै ।१५
सुपरीक्षितरक्षितान्तसीमां लघुकोष्ठस्तु मृगाटवीमुपेयात् ॥

३७ कारयेद्वनशोधनमादौ मातुरन्तिकमपि प्रविविक्षुः ।
आप्तशस्त्यनुगतः प्रविशेत्तत्सङ्कटे च गहने न च तिष्ठेत् ॥

He should only employ someone as personal attendant who has been thoroughly examined, who is known never to have committed a crime, who is trusted, and whose familial antecedents are well known. He must keep his distance from all those who are unrighteous, violent, known for their criminal behavior, who have previously been banished, or who have come over from the enemy side.

The king should never board a boat that is decrepit, or tossed about by strong winds, or whose sailors have not been thoroughly examined, or which is tied to another boat.

On very hot days—after seeing to it that his full trustworthy army is arrayed on the banks, and after eradicating any large fishes or crocodiles—he may go for a swim accompanied by his close friends. 34

Avoiding dense thickets, the king should visit an outdoor forest garden, which has been cleared of all danger, and enjoy himself in a pleasant way befitting his age. But he should not let the passionate pleasures of the senses intoxicate him. 35

When hunting, his belly should not be full, and he should travel on a horse that is both well-trained and swift. He should visit a hunting ground that has its outer perimeter carefully examined and guarded. It should be properly arranged and easy to move around in to facilitate aiming at targets. 36

He should have his people safeguard even his mother's residence before he goes to meet her, and he should only enter in the company of trusted armed guards. He should never spend time—even with her—in an unsafe or desolate place. 37

87

३८ पांसूत्करोत्कर्षिणि वाति वाते संसक्तधाराजलदे च काले ।
अत्यातपे वापि तथान्धकारे स्वस्थस्तु सन्न क्वचिदभ्युपेयात् ॥

३९ निर्गमे च प्रवेशे च राजमार्गं समन्ततः ।
प्रोत्सारितजनं गच्छेत्सम्यगावि‌ष्कृतोन्नतिः ॥

४० यात्रोत्सवसमाजेषु जनसंबाधशालिनः ।
प्रदेशान्नावगाहेत नातिवेलं च संपतेत् ॥

४१ निषेवि‌तो वर्षवरैः कञ्चुकोष्णीषधारिभिः ।
अन्तःपुरेषु विचरेत्कुब्जकैरातवामनैः ॥

४२ नीचैरन्तःपुरामात्याः शुचयश्चिन्तवेदिनः ।
शस्त्राग्निविषवर्जं हि नर्मयेयुर्महीपतिम् ॥

४३ अन्तर्वंशिकसैन्यं हि सन्नद्धं साधुसम्मतम् ।
रक्षेदायुक्तकुशलमन्तःपुरगतं नृपम् ॥

४४ आशीतिकाश्च पुरुषाः पञ्चाशत्काश्च योषितः ।
पश्येयुरवरोधानां शौचमागारिकाश्च ये ॥

४५ रूपाजीवाः स्त्रियः स्नाताः परिवर्तितवाससः ।
राजानमुपतिष्ठेयुर्विशुद्धस्रग्विभूषणाः ॥

४६ कुहकैर्जटिलैश्चापि मुण्डैश्चाभ्यन्तरो जनः ।
संसर्गं न क्वचिद्गच्छेद्दासीजनैस्तथा ॥

४७ निर्गच्छेत्प्रविशेच्चापि सर्वत्राभ्यन्तरो जनः ।
विज्ञातद्रव्यसञ्चारी करणेनोपलक्षितः ॥१६

88

Whenever the wind blows hard, kicking up dust and rubble, whenever storm clouds rain incessantly, whenever it is excessively hot or dark, the king should stay safe and go nowhere. 38

Whenever he is leaving or returning, the royal road should be cleared of people, in order to fully display his grandeur. When there are pilgrimages or festivals, the king should not make an appearance in crowded places, and he should not go anywhere afterhours. He should only wander about 40 the harem accompanied by eunuchs wearing armor and turbans, hunchbacks, Kirata dwarves, and midgets.[2] Harem ministers who are pure and who know his heart should humbly entertain the king, without using weapons, fire, or poison in their tricks. A division of the army with kinship ties to the king, tightly organized and highly esteemed—with each member skilled in his role—should guard the king while in the harem. Attendants of the harem's inner rooms—eighty years of age in the case of males, and fifty in the case of females—should monitor the women's purity and loyalty.

Beautiful women, who have bathed and changed their clothes, wearing fresh garlands and ornaments, should attend upon the king. The attendants of the harem's 45 interior should have absolutely no contact with magicians, mendicants—whether bald or with dreadlocks—or common prostitutes. Whenever the harem attendants enter or exit, their destination and belongings must be thoroughly examined, and they must also present a pass issued by the guards.

The king should never meet with a follower who has fallen

४८ न चानुजीविनं पश्येदकल्यं पृथिवीपतिः ।
अन्यत्रात्ययिकाद्रोगात्सर्वस्यैवातुरो गुरुः ॥१७

४९ स्नातानुलिप्तः सुरभिः स्रग्वी रुचिरभूषणः ।
स्नातां विशुद्धवसनां पश्येद्देवीं सुभूषणाम् ॥

५० न च देवीगृहं गच्छेदात्मीयात्सन्निवेशनात् ।
अत्यन्तं वल्लभो ऽस्मीति विस्रम्भं स्त्रीषु न व्रजेत् ॥

५१ देवीगृहं गतो भ्राता भद्रसेनममारयत् ।
मातुः शय्यान्तरालीनः कारूशं चौरसः सुतः ॥

५२ लाजान्विषेण संयोज्य मधुनेति विलोभ्य तम् ।
देवी तु काशिराजेन्द्रं निजघान रहोगतम् ॥

५३ विषदिग्धेन सौवीरं मेखलामणिना नृपम् ।
नूपुरेण च वैरूप्यं जारूष्यं दर्पणेन च ॥१८

५४ वेण्यां शस्त्रं समाधाय तथा चापि विडूरथम् ।
अहिवृत्तं परिहरेच्छत्रौ चापि प्रयोजयेत् ॥१९

५५ यस्य दाराः सुगुप्ताः स्युः पुरुषैराप्तकारिभिः ।
सर्वभोगान्वितं तस्य हस्ते लोकद्वयं स्थितम् ॥

५६ धर्ममिच्छन्नरपतिः सर्वदारानानुक्रमात् ।
गच्छेदनुदिनं नित्यं वाजीकरणबृंहितः ॥

ill. However, if a follower falls mortally ill in the course of his duties, then the sick man becomes worthy of precedence over everyone.

The king should approach the queen when he has bathed, applied fragrant creams, and dressed in garlands and shiny ornaments. The queen should bathe, wear clean clothes, and put on her loveliest ornaments. However, the king should never proceed directly from his own residence to the queen's quarters. Even if he feels very loved, he should not trust women.

50

Bhadrasena was killed by his brother, hiding in the queen's quarters.[3] Karusha was killed by his own son, hiding under his mother's bed. The queen mixed poison with puffed rice, using honey to make it seem tasty, and killed the king of Kashi in private. The king of Sauvira was killed by his queen with a poison-laced gem from her girdle. Vairupya was killed in a similar fashion with an anklet-jewel. Jarushya was slain by a poisoned mirror. Viduratha's queen killed him with a dagger hidden in her braid. The king should root out such wily tactics; indeed, he should deploy them against his enemies.

If his wives are well guarded by trustworthy attendants, a king holds both the mundane and heavenly worlds, with all their pleasures, in the palm of his hand. In the interests of dharma, the king should go to his wives in due order from one night to the next, after fortifying himself with aphrodisiacs.

55

At day's end, after giving due consideration to all the elements of his affairs, he should dismiss everyone and focus on erotic enjoyments with his women. He should

५७ विचार्य कार्यावयवान्दिनक्षये विसृज्य लोकं प्रमदाकृतक्रियः ।
अशस्त्रबन्धेन हि साधु पाणिना स्वपेदसक्तं परमात्परक्षितः ॥

५८ नयेन जाग्रत्यनिशं नरेश्वरे सुखं स्वपन्तीह निराधयः प्रजाः ।
प्रमत्तचित्ते स्वपति त्रसद्द्वयात्प्रजागरेणास्य जगत्प्रबाध्यते ॥२०

५९ इति स्म पूर्वे मुनयो बभाषिरे नृपस्य राज्यस्य च साधु रक्षणम् ।
तदेतदेवं परिपालयन्नयान्नरेश्वरः पालनकल्यतां व्रजेत् ॥

then sleep, but not too deeply, with his hand ever clasping his unsheathed weapon, with supremely trustworthy men guarding him.   57

When the king is ever wakeful in his political strategy, the subjects sleep happily, free from care. But if the king falls asleep politically, his mind intoxicated with sensuality, the people live in fear of dangers, and the world is tormented by sleeplessness.   58

Thus have the ancient sages told of the proper protection of a king and his kingdom. When he protects the people in this fashion, according to proper politics, the lord of men becomes a stalwart protector indeed.   59

अष्टमः सर्गः

मण्डलयोनिप्रकरणम्

१ उपेतः कोशदण्डाभ्यां सामात्यः सह मन्त्रिभिः ।
दुर्गस्थश्चिन्तयेत्साधु मण्डलं मण्डलाधिपः ॥

२ रोचते सर्वभूतेभ्यः शशीवाखण्डमण्डलः ।
सम्पूर्णमण्डलस्तस्माद्विजिगीषुः सदा भवेत् ॥

३ रथीव राजते राजा विशुद्धे मण्डले चरन् ।
अशुद्धे मण्डले सर्वं शीर्यते रथचक्रवत् ॥

४ अमात्यराष्ट्रदुर्गाणि कोशो दण्डश्च पञ्चमः ।
एताः प्रकृतयस्तज्ज्ञैर्विजिगीषोरुदाहृताः ॥

५ एताः पञ्च तथा मित्रं सप्तमः पृथिवीपतिः ।
सप्तप्रकृतिकं राज्यमित्युवाच बृहस्पतिः ॥

६ सम्पन्नस्तु प्रकृतिभिर्महोत्साहः कृतश्रमः ।
जेतुमेषणशीलश्च विजिगीषुरिति स्मृतः ॥

७ कौलीन्यं वृद्धसेवित्वमुत्साहः स्थूललक्षता ।
चित्तज्ञता बुद्धिमत्त्वं प्रागल्भ्यं सत्यवादिता ॥

८ आदीर्घसूत्रताक्षौद्रं प्रश्रयः स्वप्रधानता ।
देशकालज्ञता दार्ढ्यं सर्वक्लेशसहिष्णुता ॥

९ सर्वविज्ञानिता दाक्ष्यमूर्जः संवृत्तमन्त्रता ।
अविसंवादिता शौर्यं भक्तिज्ञत्वं कृतज्ञता ॥

CHAPTER 8

The Mandala's Center

Well-equipped with a treasury and the rod of coercion, the lord of the mandala should gather his ministers and counselors inside a fortification and carefully consider his mandala.[1] A king with intact mandala becomes delightful to all beings like a full moon with unbroken orb. Therefore an expansionist king should always keep his mandala complete.[2] The king bestrides a fully safeguarded mandala like a glorious charioteer, but everything falls apart in an unsafeguarded mandala, like a chariot-wheel whose axle is broken.

Authorities state that the seven key state-elements for a conqueror are minister, kingdom, fortification, treasury, rod of coercion, ally, and king. Thus, Brihaspati has said that the state consists of these seven elements. An "expansionist king" is known as someone in possession of these seven elements as well as great determination, who makes every effort and is naturally ambitious for victory. The essential virtues of a conqueror are good lineage, devotion to elders, determination, generosity, intuition, intelligence, maturity, truthfulness, timeliness, magnanimity, courtesy, self-reliance, awareness of time and place, steadiness, ability to endure all calamities, comprehensive understanding, dexterity in action, maintaining secrecy in strategy, consistency, heroism, recognition of loyalty, gratitude, care for those who seek refuge, aggression, constancy, following the *śāstras* in his practice, accomplishment in

5

१० शरणागतवात्सल्यममर्षित्वमचापलम् ।
स्वकर्मदृष्टशास्त्रत्वं कृतित्वं दीर्घदर्शिता ॥

११ जितश्रमत्वं वाग्मित्वमक्रूरपरिवारता ।
प्रकृतिस्फीतता चेति विजिगीषोर्गुणोदयः ॥१

१२ सर्वैर्गुणैर्विहीनोऽपि स राजा यः प्रतापवान् ।
प्रतापयुक्तात्त्रस्यन्ति परे सिंहान्मृगा इव ॥२

१३ प्रतापयुक्तो नृपतिः प्राप्नोति महतीं श्रियम् ।३
तस्मादुत्थानयोगेन प्रतापं जनयेत्प्रभुः ॥४

१४ एकार्थाभिनिवेशित्वमरिलक्षणमुच्यते ।
दारुणस्तु स्मृतः शत्रुर्विजिगीषुगुणान्वितः ॥

१५ लुब्धः क्रूरोऽलसोऽसत्यः प्रमादी भीरुरस्थिरः ।
मूढो योधावमन्ता च सुखोच्छेद्यो रिपुः स्मृतः ॥

१६ अरिमित्रमरेर्मित्रं मित्रमित्रमतःपरम् ।
तथारिमित्रमित्रं च विजिगीषोः पुरः स्थिताः ॥५

१७ पार्ष्णिग्राहस्ततः पश्चादाक्रन्दस्तदनन्तरः ।
आसारावनयोश्चेति विजिगीषोस्तु पृष्ठतः ॥

१८ अरेश्च विजिगीषोश्च मध्यमो भूम्यनन्तरः ।
अनुग्रहे संहतयोर्व्यस्तयोर्निग्रहे प्रभुः ॥६

१९ मण्डलाद्बहिरेतेषामुदासीनो बलाधिकः ।७
अनुग्रहे संहतानां व्यस्तानां च वधे प्रभुः ॥

learning, farsightedness, indefatigability, eloquence, exclud- 10
ing cruel people from his retinue, and establishing prosperous state-elements.

Even if devoid of all virtues, a king who is valorous will
terrify his enemies, as a lion terrifies deer. A king accomplished in valor attains great royal majesty. Therefore,
through energetic activity, the king must strive to cultivate
valor. An enemy is defined as someone occupied with the
same objective as the king; he is considered fearsome when
he possesses the same virtues as the conqueror. On the other
hand, an enemy who is greedy, cruel, lazy, untruthful, reckless, cowardly, unstable, stupid, and contemptuous of his
warriors, is regarded as easy to eliminate. 15

In front of the conqueror, in successive concentric mandalas, stand: the enemy, the friend, the enemy's friend, the
friend's friend, and lastly, the enemy's friend's friend. At
the back of the conqueror are the "rear adversary," that is,
an enemy who attacks from the rear, the "rear supporter," a
friend who attacks the rear adversary, and then two "backup
forces," who support the rear adversary and rear supporter,
respectively.[3] The king whose land is contiguous to both
the conqueror and his enemy is known as the "intermediate
one." He can favor the conqueror or his enemy when they are
united, and destroy them both if they are disunited. Beyond
all these lies the "neutral one," who is more powerful than all
of the above. He can favor the conqueror, his enemy, or the
intermediate one when they are united, and holds the power
of life and death over everyone when they are disunited.

२० मूलप्रकृतयस्त्वेताश्चतस्रः परिकीर्तिताः ।
आहैव मन्त्रकुशलश्चतुष्कं मण्डलं मयः ॥ ८

२१ विजिगीषुररिरिमित्रं पार्ष्णिग्राहोऽथ मध्यमः ।
उदासीनः पुलोमेन्द्रौ मण्डलं षट्कमूचतुः ॥

२२ उदासीनो मध्यमश्च विजिगीषोश्च मण्डलम् ।
उशना मण्डलमिदं प्राह द्वादशराजकम् ॥

२३ द्वादशानां नरेन्द्राणामरिमित्रे पृथक्पृथक् ।
षट्त्रिंशत्कमिति प्राहुस्ते च ते च महर्षयः ॥ ९

२४ द्वादशानां नरेन्द्राणां पञ्च पञ्च पृथक्पृथक् ।
अमात्याद्याश्च प्रकृतीरामनन्तीह मानवाः ॥

२४ मौला द्वादश चैवैता अमात्याद्यास्तथा च याः ।
सप्ततिर्द्व्यधिका ह्येषां सर्वप्रकृतिमण्डलम् ॥

२६ संयुक्तस्त्वरिमित्राभ्यामुभयारिस्तथा सुहृत् ।
मौला द्वादश राजान इत्यष्टादशकं गुरुः ॥

२७ अष्टादशानामेतेषाममात्याद्याः पृथक्पृथक् ।
अष्टोत्तरशतं ह्येतन्मण्डलं कवयो विदुः ॥

२८ एतेऽष्टादश चैतेषां शत्रुमित्रे पृथक्पृथक् ।
चतुष्पञ्चाशत्कमिति विशालाक्षः प्रभाषते ॥

२९ चतुष्पञ्चाशतो राज्ञाममात्याद्याः पृथक्पृथक् ।
सचतुर्विंशतीदं हि मण्डलं त्रिशतं मतम् ॥

The main elements of the mandalas are said to be these four: expansionist king, enemy, intermediate one, and neutral one. That the mandala has four constituents is in fact the opinion of the expert on strategy Maya. However, 20 the scholars Puloma and Indra say that the realm has six: expansionist king, enemy, friend, rear adversary, intermediate one, and neutral one. Ushanas says the realm comprises twelve states: the neutral one and the intermediate one along with the ten parties that extend from the expansionist king. Great sages proclaim the view that beyond the twelve kings specified above, along with further permutations of friend and enemy, the total number of constituents is thirty-six.

The followers of Manu hold that when we include the ministers and other elements of the mandala—which includes twelve kings—we must multiply by five to get a total number of sixty. Finally, when we add the principal twelve kings to the number of the ministers and other elements, we get a figure of seventy-two for the mandala with all its elements. The guru Brihaspati considers that these main twelve kings 25 each have a common enemy and friend—when they are united—and that they also share friends and enemies with these friends and enemies, so that the mandala comprises eighteen. And the sages teach that each set of eighteen added together, along with each of their five principal allies, gives a total number of one hundred and eight. Vishalaksha says that the eighteen, combined with their respective friends and enemies, yields a number of fifty-four. These fifty-four kings along with their ministers make the mandala in fact consist of three hundred and twenty-four elements.

३० सप्तप्रकृतिकं यत्तु विजिगीषोररेश्च तत् ।
    चतुर्दशकमेवेह मण्डलं परिचक्षते ॥

३१ मण्डलं त्रिकमित्याहुर्विजिगीष्वरिमध्यमाः ।
    मित्रयुक्ताः पृथक्चैते षट्कमित्यपरे जगुः ॥

३२ अमात्याद्याः प्रकृतय एकैकस्यैव भूपतेः ।
    मण्डलं मण्डलविदः षट्त्रिंशत्कं प्रचक्षते ॥

३३ सप्तप्रकृतिकाः सर्वे विजिगीष्वरिमध्यमाः ।
    एकविंशतिरित्याहुः परे च नयवादिनः ॥१०

३४ चत्वारः पार्थिवा मौलाः पृथग्भिन्नैः सहाष्टकम् ।
    अमात्यादिभिरेते च जगत्यक्षरसम्मिताः ॥

३५ विजिगीषोः पुरस्ताच्च ये च पश्चात्प्रकीर्तिताः ।
    दशकं मण्डलमिदं मण्डलज्ञाः प्रचक्षते ॥

३६ दशानां भूमिपालानाममात्याद्याः पृथक्पृथक् ।
    मण्डलं मण्डलविदः षष्टिसंख्यं प्रचक्षते ॥

३७ प्राग्यौ द्वौ विजिगीषुश्च पश्चिमौ चेति पञ्चकम् ।
    अमात्याद्याः पृथक्चैषां त्रिंशत्कं हि प्रचक्षते ॥

३८ अरेरप्येवमेवेति दृष्टं दृष्टिमतां वरैः ।
    पञ्चकं मण्डलं न्याय्यं त्रितयं च मनीषिभिः ॥

३९ द्वे एव प्रकृती न्याय्ये इत्युवाच पराशरः ।
    अभियोत्तृप्रधानत्वात्तथान्यो योऽभियुज्यते ॥

Since the expansionist king and his enemy have territories consisting of seven elements each, the mandala holds fourteen elements. The mandala includes a triad: the expansionist king, his enemy, and the intermediate one. Since each of these also has a friend, therefore other authorities say the mandala is six. Each individual king has his ministers and other state-elements, and therefore the specialists in mandalas say that the realm comprises thirty-six elements. According to other interpreters of politics, the expansionist king, enemy, and intermediate one each have seven state-elements; therefore they say the realm comprises twenty-one elements. The four main kings each have an ally, which brings the number to eight; with each one's ministers and other state-elements, the number becomes equal to the number of syllables in a *jagatī* quatrain: forty-eight.

Some scholars of mandalas consider the realm to be tenfold, as including all the rulers in front of and behind the expansionist king. Therefore, with each of the ten kings' ministers and other state-elements, these scholars say the realm comprises sixty elements.

The ruler along with the two realms to his east, and the two to his west, makes five. Considering each of their ministers and other state-elements, this equals thirty. Wise men of vision observe that the enemy has likewise five associated territories, which should be added to the thirty comprising the realm.

Parashara says that mandalas have only two main elements to be recognized: the principal one is the attacker, and the other, the one attacked. The expansionist king and the enemy attack each other reciprocally so that the two

101

४० परस्पराभियोगेन विजिगीषोररेस्तथा ।
अरित्वविजिगीषुत्वे एका प्रकृतिरित्यतः ॥

४१ इतिप्रकारं बहुधा मण्डलं परिचक्षते ।
सर्वलोकप्रतीतं हि स्फुटं द्वादशराजकम् ॥

४२ अष्टशाखं चतुर्मूलं षष्टिपत्रं द्वये स्थितम् ।
षड्पुष्पं त्रिफलं वृक्षं यो जानाति स नीतिवित् ॥

मण्डलशोधनप्रकरणम्¹¹

४३ पार्ष्णिग्राहस्तदासारः शत्रुमित्रे प्रकीर्तिते ।
आक्रन्दोऽथ तदासारो विजिगीषोरुदाहृते ॥

४४ पुरो यायाद्विगृह्यैव मित्राभ्यां पश्चिमावरी ।
पश्चिमाविव पूर्वाभ्यामरिं तन्मित्रमेव च ॥

४५ अरिमित्रस्य मित्रं तु कृतकृत्येन भूयसा ।
संस्तम्भ्योभयमित्रेण पश्चाद्गृच्छेन्नरेश्वरः ॥

४६ आक्रन्देनात्मना चैव पार्ष्णिग्राहं प्रपीडयेत् ।
आक्रन्देन तदासारमाक्रन्दासारभागिना ॥

४७ मित्रेण चात्मना चैव कुर्वीतोद्धरणं रिपोः ।
मित्रेण हि समित्रेण रिपुमित्रं प्रपीडयेत् ॥

४८ अरिमित्रस्य मित्रस्य पीडनं पृथिवीपतिः ।
कुर्वीतोभयमित्रेण मित्रमित्रेण चैव हि ॥

४९ अनेन क्रमयोगेन विजिगीषुः सदोत्थितः ।
पीडयेदहितं शत्रुं मित्राणामन्तरान्तरा ॥

elements, conqueror and enemy respectively, should really
be considered as one.   40

The mandalas are explained in many such fashions, but
the unit of twelve kings is clear and known to everyone. The
mandala is a tree with eight branches. It has four roots. It has
sixty leaves, which are set on two trunks. It has six flowers,
and finally, three fruits.[4] He who understands this knows
political science.

Securing the Mandala

The enemy's friends are known as the rear adversary and
the latter's backup forces. The conqueror's friends are his
rear supporter and the rear supporter's backup forces. When
the conqueror does battle in front, he should mobilize his
friends to initiate hostilities with his enemy's allies to the
rear. When he does battle toward the rear, he should mobilize his friends in front so as to initiate hostilities with the
enemy and his friends. The king should go forth in battle
only after neutralizing the enemy's friend's friend by means
of a common friend who is more powerful and more accomplished.   45

He should attack the rear adversary both on his own and by
means of his rear supporter. He should use his rear supporter
and the latter's backup force against the enemy's backup
force. He should destroy the enemy both on his own and with
the help of an ally. He should afflict the enemy's friend by
means of his own friend and friend's friend. Further, the king
should engineer the calamity of the enemy's friend's friend

103

५० पीड्यमानो ह्युभयतः सदोद्युक्तैर्मनीषिभिः ।
रिपुरुच्छेदमायाति तद्द्वेशे वावतिष्ठते ॥

५१ सर्वोपायेन कुर्वीत सामान्यं मित्रमात्मसात् ।
भवन्ति मित्रादुच्छिन्नाः सुखोच्छेद्या हि विद्विषः ॥

५२ कारणेनैव जायन्ते मित्राणि रिपवस्तथा ।
रिपवो येन जायेरन्कारणं तत्परित्यजेत् ॥

५३ प्राधान्येन हि सर्वत्र सर्वाः संरञ्जयेत्प्रजाः ।
तासां संरञ्जनाद्राजा सर्वाङ्गीं श्रियमश्नुते ॥१२

५४ दूरेचरान्माण्डलिकांस्तथान्यान्दुर्गवासिनः ।
मित्रीकुर्वीत तत्प्राणाः साधयन्तीह मण्डलम् ॥

५५ चलेच्चेदूर्जितबलो मध्यमो विजिगीषया ।
एकीभूयारिणा तिष्ठेदशक्तः सन्धिना नमेत् ॥

५६ विजिगीषत्युदासीने सर्वे मण्डलिनः सह ।१३
सङ्घधर्मेण तिष्ठेयुः सन्नमेयुरशक्तयः ॥

५७ समुत्पन्नेषु कृच्छ्रेषु सम्भूय स्वार्थसिद्धये ।
आपत्प्रतरणं सम्यक्सङ्घधर्म इति स्थितिः ॥

५८ सहजः कार्यजश्चैव द्विविधः शत्रुरिष्यते ।
सहजः स्वकुलोत्पन्न इतरः कार्यजः स्मृतः ॥

५९ उच्छेदनं चापचयः पीडनं कर्शनं तथा ।
इति विद्याविदः प्राहुः शत्रौ वृत्तं चतुर्विधम् ॥

by means of a common friend and a friend's friend. Through this order of hostilities, the ever-active conqueror should afflict his vicious enemy, along with the latter's successively arrayed allies. When the enemy is afflicted on both sides by ever-engaged wise men, he either meets ruin or remains under the conqueror's control. Using all available means, the conqueror should annex the territory of an ally common to both himself and the enemy, for enemies severed from their allies are easy to destroy.

Friends and enemies alike are produced by some cause. The causes through which enemies are produced must be eliminated. First and foremost, the king should gratify his subjects. The king thereby enjoys comprehensive royal majesty. He should make friends with rulers of far-off realms and those who dwell in forts. Kings vitalized by such allies are able to perfect their realm. If the intermediate king launches an attack, once his forces are fortified by allies, the expansionist king should resist him in union with his enemy. If he is not strong enough to resist, then he should bow down in submission and forge an alliance.

If the neutral one attacks, all the kings should unite, following the law of confederation, but again, they should all bow down in submission if their power is insufficient. Coming together when problems arise to accomplish their own goals, and to fully persist through calamity, is what is meant by "the law of confederation."

There are two kinds of enemy, natural and artificial. The first is a product of ancestral enmity; the other type comes from rivalry over a specific objective. The four expedients for dealing with an enemy, specified by the scholars of

६० उच्छेदनं तु विज्ञेयं सर्वप्रकृतिनाशनम् ।
नाशो योग्यनरादीनां बुधैरपचयः स्मृतः ॥

६१ रेचनं कोशदण्डाभ्यां महामात्रवधस्तथा ।
एतत्कर्शनमित्याहुराचार्याः पीडनं परम् ॥

६२ समाश्रयविहीनो वा दुर्बलं वा समाश्रितः ।
शक्योऽरिः सम्पदा युक्त उच्छेत्तुं भूम्यनन्तरः ॥१४

६३ कर्शनं पीडनं काले कुर्वीताश्रयमानिनः ।
समाश्रयं दुर्गमाहुर्मित्रं वा साधुसम्मतम् ॥

६४ विभीषणस्य सोदर्यस्तथा सूर्यसुतस्य च ।
सर्वतन्त्रापहारित्वात्तथोच्छेद्यो निजो रिपुः ॥

६५ छिद्रं कर्म च वित्तं च विजानाति निजो रिपुः ।१५
दहत्यन्तर्गतश्चैव शुष्कं वृक्षमिवानलः ॥

६६ बलिना विगृहीतस्य जिगीषुः कृच्छ्रवर्तिनः ।
कुर्वीतोपचयं शत्रोरात्मोच्छित्तिविशङ्कया ॥१६

६७ यस्मिन्नुच्छिद्यमाने तु रिपुरन्यः प्रवर्तते ।
न तस्योच्छित्तिमातिष्ठेत्कुर्वीतैनं स्वगोचरम् ॥

६८ वंशागतो रिपुर्यश्च विचलेदुरवग्रहः ।१७
तस्य संयमनायाशु तत्कुलीनं समुन्नयेत् ॥

६९ विषं विषेण व्यथते वज्रं वज्रेण भिद्यते ।
गजेन्द्रो दृष्टसारेण गजेन्द्रेणैव वध्यते ॥

106

governance, are "dissevering," "despoiling," "afflicting," and "depleting." "Dissevering" means destroying all his state-elements. Wise men call the destruction of his men and draft animals "despoiling." The teachers say that "depleting" means draining his treasury and his coercive power, while "afflicting" means assassinating high officials, and so on. If he lacks support in the form of fortifications and allies, or if his fortifications and allies are weak, a wealthy enemy from an adjacent territory can be cut off from his resources. The expansionist king should deplete the resources of an enemy who is arrogant about his means of support and afflict him at an opportune moment. Wise men agree that the means of support consist of fortifications and allies. Vibhishana's brother Ravana and the sun god Surya's son Valin were rendered vulnerable by their own brothers, through having all their powers confiscated.[5] In this exact way one should make one's own enemy susceptible to destruction.

The natural enemy knows one's wealth, activities, and weak points; when he penetrates, he burns like fire inside a dried-out tree. When an enemy is attacked by a stronger adversary and finds himself in dire straits, one should offer support, otherwise there is the lurking danger of one's own destruction later. When one enemy is destroyed, another is born. Therefore never countenance the destruction of an enemy, and instead seek to bring him into the fold. If an enemy from one's own extended family launches hostilities and becomes difficult to control, then induce another one of his relatives to swiftly contain him. Poison fights poison; diamond cuts diamond; only a strong bull elephant can subdue another; fish devour fish, and kinsmen, their

७० मत्स्यो मत्स्यमुपादत्ते ज्ञातिर्ज्ञातिमसंशयम् ।
रावणोच्छित्तये रामो विभीषणमपूजयत् ॥

७१ यस्मिन्मण्डलसंक्षोभः कृते भवति कर्मणि ।
न तत्कुर्वीत मेधावी प्रकृतीरनुरञ्जयेत् ॥

७२ साम्ना दानेन मानेन प्रकृतीरनुरञ्जयेत् ।
आत्मीया भेददण्डाभ्यां परकीयास्तु भेदयेत् ॥

७३ आकीर्णं मण्डलं सर्वं मित्रैररिभिरेव च ।
सर्वः स्वार्थपरो लोकः कुतो मध्यस्थता क्वचित् ॥

७४ भोगप्राप्तं विकुर्वाणं मित्रमप्यवपीडयेत् ।
अत्यन्तविकृतं हन्यात्स पापीयात्रिपुर्मतः ॥

७५ वर्तते पक्षपातेन मित्रं चेदुभयात्मकम् ।
वज्रीव हि त्रिशिरसं तदुच्छिन्द्यात्कृतत्वरः ॥

७६ अमित्रानपि कुर्वीत मित्राण्युपचयावहान् ।
अहिते वर्तमानानि मित्राण्यपि परित्यजेत् ॥

७७ स बन्धुर्योऽनुबध्नाति हितेष्वत्याहितादरः ।
अनुरक्तं विरक्तं च तन्मित्रमुपकारि यत् ॥

७८ मित्रं विचार्य बहुशो ज्ञातदोषं परित्यजेत् ।
त्यजन्नभूतदोषं हि धर्मार्थावुपहन्ति सः ॥

७९ स्वयं दोषगुणान्वेषी भवेत्सर्वत्र सर्वदा ।
स्वयं ज्ञातेषु दोषेषु शस्यं स्याद्दण्डपातनम् ॥

८० न ह्यविज्ञाय तत्त्वेन दोषं कुप्येत्कथंचन ।
भुजङ्गमिव मन्यन्ते निर्दोषक्रोधिनं जनाः ॥

kinsmen without a doubt. To destroy Ravana, Rama took
recourse to his brother Vibhishana.   70

A wise man should undertake no action that might produce
unrest in his realm. He should please the people, by conciliation, bestowing gifts, and granting honors. He should divide
the enemy's people by violence and sowing dissension. The
entire realm is bestrewn with both friends and enemies. All
pursue their own interests, so how can there be any neutral-
ity? If someone is arrogant in his success and commits an
outrage, you should injure him, even if he is an ally. If he
commits a severe outrage, he becomes a most wicked enemy
and should be killed. If a common ally displays partiality to
the enemy, then destroy him at once, the way Indra wielder
of the lightning-bolt destroyed Trishiras.[6]   75

Make allies of enemies if they can contribute to your
prosperity, but abandon even allies if they act against your
interests. He is a friend who befriends your interests and
works for your benefit. Whether loyal or disloyal, the
one who helps you is a friend. Only after much deliberation should one abandon a friend, and only when his faults
have been made known. When one abandons a faultless
person, dharma is destroyed along with one's material
welfare.

The king should always and everywhere examine virtues
and vices. Punishment is praiseworthy when it falls on
those whose faults one has known for oneself. The
king should never get angry about a fault without
having ascertained the substance of the matter. People
consider him a snake if he gets angry at an innocent person.
The king should know the distinctions among friends: some 80

८१ मित्राणामन्तरं विद्यान्मध्यज्यायःकनीयसाम् ।१८
मध्यज्यायःकनीयांसि कार्याणि च पृथक्पृथक् ॥

८२ न हि मिथ्याभियुञ्जीत शृणुयाच्चापि तद्विधम् ।
मित्रभेदं च ये कुर्युस्तान्समस्तान्परित्यजेत् ॥

८३ प्रायोगिकं मात्सरिकं माध्यस्थं पाक्षपातिकम् ।
सोपन्यासं च जानीयाद्वचः सानुशयं तथा ॥१९

८४ प्रकाशपक्षग्रहणं न कुर्यात्सुहृदां स्वयम् ।
अन्योन्यमत्सरं चैषां स्वयमेवाशु वारयेत् ॥

८५ कार्यस्य हि गरीयस्त्वान्नीचानामपि कालवित् ।
सतोऽपि दोषान्प्रच्छाद्य गुणानप्यसतो वदेत् ॥

८६ प्रायो मित्राणि कुर्वीत सर्वावस्थानि भूपतिः ।
बहुमित्रो हि शक्नोति वशे स्थापयितुं रिपून् ॥

८७ न तत्र तिष्ठति भ्राता न पितान्योऽपि वा जनः ।२०
पुंसामापत्प्रतीकारे सन्मित्रं यत्र तिष्ठति ॥

८८ अमित्रान्सर्वतो मित्रैर्निगृह्णीयाद्दृढव्रतैः ।
इति मण्डलवृत्तं तन्मण्डलज्ञाः प्रचक्षते ॥

८९ मित्रोदासीनरिपव एतन्मात्रं तु मण्डलम् ।
सम्यक्साधनमेतेषामिति मण्डलशोधनम् ॥

९० इति स्म राजा नयवर्त्मना व्रजन्समुद्यमी मण्डलशुद्धिमाचरेत् ।
विराजते साधु विशुद्धमण्डलः शरच्छशीव प्रतिरञ्जयन्प्रजाः ॥

are superior, some middling, and some inferior; just as their work is respectively superior, middling, and inferior.

He should not accuse anyone falsely or listen to false allegations. All those who create rifts among friends should be abandoned. He should be able to interpret people's speech, in terms of whether it is informed by political expedient, enmity, impartiality, partiality, insinuation, or remorse. Among his friends, he should not openly take sides against anyone, and he should promptly prevent their mutual enmity.

Understanding the significance of the moment, and in view of the importance of the task, the king should extoll his low-level retainers' virtues, even if they are not real, and cover up their faults, even if they are very real. In general, 85 the king should secure friends of every station. A king with many friends can keep his enemies in check. A brother, a father, or really any other person, is not there for you like a true friend when it comes to quelling a calamity. The basic law of realms, promulgated by authorities on mandalas, is that one should always attack one's enemies using allies who hold fast to their promises. The realm is composed entirely of friends, neutrals, and enemies. If one can master them well, one subdues the entire mandala.

The king should follow the path of politics, maintain his efforts, and sanitize his mandala, so that he maintains his grip on a resplendent realm and delights his people; glimmering like the autumnal moon with its resplendent orb that delights people. 90

नवमः सर्गः

सन्धिविकल्पप्रकरणम्

१ बलिना विगृहीतः सन्नृपो ऽनन्यप्रतिकियः।१
आपन्नः सन्धिमन्विच्छेत्कुर्वाणः कालयापनम्॥

२ कपाल उपहारश्च सन्तानः सङ्गतस्तथा।
उपन्यासः प्रतीकारः संयोगः पुरुषान्तरः॥

३ अदृष्टनर आदिष्ट आत्मामिष उपग्रहः।
परिक्रयस्तथोच्छिन्नस्तथा च परदूषणः॥

४ स्कन्धोपनेयः सन्धिश्च षोडशः परिकीर्तितः।
इति षोडशकं प्राहुः सन्धिं सन्धिविचक्षणाः॥

५ कपालसन्धिर्विज्ञेयः केवलं समसन्धिकः।
सम्प्रदानाद्भवति य उपहारः स उच्यते॥

६ सन्तानसन्धिर्विज्ञेयो दारिकादानपूर्वकः।
सद्भिः सङ्गतसन्धिस्तु मैत्रीपूर्व उदाहृतः॥

७ यावदायुःप्रमाणस्तु समानार्थप्रयोजनः।
सम्पत्तौ च विपत्तौ च कारणैर्यो न भिद्यते॥२

८ सङ्गतः सन्धिरेवेह प्रकृष्टत्वात्सुवर्णवत्।
अपरैः सन्धिकुशलैः काञ्चनः स उदाहृतः॥

९ भव्यामेकार्थसिद्धिं तु समुद्दिश्य क्रियेत यः।
स उपन्यासकुशलैरुपन्यास उदाहृतः॥

१० मयास्योपकृतं पूर्वमयं प्रतिकरिष्यति।
इति यः क्रियते सन्धिः प्रतीकारः स उच्यते॥

112

CHAPTER 9

Tactic One: Types of Alliances

When the king is attacked by a more powerful enemy—in dire straits and without any other recourse—he should seek an alliance and then bide his time.

Scholars of alliances specify sixteen types, known as: potsherd, gift, offspring, united, deposit, recompense, union, other man, unseen man, ordered, one's own meat, propitiation, buying off, cut off, despoiling the enemy, and installment plan.

The alliance known as potsherd is one that takes place only between equals, while the gift alliance happens through donation. Gift is preceded by bestowing one's daughters in marriage. The united alliance is preceded by a friendship formed among good men; it lasts for life, involves the sharing of common goals, and is never broken for any reason, whether in prosperity or calamity. Because of its superiority, the united alliance is like gold, and therefore other scholars call it the golden alliance. Scholars knowledgeable about deposits understand a deposit alliance as one formed after identifying a shared future prospect of success.

The recompense alliance is formed based on the thought: "I did him a favor before, and he will do the same for me." Thinking, "I will do him a favor and he will do the same for me," Rama made the recompense alliance with Sugriva.[1] When two people undertake an expedition, after identifying a common objective, this combined undertaking is known

5

10

११ उपकारं करोम्यस्य ममाप्येष करिष्यति ।
अयं चापि प्रतीकारो रामसुग्रीवयोरिव ॥

१२ एकार्था सम्यगुद्दिश्य यात्रां यत्र हि गच्छतः ।
स संहतप्रयाणस्तु सन्धिः संयोग उच्यते ॥

१३ आवयोर्योधमुख्याभ्यां मदर्थः साध्यतामिति ।
यस्मिन्पणः प्रक्रियते स सन्धिः पुरुषान्तरः ॥

१४ त्वयैकेन मदीयार्थः सम्प्रसाध्यस्त्वसाविति ।
यत्र शत्रुः पणं कुर्यात्सोऽदृष्टपुरुषः स्मृतः ॥

१५ यत्र भूम्येकदेशेन पणेन रिपुरूर्जितः ।
सन्धीयते सन्धिविद्भिरादिष्टः स उदाहृतः ॥

१६ स्वसैन्येन तु सन्धानमात्मामिष इति स्मृतः ।
क्रियते प्राणरक्षार्थं सर्वदानमुपग्रहः ॥

१७ कोशांशोनाथ कुप्येन सर्वकोशेन वा पुनः ।
शेषप्रकृतिरक्षार्थं परिक्रय उदाहृतः ॥

१८ भुवां सारवतीनां तु दानादुच्छिन्न उच्यते ।
सर्वभूम्युत्थितफलदानेन परदूषणः ॥

१९ परिच्छिन्नं फलं यत्र स्कन्धस्कन्धेन नीयते ।
स्कन्धोपनेयं तं प्राहुः सन्धिं सन्धिविदो जनाः ॥

२० परस्परोपकारश्च मैत्रः सम्बन्धजस्तथा ।
उपहारश्च विज्ञेयाश्चत्वारोऽन्ये तु सन्धयः ॥

२१ एक एवोपहारस्तु सन्धिरेतन्मतं हि नः ।
उपहारस्य भेदास्तु सर्वेऽन्ये मैत्रवर्जिताः ॥

२२ अभियोक्ता बली यस्मादलब्ध्वा न निवर्तते ।
उपहाराद्दते तस्मात्सन्धिरन्यो न विद्यते ॥

114

as the union alliance. When someone makes a wager with another party along the lines of: "Let us have our two chief warriors work together to accomplish my objective," this is called the other man alliance. The unseen man alliance is based on the enemy's wager that: "You alone will end up having to accomplish my objective."[2] When an alliance is concluded after enriching the enemy by handing over a portion of one's territory, the scholars call this the ordered alliance.

When a king hands himself over along with his army, it is known as one's own meat. When he hands over everything to protect his own life, it is known as propitiation. When he hands over part of his treasury, precious metals, or even his entire treasury to protect the other state-elements, this alliance is known as buying off. When he gives over his richest lands, this is known as the cut off alliance. When he gives the entire yield of his lands it is called despoiling the enemy. Where the tribute designated is paid bit by bit in installments, the scholars of alliances call this the installment plan.

According to others there are only four types of alliance: recompense, which is based on mutual benefit; union, which is based on friendship; offspring, which is based on familial relationship; and the gift alliance. In our view, however, there is only one type of alliance, namely the gift, since, excluding union, which is based on friendship, all the others are varieties of the gift. A powerful attacker does not turn back without having received tribute, therefore there is really no alliance other than the gift.

There are twenty types of person with whom one should

२३ बालो वृद्धो दीर्घरोगी तथा ज्ञातिबहिष्कृतः ।
भीरुको भीरुकजनो लुब्धो लुब्धजनस्तथा ॥

२४ विरक्तप्रकृतिश्चैव विषयेष्वतिसक्तिमान् ।
अनेकचित्तमन्त्रश्च देवब्राह्मणनिन्दकः ॥

२५ दैवोपहतकश्चैव दैवचिन्तक एव च ।
दुर्भिक्षव्यसनोपेतो बलव्यसनसङ्कुलः ॥

२६ अदेशस्थो बहुरिपुर्युक्तः कालेन यश्च सः ।
सत्यधर्मव्यपेतश्च विंशतिः पुरुषा अमी ॥

२७ एतैः सन्धिं न कुर्वीत विगृह्णीयात्तु केवलम् ।
एते विगृह्यमाणा हि ध्रुवं यान्ति रिपोर्वशम् ॥

२८ बालस्य ह्याप्रभावत्वान्न लोको योद्धुमिच्छति ।[3]
योद्धुं स्वयमशक्तस्य परार्थे को हि युध्यते ॥[4]

२९ उत्साहशक्तिहीनत्वाद्वृद्धो दीर्घामयस्तथा ।
स्वैरेव परिभूयेते द्वावप्येतावसंशयम् ॥

३० सुखोच्छेद्यो हि भवति सर्वज्ञातिबहिष्कृतः ।
त एवैनं विनिघ्नन्ति ज्ञातयस्त्वात्मसात्कृताः ॥[5]

३१ भीरुर्युद्धपरित्यागात्क्षिप्रमेव विनश्यति ।
वीरोऽप्यवीरपुरुषः सङ्ग्रामे तैर्विमुच्यते ॥

३२ लुब्धस्यासंविभागित्वान्न युध्यन्तेऽनुजीविनः ।
लुब्धानुजीवी तैरेव दानभिन्नैर्निहन्यते ॥

not conclude an alliance: a child, an elderly person, someone afflicted with a chronic disease, someone banished by his relatives, a coward, someone whose followers are cowards, a greedy person, someone whose followers are greedy, someone whose state-elements have become disaffected, someone excessively attached to sensual pleasures, a person whose thoughts and strategy are confused, a reviler of gods and Brahmans, someone afflicted with evil destiny, someone obsessed with destiny and divination, someone whose country is beset with famine, someone whose army is riddled with vice, someone not residing in his own territory, someone   25
with many enemies, someone unable to seize the moment, and someone bereft of dharma and truthfulness. One should not conclude an alliance with these types of people, but only attack them. These types of people, when attacked, swiftly fall under their enemy's power.

Because a child lacks power, no one wants to fight on his behalf. When he is incapable of fighting on his own, who will fight for him? Because they lack the power of determination, neither an elderly person nor someone suffering from chronic disease is worth fighting for—both will doubtlessly be defeated anyway by their own people.

Someone banished by his relatives is easy to destroy. His relatives will take the conqueror's side and annihilate him on their own. A cowardly person collapses on his own by aban-   30
doning the fight. Even a valiant person whose soldiers are cowards finds himself abandoned in battle. Because a greedy person does not share the spoils of battle, his followers will not fight for him. The followers of a greedy man will even kill him themselves when enticed to dissension by bribes.

३३ सन्त्यज्यते प्रकृतिभिर्विरक्तप्रकृतिर्युधि ।
सुखाभियोगो भवति विषयेष्वतिसक्तिमान् ॥

३४ अनेकचित्तमन्त्रश्च द्वेष्यो भवति मन्त्रिणाम् ।
अनवस्थितचित्तत्वात्कार्ये तैः समुपेक्ष्यते ॥

३५ सदा धर्मबलीयस्त्वाद्देवब्राह्मणनिन्दकः ।
विशीर्यते स्वयं ह्येव दैवोपहतकस्तथा ॥

३६ सम्पत्तौ च विपत्तौ च दैवमेव हि कारणम् ।६
इति दैवपरो ध्यायन्नात्मना न विचेष्टते ॥

३७ दुर्भिक्षव्यसनी चैव स्वयमेवावसीदति ।
बलव्यसनयुक्तस्य योद्धुं शक्तिर्न विद्यते ॥

३८ अदेशस्थो हि रिपुणा स्वल्पकेनापि हन्यते ।
ग्राहोऽल्पीयानपि जले गजेन्द्रमपकर्षति ॥७

३९ बह्वमित्रस्तु सन्त्रस्तः श्येनमध्ये कपोतवत्
येनैव गच्छति पथा तेनैवाशु विनश्यति ॥

४० अकालयुक्तसैन्यस्तु हन्यते कालयोधिना
कौशिकेन हतज्योतिर्निशीथ इव वायसः ॥

४१ सत्यधर्मव्यपेतेन न सन्दध्यात्कथंचन ।
स सन्धितो ऽप्यसाधुत्वादचिराद्याति विक्रियाम् ॥८

118

Someone whose state-elements are disaffected quickly finds himself abandoned in battle by them. Someone given over to sensual pleasures is easy to attack. Someone whose thoughts and strategy are confused is hated by his counselors; they ignore him as they go about their tasks because his thinking is muddled. Dharma is most powerful, and hence revilers of gods or Brahmans will always destroy themselves on their own, crushed by destiny. Brooding that "destiny   35 alone is the cause of prosperity and downfall," the person obsessed with destiny does nothing himself. Someone whose land is beset with famine collapses on his own, while someone whose army is riddled with vice has no power to wage war.

Even a feeble enemy can overcome someone not residing in his own territory, just as even a small crocodile can drag an elephant away into the water. Someone with many enemies—terrorized like a pigeon among hawks—meets his destruction no matter which path he takes. A warrior who observes the proper moment can kill someone whose army is unable to seize the proper moment, just as an owl can kill a crow unable to see without light at night. One should   40 never form an alliance with someone who lacks dharma and truthfulness. Such a person, even when firmly united in an alliance, quickly transgresses it out of wickedness.

There are seven types of person worthy of alliance: a truthful person, a noble person, a righteous person, an ignoble person, someone with a league of powerful brothers, someone with a powerful army, and someone who has accumulated many victories in battle.

When a truthful person who keeps his promises enters into

119

४२ सत्यार्यौ धार्मिकानार्यौ भ्रातृसङ्घातवान्बली ।
अनेकविजयी चेति सन्धेयाः सप्त कीर्तिताः ॥

४३ सत्योऽनुपालयन्सत्यं सन्धितो नैति विक्रियाम् ।
प्राणबाधेष्वपि व्यक्तमार्यो नायात्यनार्यताम् ॥

४४ धार्मिकस्याभियुक्तस्य सर्व एव हि युध्यते ।
प्रजानुरागाद्धर्माच्च दुःखोच्छेद्यो हि धार्मिकः ॥

४५ सन्धिः कार्यो ह्यनार्येण संप्राप्योत्सादयेद्धि सः ।९
रेणुकायाः सुत इव मूलेष्वपि न तिष्ठति ॥

४६ सङ्घातवान्यथा वेणुर्निबिडः कण्टकैर्वृतः ।
न शक्यते समुच्छेत्तुं भ्रातृसङ्घातवांस्तथा ॥

४७ समाक्रान्तस्य बलिना सर्वयत्नवतोऽपि हि ।
हरिणस्येव सिंहेन शरणं नैव विद्यते ॥

४८ ईषदायच्छमानोऽपि सिंहो मत्तानपि द्विपान् ।
निहन्ति बलवांस्तस्मात्सन्धेयः शिवमिच्छता ॥

४९ बलिना सह योद्धव्यमिति नास्ति निदर्शनम् ।
प्रतिवातं न हि घनः कदाचिदुपसर्पति ॥१०

५० बलीयसि प्रणमतां काले विक्रामतामपि ।
सम्पदो नापगच्छन्ति प्रतीपमिव निम्नगाः ॥

५१ जमदग्नेः सुतस्येव सर्वः सर्वत्र सर्वदा ।
अनेकयुद्धजयिनः प्रतापादेव भिद्यते ॥

५२ अनेकयुद्धविजयी सन्धानं यस्य गच्छति ।
तत्प्रतापेन तस्याशु वशं गच्छन्ति विद्विषः ॥

५३ न जातु गच्छेद्विश्वासं सन्धितो ऽपि हि बुद्धिमान् ।११
अद्रोहे समयं कृत्वा वृत्रमिन्द्रः पुरावधीत् ॥

an alliance, he will not transgress it. A noble person, even when his life is in danger, will preserve his nobility. When a righteous person is attacked, everyone fights on his behalf. A righteous person is difficult to destroy precisely because of his righteousness and the people's loyalty to him. An alliance must be made even with an ignoble person, otherwise he will attack and destroy you down to the root, just as Renuka's son Parashurama wiped out the Kshatriyas down to the root.[3] Just as a sturdy piece of bamboo surrounded by a thorny bush   45 cannot be broken, so a man sturdily in league with powerful brothers cannot be broken.

When you are attacked by a powerful enemy, there is no refuge in this world—for all your efforts—as when a deer is attacked by a lion. Even when a powerful enemy wants to seize only a small portion of the kingdom, he will kill you the way a lion will kill even raging elephants. Therefore you should make an alliance. There is no support for the proposition that one should fight against a more powerful enemy. Indeed, a cloud never drifts against the wind. When men of valor bow down at an opportune moment before a more powerful adversary, their riches do not drain away, just as rivers do not flow backward.   50

Someone who, like the son of Jamadagni,[4] is victorious in many battles finds that everyone everywhere is ever broken by the mere aura of his power. When you conclude an alliance with someone victorious in many battles, the mere aura of his power will quickly bring the enemy under your control. A prudent king, however, should never be trusting even after entering into an alliance. Indra killed Vritra once upon a time after making a peace agreement.[5] A son changes his nature

५४ विकारं याति पुत्रोऽपि राज्यालीढस्तथा पिता ।
तल्लोकवृत्तान्नृपतेरन्यद्वृत्तं प्रचक्षते ॥

५५ अभियुक्तो बलवता तिष्ठन्दुर्गे प्रयत्नवान् ।
तद्बलीयस्तराह्वानं कुर्वीतात्मविमुक्तये ॥

५६ स्वशक्त्युत्साहमुद्वीक्ष्य विगृह्णीयान्महत्तरम् ।
केसरीव द्विपमिति भरद्वाजः प्रभाषते ॥

५७ एकोऽपि सिंहः साहसं यूथं मश्राति दन्तिनाम् ।
तस्मात्सिंह इवोदग्रमात्मानं वीक्ष्य सम्पतेत् ॥१२

५८ ज्यायांसमल्पसैन्यस्य बलाद्विक्रम्य निघ्नतः ।
प्रतापसिद्धाः सर्वत्र भवन्ति रिपवो वशे ॥

५९ सन्धिमिच्छेत्समेनापि सन्दिग्धो विजयो युधि ।
न हि संशयितं कुर्यादित्युवाच बृहस्पतिः ॥

६० आ सम्प्रवृद्धेरभिवृद्धिकामः समेन सन्धानमिहोपगच्छेत् ।१३
अपक्वयोर्वा घटयोरवश्यमन्योन्यभेदी समसन्निपातः ॥

६१ युद्धे विनाशो नियतः कदाचिदुभयोरपि ।
सुन्दोपसुन्दावन्योन्यं समवीर्यौ हतौ न किम् ॥

६२ विहीनोऽपि हि सन्धेयो व्यसने रिपुरागतः ।
पतन्दुनोति हिमवत्तोयबिन्दुरिव क्षते ॥१४

122

when seduced by kingship, and so does a father. They say a king's mode of life has to be totally different from ordinary people.[6]

When attacked by a powerful enemy, the king should remain vigilant in his fort and then call on an ally more powerful than the attacker to liberate him. The king should examine his own power of determination, and then attack a more powerful enemy with all his force, as a lion attacks an elephant. This is the opinion of Bharadvaja. A single lion can shatter a herd of elephants a thousand strong. Therefore, after discerning himself to be fiercely powerful, a besieged king should pounce on his foe like a lion. 55

When he gathers an army, shows his valor, and violently kills a stronger foe, then all his other enemies everywhere will be overwhelmed by the aura of his power. Since victory in battle is doubtful, however, he should seek an alliance even with someone of equal might. Brihaspati says one should never do anything with an uncertain outcome. An expansionist king seeking increase should form an alliance with someone of equal might until he gains profound prosperity. The conflict of equal powers is without doubt mutually destructive, like smashing together two clay jars that have not been properly fired. 60

Sometimes both parties are destroyed in battle. Did not the demons of equal might, Sunda and Upasunda, kill one another?[7] When in distress, one should make an alliance even with a weaker enemy who has approached you, for he can harm you if he falls upon you, like a drop of ice-cold water from the Himalaya mountain can aggravate a wound when it falls. If a weaker party does not want an alliance,

६३ न सन्धिमिच्छेद्धीनश्चेत्तत्र हेतुरसंशयः।
तस्य विस्रम्भमालभ्य प्रहरेत्तत्र निःस्पृहः॥१५

६४ बलीयसाभिसन्धाय तं प्रविश्य प्रयत्नवान्।१६
तथासावुपगन्तव्यो यथा विस्रम्भमाप्नुयात्॥

६५ विस्रम्भे नित्यमुद्युक्तो निगूढाकारचेष्टितः।
प्रियाण्येवाभिभाषेत यत्कार्यं कार्यमेव तत्॥

६६ विस्रम्भात्प्रियतामेति विस्रम्भात्कार्यमृच्छति।१७
विस्रम्भेण हि देवेन्द्रो दितेर्गर्भमपातयत्॥

६७ युवराजेन सन्धाय प्रधानपुरुषेण वा।
अन्तःप्रकोपं जनयेदभियोक्तुः स्थिरात्मनः॥१८

६८ अर्थोत्सर्गेण महता लेखैश्चाप्यात्मसंहितैः।१९
प्रधानपुरुषस्येह प्रकुर्वीतार्थदूषणम्॥

६९ दूषिते हि महामात्रे रिपुरुग्रोऽपि धीमता।
स्वपक्षे यात्यविश्वासमित्थंभूतश्च निष्क्रियः॥२०

७० अरेरमात्यान्सन्धाय तदारम्भं शमं नयेत्।
भिषग्भेदेन वा शत्रुं रसदानेन शातयेत्॥

७१ अरेः सर्वप्रयत्नेन पश्चात्कोपं प्रकल्पयेत्।
पश्चात्कोपमथानिष्टमनुसृत्य प्रधर्षयेत्॥२१

७२ तद्देशकृतसंवासैश्चरैर्नैमित्तिकैरपि।
उपोढव्यसनादेशं कारयेत्सिद्धलक्षणैः॥

there must be some reason. The conqueror should therefore cultivate his trust—and then annihilate him without a
second thought.

When a powerful conqueror forms an alliance with a more
powerful adversary, he should obey him studiously to gain
his trust. A trustworthy person is always on task, concealing
gestures and activities that might give away secret strate-
gies. He should say only what is pleasing and do whatever
needs to be done. Through trustworthiness, you gain affection; through trustworthiness you accomplish your aims.
Through trustworthiness, Indra lord of gods smashed Diti's   65
womb, causing her to miscarry.[8]

When attacked, the king should enter into an alliance
with the prince regent or the chief minister of the resolute
attacker. In this way he should create dissension before coun-
terattacking. Through hefty bribes and forged documents,
he should implicate the enemy's chief minister in treachery.
When a wise king has implicated the chief minister in treachery, even a fierce enemy is paralyzed because his people
are rendered untrustworthy. By making alliances with his
enemy's ministers, the king should extinguish his enemy's
efforts. Or else by inciting the enemy's doctors to rebellion,
he should get them to administer poison.   70

He should make every effort to provoke the enemy's
enemies to the rear. After creating a volatile situation among
them, the king should attack the enemy. He should employ
spies living in the enemy's territory in the convincing guise
of astrologers, instructing them to predict disaster as the
outcome of his undertakings.

A king who has applied discernment in his examination of

७३ क्षयव्ययायासवधादिदोषव्यपेक्षयान्वीक्षितसाधुकृत्यः।
कामं तु पीडामपि काञ्चिदिच्छेन्न विग्रहं तत्प्रभवा हि दोषाः॥

७४ कलत्रमात्मा सुहृदो धनानि वृथा भवन्तीह निमेषमात्रात्।२२
मुहुर्मुहुश्चाकुलितानि तानि तस्मान्न विद्वानतिविग्रही स्यात्॥

७५ सुहृद्धनं तथा राज्यमात्मानं कीर्तिमेव च।
युधि सन्देहदोलास्थं को हि कुर्यादबालिशः॥२३

७६ साम्ना प्रदानेन विभेदनेन सन्धापयेत्साध्वभियुज्यमानः।२४
सन्धित्सुरारात्समसैन्यचक्रं सामन्तमायान्तमपेतसन्धिम्॥२५

७७ स्वगुप्तिमाधाय सुसंहतेन बलेन धीरो विचरन्नरातिम्।
सन्तापयेद्येन सुसंप्रतप्तस्तप्तेन सन्धानमुपैति तप्तः॥२६

७८ इति स्म सन्धिं खलु सन्धिवित्तमा बभाषिरे पूर्वतना महर्षयः।
तदेतदेवं विनयेन्नरेश्वरः संवीक्ष्य कार्यं गुरु चेतरद्विधा॥२७

right conduct would readily choose any hardship over going to war, since war entails destruction, wastage, suffering, death, and other hardships. War is the source of all troubles. 73

In war, one's wife, oneself, friends, wealth, and everything can all come to naught in the blink of an eye. Such calamities arise again and again. Therefore a wise man should not be a warmonger. 74

A war puts oneself, one's friends, wealth, kingdom, and glory in danger's balance. Who other than a fool would do it? 75

When a king is attacked, he should push his neighboring enemy toward an alliance through conciliation, donation, and sowing dissension. He should pursue alliance with an enemy who is approaching nearby, who has an equivalent military, and with whom he has not already forged an alliance. 76

The prudent king should advance on the enemy with an impregnable army that is heavily secured in order to torment him. A piece of metal fuses with another piece of metal only when both have been thoroughly heated. 77

This is what the ancient sages, the most learned scholars on the matter of alliances, have said about alliances. After thoroughly examining the weighty matter of what is to be done—as exemplified here—the king should apply the tactic of alliance, or else adopt a duplicitous strategy. 78

दशमः सर्गः

विग्रहविकल्पप्रकरणम्

१ अमर्षोपगृहीतानां मन्युसन्तप्तचेतसाम् ।
   परस्परापकारेण पुंसां भवति विग्रहः ॥

२ आत्मनोऽभ्युदयाकाङ्क्षी पीड्यमानः परेण वा ।
   देशकालबलोपेतः प्रारभेतैव विग्रहम् ॥

३ राज्यस्त्रीस्थानदेशानां ज्ञानस्य च बलस्य च ।९
   अपहारो मदो मानः पीडा वैषयिकी तथा ॥

४ ज्ञानार्थशक्तिधर्माणां विघातो दैवमेव च ।
   मित्रार्थं चावमानश्च तथा बन्धुविनाशनम् ॥

५ भूतानुग्रहविच्छेदस्तथा मण्डलदूषणम् ।
   एकार्थाभिनिवेशित्वमिति विग्रहयोनयः ॥

६ राज्यस्त्रीस्थानदेशानां दानेन च दमेन च ।
   विग्रहस्य तु युक्तिज्ञैरिति प्रशमनं स्मृतम् ॥

७ एतदेव तु विज्ञेयं स्वार्थधर्मविघातजे ।
   विषयध्वंसजे शत्रोर्विषयप्रतिपीडनम् ॥

CHAPTER 10

Tactic Two: Types of War

War comes about as a result of mutual injury between men seized by enmity, their minds inflamed with rage. But a king should only undertake war in the quest for political advancement or after being attacked by an enemy, and only if he possesses favorable terrain, timing, and forces. The sources of war are usurpation of the kingdom; abduction of women; occupation of fortifications; occupation of territories; seizure of the means of knowledge; seizure of the army; recklessness, arrogance, or exploitation of one's territory; damage to knowledge;[1] damage to economic interests; damage to royal power; affront to moral order; reasons of fate; the interests of one's allies; to remedy dishonor; because one's kinsmen have been killed; because of withdrawal of favor to people one has vowed to favor; because of subverting the mandala's stability;[2] or because of vying for the same objective.[3]

Scholars hold that war can be stopped by returning the kingdom, women, and lands that have been appropriated, or through restraint. Similar methods of recompense and restraint should be understood to apply to war arising from damage to one's economic interests or the moral order. But if the enemy destroys the king's territorial interests, then he should respond by destroying the enemy's territorial interests in return.[4]

When war arises through seizure of the means of

८   ज्ञानापहारसम्भूते ज्ञानशक्तिविघातजे ।२
शमस्तदर्थत्यागेन क्षान्त्या वोपेक्षणेन वा ॥

९   अधर्मद्रोहसंयुक्ते मित्रजातेऽप्युपेक्षणम् ।
आत्मवन्मित्रजाते तु प्राणानपि परित्यजेत् ॥

१०   अपमानात्तु सम्भूतं मानेन प्रशमं नयेत् ।
सामपूर्व उपायो वा प्रणामो वाभिमानजे ॥

११   रहस्येन प्रयोगेण रहस्यकरणेन वा ।
विग्रहं शमयेद्धीरो बन्धुनाशसमुद्भवम् ॥

१२   येन पीडा न जायेत तादृशं तु विचक्षण: ।
कुर्यादर्थपरित्यागमेकार्थाभिनिवेशजे ॥

१३   धनापहारजे जातु विरोधं न समाचरेत् ।
कदाचिद्विग्रहे पुंसां सर्वनाशोऽपि जायते ॥

१४   दृष्टोपन्यासयुक्तेन सम्प्रदानादिकेन च ।
महाजनसमुत्पन्नं भेदेन प्रशमं नयेत् ॥

१५   भूतानुग्रहविच्छेदजातस्यान्तं व्रजेद्दृशी ।३
दैवमेव तु दैवोत्थे शमनं साधुसम्मतम् ॥

१६   मण्डलक्षोभसम्भूतमुपायैः प्रशमं नयेत् ।
सापत्नं वास्तुजं स्त्रीजं वाग्घातमपराधजम् ॥

१७   वैरप्रभेदनिपुणैर्वैरं पञ्चविधं स्मृतम् ।
जातं भूम्युपरोधेन तथा शक्तिविघातजम् ॥

knowledge, through damage to knowledge, or through damage to royal power, the method of quelling it is to grant what the enemy wants, to practice tolerance, and to practice disregard.[5] One should ignore a war started by an unrighteous, rebellious ally. But if a war is launched by an ally who is like a second self, one should give up even one's life to help him. A war caused by dishonor should be stopped through a show of respect; it can also be stopped through conciliation and related methods, as well as by paying homage.[6]   10

A steadfast king should conclude a war originating from the assassination of his kinsman through the application of covert stratagems or covert use of force. In the case of a war arising from vying for the same object, a prudent ruler should abandon that object so long as no serious loss is sustained. In the case of hostilities arising from appropriation of wealth, one should not enter into conflict, since in some cases war between men leads to total destruction.[7]

A war initiated by prominent men should be stopped by means of public gifts and offerings tied to sowing dissension.[8] When conflict arises from withdrawal of favor to people one has vowed to favor, one must dominate the scene and see a war to its end. When there is conflict for reasons of destiny, it can only be concluded by divinatory intervention—such is the opinion of wise men.[9]   15

One should quell a conflict arising from internal disturbance among the state-elements, by using the primary methods: conciliation, donation, sowing dissension, and coercion.[10] There are five types of hostility acknowledged by experts in the matter, depending on whether hostility arises from rivalry, property in land, women, hostile words, or is

१८ भूम्यनन्तरजातं च मण्डलक्षोभजं तथा ।
चतुर्विधं वैरजातं बाहुदन्तिसुतोऽब्रवीत् ॥

१९ कुलापराधजे प्राहुर्वैरे द्वे एव मानवाः ।
किञ्चित्फलं निष्फलं च सन्दिग्धफलमेव च ॥

२० तदात्वे दोषजननमायत्यां चापि निष्फलम् ।
आयत्यां च तदात्वे च दोषस्य जननं तथा ॥

२१ अपरिज्ञातवीर्येण परेण स्तोभितो अपि वा ।४
परार्थं स्त्रीनिमित्तं च दीर्घकालं द्विजोत्तमैः ॥

२२ अकाले दैवयुक्तेन बलोद्धृतसखेन च ।५
तदात्वे फलसंयुक्तमायत्यां फलवर्जितम् ॥

२३ आयत्यां फलसंयुक्तं तदात्वे निष्फलं तथा ।
इतीमं षोडशविधं न कुर्यादेव विग्रहम् ॥

२४ तदात्वायतिसंशुद्धमारभेत विचक्षणः ।
तदात्वायतिशुद्धानि सर्वकर्माणि चिन्तयेत् ॥

२५ तदात्वायतिसंशुद्धमातिष्ठन्नैति वाच्यताम् ।
साधु लोकद्वयग्राहि विद्वान्कर्म समाचरेत् ॥
परित्यजेदिमं लोकं नार्थलेशोपलोभितः ।६

२६ परलोकविरुद्धानि कुर्वाणं दूरतस्त्यजेत् ।
इत्यागमप्रमाणत्वात्साधु कल्याणमाचरेत् ॥

born of a crime. The son of Bahudanti says that hostilities are of four types: arising from seizure of land; arising from damage to royal power; arising from hostile neighbors; and arising from internal disturbance among the state-elements. The followers of Manu acknowledge two types of hostilities: inherited, and born of an offense.

There are sixteen types of war that one should not undertake: war of little benefit; war of no benefit; war of doubtful benefit; war producing immediate problems and no future benefit; war producing immediate as well as future problems; war with an enemy whose power is unknown; war in which one has been cornered by an adversary; war waged on behalf of others; war for the sake of women; protracted war; war against exalted Brahmans; war out of season; war against someone with destiny on his side; war against someone with powerful allies; war with immediate benefit, but no future benefit; and lastly, war with future benefits, but no immediate benefit. 20

A prudent king should undertake actions that are fully sound both at present and in the future. He should focus on both present and future soundness in all his actions. When he maintains policies that are fully sound both at present and in the future, he never attracts opprobrium. Likewise, a wise man undertakes actions that satisfy both the earthly and heavenly worlds. One should not forfeit this world, lured by a trace of material gain. Likewise, one should reject and keep at a distance anyone offending against the world beyond. Thus, with scripture as infallible guide, one should act in a thoroughly righteous way. 25

When his army is content and well fed; when his state-

२७ यदा मन्येत मतिमान्हृष्टं पुष्टं स्वकं बलम् ।
परस्य विपरीतं च तदा विग्रहमाचरेत् ॥

२८ स्फीतं यदानुरक्तं च भवेत्प्रकृतिमण्डलम् ।
परस्य विपरीतं च तदा विग्रहमाचरेत् ॥

२९ उपनामि यदा दैवं सुव्यक्तमुपलक्षितम् ।
परस्य विपरीतं तु तदा विग्रहमाचरेत् ॥

३० मित्रमाक्रन्द आसारो यदा स्युर्दृढभक्तयः ।
परस्य विपरीताश्च तदा विग्रहमाचरेत् ॥

३१ भूमिर्मित्रं हिरण्यं च विग्रहस्य फलं त्रयम् ।
यदैतन्नियतंभावि तदा विग्रहमाचरेत् ॥

३२ गुरु वित्तं ततो मित्रं तस्माद्भूमिर्गरीयसी ।
भूमेर्विभूतयः सर्वास्ताभ्यो बन्धुसुहृद्गणाः ॥

३३ सर्वसम्पत्समे शत्रावुपायान्निक्षिपेद्बुधः ।
उपायैरप्रतिव्यूढे समे दण्डः प्रशस्यते ॥

३४ आगतं विग्रहं विद्वानुपायैः प्रशमं नयेत् ।
विजयस्य ह्यनित्यत्वाद्रभसेन न सम्पतेत् ॥

३५ समाक्रान्तो बलवता काङ्क्षन्नभ्रंशिनीं श्रियम् ।
श्रयेत वैतसीं वृत्तिं न भौजङ्गीं कदाचन ॥

३६ क्रमाद्वेतसवृत्तिः सन्प्राप्नोति महतीं श्रियम् ।
भुजङ्गवृत्तिराप्नोति वधमेव तु केवलम् ॥

३७ मत्तप्रमत्तवत्स्थित्वा ग्रसेतोत्प्लुत्य पण्डितः ।
अपरिभ्रश्यमानं हि क्रमप्राप्तं मृगेन्द्रवत् ॥

elements are prosperous and devoted to him; when the signs of favorable destiny are clearly discerned; when his ally, rear supporter, and backup forces are firmly loyal—when the opposite is true of the enemy, in every respect—an intelligent king can launch a war. The fruits of war are three: land, 30 allies, and gold. When these are certain to be forthcoming, he can launch a war. Wealth is important, allies are more important, and land is the most important of all. From land all kinds of riches flow, and from these riches in turn flow hordes of family and friends.

When the adversary is equal to him in all endowments, the king should apply the first three methods: conciliation, donation, and sowing dissension. When these are exhausted, then violence is acceptable. When war has been thrust upon him, a prudent king will also apply the first three methods to end it. Since victory is never certain, one should not take up arms heedlessly.

When attacked by a powerful foe, a king should seek to make his royal power indestructible by adopting the way of the bamboo, which bends and does not break.[11] One should never adopt the way of the snake, which hisses and bites when provoked.[12] From adopting the way of the bamboo in 35 due course, one attains great royal power. He who adopts the way of the snake attains only death.[13]

The wise king should wait for the opportune moment, pretending to be drunk or crazy; then—when he has the enemy right where he wants him, so that he cannot escape—he should pounce like a lion and devour him. The intelligent king should contract like a tortoise and endure injuries, but when the opportune moment arrives, he should rise up like

३८ कौर्मं सङ्कोचमास्थाय प्रहारमपि मर्षयेत्।
कालेे प्राप्ते तु मतिमानुत्तिष्ठेत्क्रूरसर्पवत्॥
काले सहिष्णुर्गिरिवदसहिष्णुश्च वह्निवत्।

३९ स्कन्धेनापि वहेत्काले प्रियाणि समुदाहरन्।
सम्प्राप्ते चैव काले तु भिन्द्याद्घटमिवाश्मनि॥

४० नित्यं स्वार्थपरो लोकः स्वार्थसिद्धिर्यथा भवेत्।
तथा तस्य प्रतीकारं यथोक्तं समुपाचरेत्॥

४१ प्रसादवृत्त्याहितलोकवृत्त्या प्रविश्य शत्रोर्हृदयं निरन्तरम्।
नयाग्रहस्तेन हि कालमास्थितः प्रसह्य कुर्वीत कचग्रहं श्रियः॥

४२ कुलोद्गतं सम्यगुदारविक्रमं स्थिरं कृतज्ञं मतिमन्तमूर्जितम्।७
अतीव दातारमुपेतवत्सलं सुदुष्प्रसाधं प्रवदन्ति विद्विषम्॥

४३ असत्यता निष्ठुरताकृतज्ञता भयं प्रमादोऽलसता विषादिता।
वृथाभिमानोऽपि च दीर्घसूत्रता तथाऽज्ञनाक्षादि विनाशनं श्रियः॥

४४ इति स्म दोषान्वितमाशु विद्विषं
त्रिशक्तियुक्तो विजिगीषया व्रजेत्।
अतोऽन्यथासाधुजनस्य सम्मतः
करोत्यविद्वाननुपघातमात्मनः॥

४५ समन्वितो राज्यपदोत्त्रिनीषया मनीषयान्वीक्षितमण्डलक्रियः।८
इमं नृपो विग्रहमार्गमास्थितः स्थिरोद्यमः सम्प्रयतेत सिद्धये॥

a vicious serpent. At certain times, he should be as patient as a mountain; at others, as merciless as fire. He should be prepared even to carry his enemies on his shoulders, all the while speaking sweet words. But when the right time comes, he should smash him like a clay pot on a stone. People always pursue their own interests and seek their own success. To counteract them, one must act as we have illustrated. 40

One should penetrate deeply into the enemy's heart through pleasing behavior and by acting as his benefactor. But at the right moment one must stretch out the hand of politics and violently grab the goddess of royal power by the hair. 41

They say an enemy is most difficult to handle when he is of noble birth, truthful, amply valorous, steadfast, grateful, intelligent, vigorous, most generous, and kind to those who approach him. 42

Untruthfulness, cruelty, ingratitude, fear, recklessness, laziness, dejection, false pride, procrastination—as well as women, gambling, and the like—are murderers of the goddess of royal power. 43

When the king perceives his enemy to be impaired by the defects described above, he should muster his three powers—of lordship, strategy, and determination—to advance swiftly and conquer him. If, encouraged by wicked people, the king is so unwise as to do otherwise, he will destroy only himself. Scrutinizing the realm's workings 44 with a serene intelligence[14]—and yearning to uphold royal power—the king should make a steadfast effort on the path of war and strive for success. 45

एकादशः सर्गः

यानासनद्वैधीभावसंश्रयविकल्पप्रकरणम्

१ उत्कृष्टबलवीर्यस्य विजिगीषोर्जयैषिणः ।
गुणानुरक्तप्रकृतेर्यात्रा यानमिति स्मृतम् ॥

२ विगृह्य सन्धाय तथा सम्भूयाथ प्रसङ्गतः ।
उपेक्षा चेति निपुणैर्यानं पञ्चविधं स्मृतम् ॥

३ विगृह्य याति हि यदा सर्वाञ्छत्रोर्गणान्बलात् ।¹
विगृह्ययानं यानज्ञास्तदाचार्याः प्रचक्षते ॥

४ अरिमित्राणि सर्वाणि स्वमित्रैः सर्वतो बलात् ।
विगृह्य वारिगमनं विगृह्यागमनं स्मृतम् ॥

५ सन्धायान्यत्र या यात्रा पार्ष्णिग्राहेण शत्रुणा ।
सन्धायगमनं प्रोक्तं तज्जिगीषोः फलार्थिनः ॥

६ एकीभूय यदेकत्र सामन्तैः सामवायिकैः ।
शक्तिशौचयुतैर्यानं सम्भूयगमनं हि तत् ॥

७ उभयारौ तु वा यानं द्वयोः प्रकृतिनाशने ।
सम्भूयगमनं प्रोक्तं हनूमत्सूर्ययोरिव ॥

138

CHAPTER 11

Tactics Three, Four, Five, and Six: Advance, Halt, Duplicity, and Taking Refuge

When the expansionist king marches forth yearning for victory, possessing superior military forces and personal heroism, while his internal state-elements are loyal to him because of his virtues, this is known as "advance." Experts hold that there are five types of advance, depending on whether the advance is: offensive, allied, collective, deceptive, or with disregard.

When one advances, forcefully launching a war against all the troops of one's enemies, scholars call this "offensive advance." It is also known as "offensive advance" when one marshals all one's allies, forcefully advancing to launch a war from every side against the enemy's allies. When the expansionist conqueror, seeking a definite result, makes an alliance with the enemy's rear adversary, it is known as "allied advance."

5

When one advances, after uniting in one location all the allied feudatories possessing the requisite military power and allegiance, this is known as "collective advance." When there is a joint advance of the conqueror and his rival against a common enemy, when both of their internal state-elements face imminent destruction—as when Hanuman and the sun god joined forces—this is also known as "collective advance."[1]

८   अल्पसारानुपादाय प्रतिज्ञाय फलोदयम् ।
गम्यते यत्पराञ्जेतुं सम्भूयगमनं हि तत् ॥२

९   अन्यत्र प्रस्थितः सङ्घादन्यत्रैव हि गच्छति ।
प्रसङ्ख्यानं तत्प्रोक्तमत्र शल्यो निदर्शनम् ॥

१०   रिपुं यातस्य बलिनः संप्राप्याविष्कृतं फलम् ।३
उपेक्ष्य तन्मित्रयानमुपेक्षायानमुच्यते ॥

११   निवातकवचान्हित्वा हिरण्यपुरवासिनः ।
उपेक्षायानमास्थाय निजघान धनञ्जयः ॥

१२   स्त्रियोऽथ पानं मृगया तथाक्षा दैवोपघातश्च बहुप्रकारः ।
इति प्रदिष्टं व्यसनं ह्यानेन समन्वितो यो व्यसनी स गम्यः ॥

१३   परस्परस्य सामर्थ्याविघातादासनं स्मृतम् ।
अरेश्च विजिगीषोश्च तत्पञ्चविधमुच्यते ॥

१४   अन्योन्याक्रान्तिकरणं विगृह्यासनमुच्यते ।
अरिं विगृह्यावस्थानं विगृह्यासनमुच्यते ॥४

१५   यदा दुर्गस्थितः शत्रुर्ग्रहीतुं न च शक्यते ।
विगृह्यैनं तदासीत च्छित्त्वास्यासारवीवधान् ॥५

१६   विच्छिन्नवीवधासारं प्रक्षीणयवसेन्धनम् ।
विरज्यमानप्रकृतिं कालेनैव वशं नयेत् ॥६

140

When the conqueror enlists the support of weaker allies by promising them rewards, in order to advance and conquer an enemy, this is also known as "collective advance."

When one originally advances in one direction, and then changes course for some purpose, this is known as "deceptive advance." Shalya, who went to join Yudhishthira and then changed sides to Duryodhana,[2] is an example. When a powerful conqueror attacks an enemy, but then disregards the clear prospects of success to attack the enemy's ally, this is called "advance with disregard." Dhananjaya practiced the "advance with disregard" when he ignored the Nivatakavachas in order to kill the residents of Hiranyapura.[3]

Women, wine, hunting, gambling, and the various disasters brought on by destiny are all forms of vice and calamity. Someone overcome by them is known as vice-ridden or calamity-ridden. One should advance upon him.

When the power of the expansionist king and his enemy cancel each other out, they practice "halt," which is of five types: "offensive halt," "allied halt," "collective halt," "deceptive halt," and "halt with disregard."

Halt employed after the expansionist king and his enemy have mounted an assault against each other is said to be "offensive halt." When the king suspends hostilities after unilaterally attacking the enemy this is also said to be "offensive halt." When an enemy is holed up in a fort and it is unfeasible to attack him, one should lay siege to the fort and then halt to cut off his backup forces and supply routes. With his supply routes and backup forces severed, and supplies of grain and fuel dwindling, his internal state-elements will become disaffected, and it is only a matter of time before the

१७ अरेश्च विजिगीषोश्च विग्रहे हीयमानयोः ।
सन्धाय समवस्थानं सन्धायासनमुच्यते ॥

१८ निवातकवचैः सार्धं रावणः शत्रुरावणः ।
ब्रह्माणमन्तरे कृत्वा सन्धायासनमास्थितः ॥

१९ उदासीने मध्यमे च समानप्रतिशङ्क्या ।
एकीभूय व्यवस्थानं सम्भूयासनमुच्यते ॥७

२० उभयारिं हि वाञ्छन्तं विनाशमुभयोरपि ।८
सम्भूयैनं प्रतिव्यूहेदधिकं सर्वसम्पदा ॥९

२१ यियासोरन्यमन्यत्र प्रसङ्गेन हि केनचित् ।
आसनं यत्तदर्थज्ञैः प्रसङ्गासनमुच्यते ॥

२२ अथोपेक्ष्यारिमधिकमुपेक्षासनमुच्यते ।
उपेक्षां कृतवानिन्द्रः पारिजातग्रहं प्रति ॥

२३ उपेक्षितस्य वान्यैस्तु कारणेनैव केनचित् ।
आसनं रुक्मिण इव तद्ध्युपेक्षासनं स्मृतम् ॥

२४ बलिनोर्द्विषतोर्मध्ये वाचात्मानं समर्पयन् ।
द्वैधीभावेन वर्तेत काकाक्षिवदलक्षितः ॥

२५ यापयेद्वत्तमास्थाय सन्निकृष्टमरिं तयोः ।१०
उभयोरपि सम्पाते सेवेत बलवत्तरम् ॥

142

expansionist king brings him under his control. When the expansionist king and his enemy are both suffering losses in war, and they form an alliance, remaining stationary, this is called "allied halt." Ravana, who caused his enemies to cry out in terror, made an alliance with the Nivatakavachas by having the god Brahma act as his middleman.[4]

When there is a comparable fear from both the intermediate one and the neutral one, and the expansionist king and his enemy join forces to remain stationary, this is called "collective halt." When a common enemy desires to destroy them both, they should array their forces, with all their resources united in common as a greater power.   20

When the conqueror is advancing against one of his enemies, but then on some pretext or another remains stationary somewhere else, experts call this "deceptive halt." When one halts after observing that the enemy is too powerful, this is called "halt with disregard." Indra practiced disregard when someone stole the celestial *pārijāta* tree.[5] When someone is ignored by others for whatever reason and remains stationary, this is also known as "halt with disregard," such as when Rukmin was dismissed from serving in war by both the Pandavas and the Kauravas.[6]

When a king finds himself in between two powerful enemies who are both attacking, he should offer a vow of submission to both and apply duplicity, undetected like the crow's single eyeball.[7] He should studiously bide his time, paying service to the more proximate of the two enemies. When both attack simultaneously, he should serve the more powerful of the two.   25

If both enemies detect his duplicity and refuse to accept

२६ यदा द्वावपि नेच्छेतां संश्लेषं जातसंविदौ ।
तदोपसर्पस्तच्छत्रुमधिकं वा समाश्रयेत् ॥११॥

२७ द्वैधीभावो द्विधा प्रोक्तं स्वतन्त्रपरतन्त्रयोः ।
स्वतन्त्र उक्तो ह्यन्यस्तु यः स्यादुभयवेतनः ॥

२८ उच्छिद्यमानो बलिना निरुपायप्रतिक्रियः ।
कुलोद्वृत्तं सत्यमार्यमाश्रयेत बलोत्कटम् ॥

२९ तद्दर्शनोपास्तिकता नित्यं तद्भावभाविता ।
तत्कारिता प्रश्रयिता वृत्तं संश्रयिणां स्मृतम् ॥

३० विनीतवत्तत्र कालं गमयित्वा गुराविव ।
तत्सङ्घात्प्रतिपूर्णः सङ्क्रमेण स्ववशो भवेत् ॥

३१ दददुलं वा कोशं वा भूमिं वा भूमिसम्भवम् ॥१२॥
आश्रयेदभियोक्तारं विसन्धिरनपाश्रयः ॥

३२ सर्वाणि चैतान्यार्तः सन्दध्यात्त्राणार्थमात्मनः ।
युधिष्ठिर इवाप्नोति पुनर्जीवन्वसुन्धराम् ॥

३३ निष्पतेदात्मलाभे वा व्यसने वा रिपोः श्रियः ।१३॥
प्रहरेद्वा बलीयस्या सैह्या वा काल उत्थितः ॥१४॥

३४ नाकारणात्सङ्गमियाज्ज्यायसा वेतरेण वा ।
क्षयव्ययकृताद्दोषाद्विसम्भद्रोहजादपि ॥

144

his advances, he should approach a more powerful enemy of both parties and take refuge if necessary. Duplicity is said to be of two types: "independent" and "dependent upon another." The independent variety is what has been described above. The dependent variety amounts to being a de facto mercenary on the payroll of both sides.[8]

When, lacking any stratagem or countermeasure, the king is about to be destroyed by a more powerful enemy, he should take refuge in someone more formidable and high-born, who is also truthful and noble. The conduct prescribed for someone taking refuge is honoring the lord upon seeing him; always thinking and feeling what he thinks and feels; doing his bidding; and behaving courteously toward him. He should behave courteously toward his protector as toward a guru and bide his time until he recovers his power and again becomes independent.　30

When, however, he is without either ally or protector, he should take refuge in the attacker himself; offering his army, treasury, territory, or the products of his lands. When he is afflicted, he should give all these things to save his own life. Like Yudhishthira, he can come back to life and regain the earth.[9] When he comes into his own again, or finds his enemy's royal majesty compromised, he should rise up at the right moment and attack in the powerful way of the lion.

He should not take refuge in someone more powerful—or anyone else—without reason because it can lead to various evils, such as personal damage, waste of resources, and treacherous violations of trust. When making a partnership, you cannot even trust your own father.

३५ संयोगं हेतुना गत्वा पितर्यपि न विश्वसेत् ।
विश्वासमागतं सन्तं प्रायो द्रुह्यन्त्यसाधवः ॥
इति षाड्गुण्यमन्ये तु द्वैगुण्यमभिचक्षते ।

३६ यानासने विग्रहस्य रूपं सद्भिः प्रकीर्तितम् ।
सन्धेस्तु सन्धिमार्गज्ञैर्द्वैधीभावसमाश्रयौ ॥१५

३७ सोऽभिगच्छंश्च तिष्ठंश्च विग्रहं कुरुते यतः ।
ततो यानासने प्राज्ञैर्विग्रहः परिकीर्त्यते ॥

३८ असन्धाय यतो नास्ति द्वैधीभावः समाश्रयः ।
ततो द्वावपि तौ प्राज्ञै रूपं सन्धेरुदाहृतौ ॥

३९ सन्धिश्च विग्रहश्चेति द्वैगुण्यमिति चक्षते
एतौ च संश्रयश्चैव त्रैगुण्यमिति चापरे ॥

४० यस्मादन्यं संश्रयेत बाध्यमानो बलीयसा ।१६
तत्सन्धेः संश्रयो ह्यन्य इत्युवाच बृहस्पतिः ॥

४१ न्याय्यो गुणो विग्रह एक एव सन्ध्यादयोऽन्ये तु गुणास्तदुत्थाः ।
अवस्थया भेदमुपागतः सन्षाड्गुण्यमित्येव गुरोर्मतं नः ॥

Wicked people will attack a good man who is too trusting.   35

 The six tactics are sometimes thought of as just two: good men consider "advance" and "halt" to be varieties of war. The rest, "taking refuge" and "duplicity," are considered varieties of alliance by experts. Since whether he advances or stands in one place, he is still just waging war, scholars consider "advance" and "halt" aspects of war. And since there is no "duplicity" or "taking refuge" without alliance, so they also consider these two to be varieties of alliance. Some say that war and peace are the only two political tactics. Others include "taking refuge" and say there are three. Since one only takes refuge when assailed by a stronger power, Brihaspati says it is different from an alliance.   40

 The only reasonable tactic is war. Alliance and other tactics have their origin in it. Our guru's opinion is that there are six tactics that emerge from war when distinct circumstances present themselves.   41

मन्त्रविकल्पप्रकरणम्

१ षाड्गुण्यनिश्चितमतिर्गुह्यां गूढप्रचारवान् ।
मन्त्रयेतेह मन्त्रज्ञो मन्त्रज्ञैः सह मन्त्रिभिः ॥

२ मन्त्रार्थकुशलो राजा सुखं विजयमश्रुते ।१
विपरीतस्तु विद्वद्भिः स्वतन्त्रोऽप्यवधूयते ॥२

३ दुर्मन्त्रमेनं रिपवो यातुधाना इव क्रतुम् ।
समन्ततो विलुम्पन्ति तस्मान्मन्त्रपरो भवेत् ॥

४ मन्त्रयेतेह कार्याणि सहायेन विपश्चिता ।
आत्तं मूर्खमनात्तं च पण्डितं वर्जयेदिह ॥३

५ मार्गं सन्मार्गगतिभिः सिद्धये सिद्धकर्मभिः ।
पूर्वैराचरितं सद्भिः शास्त्रीयं न परित्यजेत् ॥

६ उच्छास्त्रपदविन्यासः सहसैवाभिसम्पतन् ।
शत्रुखड्गमुखग्रासमगत्वा न निवर्तते ॥

७ प्रभावोत्साहशक्तिभ्यां मन्त्रशक्तिः प्रशस्यते ।
प्रभावोत्साहवान्काव्यो जितो देवपुरोधसा ॥

८ अशिक्षितनयः सिंहो हन्तीभं केवलं बलात् ।
तं च धीरो नरस्तेषां शतानि मतिमाञ्जयेत् ॥

९ पश्यद्भिर्दूरतोऽपायान्सूपायप्रतिपत्तिभिः ।
भवन्तीह फलायैव विद्वद्भिर्मन्त्रिताः क्रियाः ॥

CHAPTER 12

Types of Strategy

A king knowledgeable about strategy, adept at covert action, and mindful of the six tactics should strategize covert actions in the company of counselors knowledgeable about strategy.[1] A king proficient in the essence of strategy easily enjoys victory, while an ignorant king, albeit independent, is throttled by learned enemies. Enemies completely destroy a ruler with bad strategy, just as evil spirits destroy a sacrifice where the sacred incantations are incorrect.[2] Therefore the king must focus on strategy, and should strategize with trusted and discerning counselors, shunning both a trustworthy fool and an untrustworthy sage.

In the pursuit of success, he should never leave the path of the *śāstra*, trod by the great men of old who never strayed from the right path and whose actions were perfect. If he suddenly falls upon his enemy in a manner contrary to the *śāstra's* teaching, he will be swallowed up in the jaws of the enemy's sword and never return. The power of strategy is considered superior to the powers of lordship and determination. The demons' priest, Ushanas Kavya, possessed lordship and determination, but was still defeated by the gods' priest, Brihaspati.

A lion unlearned in politics can kill an elephant by sheer force, yet a steadfast and intelligent man can defeat the lion, and also conquer hundreds of them. A king's actions always have successful results when learned

१० उपायपूर्वं लिप्सेत कालं वीक्ष्य समुत्पतेत् ।
पश्चात्तपाय भवति विक्रमैकरसज्ञता ॥

११ शक्याशक्यपरिच्छेदं कुर्याद्बुद्ध्या प्रसन्नया ।
केवलं दन्तभङ्गाय दन्तिनः शैलताडनम् ॥

१२ अशक्यारम्भवृत्तीनां कुतः क्लेशादृते फलम् ।
आकाशमास्वादयतः कुतस्तु कवलग्रहः ॥⁴

१३ नाग्निं पतङ्गवद्वृच्छेत्स्पृश्यमेव तु संस्पृशेत् ।
किमन्यत्स्यादृते दाहात्पतङ्गस्याग्निमृच्छतः ॥

१४ मोहात्प्रक्षिपतश्रेष्टां दुःखलभ्येषु वस्तुषु ।
भवन्ति परितापिन्यो व्यक्तं कर्मविपत्तयः ॥

१५ बुद्ध्या बोध्यानुगतया परीयात्सम्पदः पदम् ।
विशुद्धपदविन्यासः पर्वताग्रमिवोन्नतम् ॥

१६ दुरारूढं पदं राज्ञां सर्वलोकनमस्कृतम् ।
स्वल्पेनाप्यपचारेण ब्राह्मण्यमिव दुष्यति ॥

१७ आरब्धानि यथाशास्त्रं कार्याण्यमलबुद्धिभिः ।⁵
वनानीव मनोहारि प्रयच्छन्त्यचिरात्फलम् ॥

१८ सम्यगारभ्यमाणं हि कर्म यद्यपि निष्फलम् ।
न तत्तथा तापयति यथा मोहसमीहितम् ॥

१९ यत्तु सम्यगुपक्रान्तं कार्यमेति विपर्ययम् ।
पुमांस्तत्रानुपालभ्यो दैवान्तरितपौरुषः ॥

ministers—those who foresee obstacles from afar, and whose intellects discern the right method—think them through. He should seek to make gains through the correct method, and attack only after considering the right moment. Obsession with force leads to regret.   10

With a lucid mind, he should differentiate between what is possible and impossible: head-butting a mountain leads the elephant only to break its tusk. Pain alone is the outcome for those who undertake impossible tasks. What do you swallow when you try to taste the sky? Do not fall headlong into the flame like a moth. You should only reach for things that are reachable. What will a moth achieve by approaching a flame other than being burnt up? If in delusion a man strives after unreachable things, the disasters unleashed by his actions will burn him up.

Intellect coupled with a grasp of reality leads a man to the pinnacle of prosperity, just as a sure and careful step leads to the mountain's exalted summit. It is difficult to ascend to the   15 position of king, which all people revere. The slightest transgression brings infamy. Just as Brahman status is vitiated through the slightest transgression, so does infamy attach to the king. When men of pure mind undertake actions in accord with the *śāstra,* they swiftly bring forth results, just as well-tended orchards swiftly bring forth lovely fruit. When a plan properly executed yields no result, it will still not torment the mind as would a foolhardy scheme. If properly undertaken, an action will never taint a man with infamy, even when it culminates in a setback, since destiny has here merely stood in the way of human effort. A man of pure mind should still make efforts toward results. For the rest, he should

151

२० प्रयत्नस्तावदास्थेयः फलायामलबुद्धिना ।
अथर्ववेदनिपुणः शेषं दैवं समाश्रयेत् ॥

२१ आत्मानं च परं चैव वीक्ष्य धीरः समुत्पतेत् ।
एतदेव हि विज्ञानं यदात्मपरवेदनम् ॥

२२ निष्फलं क्लेशबहुलं सन्दिग्धफलमेव च ।
न कर्म कुर्यान्मतिमान्महावैरानुबन्धि च ॥

२३ तदात्वायतिसंशुद्धं सुविशुद्धक्रमागतम् ।
हितानुबन्धि च सदा कर्म सद्धिः प्रशस्यते ॥

२४ हितानुबन्धि तज्जातु गच्छेद्येन न वाच्यताम् ।
तस्मिन्कर्मणि सज्जेत तदात्वकटुकेऽपि हि ॥

२५ बुद्ध्यैवोपक्रमः श्रेयान्फलनिष्पत्तये सदा ।
क्वचित्कल्याणमित्रस्य शस्यते सिंहवृत्तिता ॥६

२६ सहसोत्प्लुत्य दुष्टेभ्यो दुष्करं सम्पदार्जनम् ।७
उपायेन पदं मूर्ध्नि न्यस्यते मत्तहस्तिनः ॥

२७ न किंचित्क्वचिदस्तीह वस्त्वसाध्यं विपश्चिताम् ।
अयोऽभेद्यमुपायेन द्रवतामुपनीयते ॥

२८ वाह्यमानमयःपिण्डं महच्चापि न कृन्तति ।८
तदल्पमपि धारावद्द्रवतीप्सितसिद्धये ॥

२९ लोकप्रसिद्धमेवैतद्द्वारि वह्नेर्नियामकम् ।
उपायोपगृहीतेन तत्तेनैव विशोष्यते ॥

३० अविज्ञातस्य विज्ञानं विज्ञातस्य विनिश्चयः ।
अर्थद्वैधस्य सन्देहच्छेदनं शेषदर्शनम् ॥

know the *Atharva Veda* well and leave things up to destiny.[3] 20

A steadfast king should come to know himself and the other, and only then attack. Understanding consists of this alone: knowledge of both self and other. An intelligent man should undertake no action that does not promise a result, while instead promising multiple hardships and a doubtful outcome, or entailing immense hostilities. Good people always praise actions that are equally beneficial both now and in the future, that are morally pure, entailing beneficial outcomes, and framed according to a sound plan. Even if an action is unpleasant in the immediate present, if it entails beneficial outcomes and does not lead to infamy, one should pursue it. An action with a carefully thought-out plan is always better when it comes to producing results. Yet sometimes the way of the lion is praiseworthy for a conqueror whose allies are strong and loyal. 25

A sudden attack to seize resources from wicked people is fraught with difficulty. Only by applying the appropriate methods can you place your foot on the head of a wild elephant.[4] There is nothing anywhere that is impossible for discerning men. Unbreakable iron can be dissolved into liquid by the right method. If you try to put a piece of iron to work—no matter how big it is—it will cut nothing on its own; but when even a tiny piece is honed into a blade, it can do whatever you want. Everyone knows that water stops fire. Yet when certain methods are applied, fire can dry up water.

The duties of a counselor are to make known what is unknown, to establish certitude about the substance of what is known, to remove doubts in the case of dilemmas,

३१ विदुषां शासने तिष्ठन्नावमन्येत कंचन ।
सर्वस्यैवोपशृणुयात्सुभाषितजिघृक्षया ॥

३२ मदोद्धृत्तः क्रियामूढो योऽतिक्रामति मन्त्रिणम् ।
अचिरात्तं वृथामन्त्रमतिक्रामन्ति विद्विषः ॥

३३ संरक्षेन्मन्त्रबीजं हि तद्बीजं हि महीभृताम् ।
तस्मिन्भिन्ने ध्रुवो भेदो गुप्ते गुप्तिरनुत्तमा ॥

३४ सिंहवच्चेष्टमानस्य काले कर्म विपश्चितः ।
क्रियमाणं स्वकुल्यास्तु विद्घुरस्य परे कृतम् ॥

३५ अपश्चात्तापकृत्सम्यगनुबन्धिफलप्रदः ।
अदीर्घकालोऽभीष्टश्च प्रशस्तो मन्त्र इष्यते ॥

३६ सहायाः साधनोपाया विभागो देशकालयोः ।
विपत्तेश्च प्रतीकारः सिद्धिः पञ्चाङ्ग इष्यते ॥

३७ अनुतिष्ठेत्समारब्धमनारब्धं प्रयोजयेत् ।
अनुतिष्ठंश्च संवृत्य विशेषेणोपपादयेत् ॥९

३८ प्रचारयेन्मन्त्रविदः कार्यद्वारेष्वनेकधा ।१०
यत्र तज्ज्ञेतेषां साम्यं तेन शीघ्रं समुत्पतेत् ॥११

३९ यत्र मन्त्रिमनःसाम्यं यत्र चेतो न शङ्कते ।
यत्र सन्तो न निन्दन्ति तत्परीयाच्चिकीर्षितम् ॥१२

४० धृतेऽपि मन्त्रे मन्त्रज्ञैः स्वयं भूयो विचारयेत् ।
तथा वर्तेत मन्त्रज्ञो यथा स्वार्थं न पीडयेत् ॥

154

and to offer a final conclusion. The king should abide by the   30
instruction of the wise and disrespect no one. He should
hear everyone's opinion in the interest of gleaning words
of wisdom. A king deluded by arrogance—who scorns wise
counsel—will be confused in his actions and have worthless
strategy. His enemies will quickly overcome him. The seed
of strategy must be safeguarded, for that is the seed of kings.
When it is exposed, all security is exposed; when guarded,
security reigns supreme.

The discerning king should act like a lion at the opportune moment. His family members may know what he is
doing while he does it, but his enemies should only come to
know of his actions once completed. Strategy is desirable
and praiseworthy when it brings no regret, leads to the right
benefits, and occasions no inordinate delay in achieving the
desired aim. Success is said to have five components: allies,   35
methods, order of time and place, disaster-prevention, and
successful conclusion.

One should tend to what has been undertaken. One should
put into action what has not been undertaken. Finally—
maintaining secrecy—one should accomplish the goal
impeccably. The king should put to work his strategy-ex-
perts to reflect on multiple paths of action. When they reach
consensus, he must spring into action.

He should only undertake plans which good men do not
revile, on which his counselors have reached consensus, and
about which he himself entertains no doubt. Even when the
experts advance a strategy, the king should reflect upon it
himself. He should be knowledgeable about strategy and
never harm his own interests.   40

४१ मन्त्रिणः स्वार्थतात्पर्याद्दीर्घमिच्छन्ति विग्रहम् ।
तेषां च भोग्यातामेति दीर्घकार्याकुलो नृपः ॥

४२ मनःप्रसादः श्रद्धा च तथा करणपाटवम् ।
सहायोत्थानसम्पच्च कर्मणां सिद्धिलक्षणम् ॥१३

४३ लघूत्थानान्यविघ्नानि सम्भवत्साधनानि च ।
कथयन्ति पुरः सिद्धिं करणान्येव कर्मणाम् ॥१४

४४ आवर्तयेन्मुहुर्मन्त्रं धारयेच्च प्रयत्नतः ।
अप्रयत्नधृतो मन्त्रः प्रचलन्नग्निवद्दहेत् ॥

४५ आप्ताप्तसन्ततेर्मन्त्रं संरक्षेत्तत्परस्तु सन् ।१५
अरक्ष्यमाणं मन्त्रं हि भिनत्त्याप्तपरम्परा ॥

४६ मदः प्रमादः कामश्च सुप्तप्रलपितानि च ।
भिन्दन्ति मन्त्रं प्रच्छन्नाः कामिन्योऽवमतास्तथा ॥

४७ निस्तम्भे निर्गवाक्षे च निष्कुड्ड्यान्तरसंश्रये ।१६
प्रासादाग्रे ह्यरण्ये वा मन्त्रयेदविभावितः ॥

४८ द्वादशेति मनुः प्राह षोडशेति बृहस्पतिः ।
उशना विंशतिरिति मन्त्रिणां मन्त्रिमण्डलम् ॥

४९ यथासम्भवमित्यन्ये तत्प्रविश्य यथाविधि ।
मन्त्रयेताहितमनाः कार्यसिद्धिविवृद्धये ॥१७

५० एकैकेनापि कार्याणि प्रविचार्य पुनः पुनः ।१८
प्रविशेत्स्वहितान्वेषी मतमेषां पृथक्पृथक् ॥

156

The counselors, intent on promoting their own interests, always want protracted war. The king becomes the counselors' plaything when he is overwhelmed by protracted campaigns. The signs of success in action are serenity of mind, faith, keen senses, and allies' collective initiative. The tools of action that bespeak imminent success are swift initiative, freedom from obstacles, and the availability of suitable methods.

The king should examine a strategy from all sides and carefully conceal it. If not carefully concealed a strategy will burn him up like a fire breaking out. He must focus keenly on guarding a strategy from the intimate associates of his intimate associates. His larger retinue will talk among themselves about a strategy and destroy it if it is not carefully guarded. Intoxication, carelessness, sensual desire, and 45 talking in one's sleep can all destroy the secrecy of a strategy, as can secret spies and jilted lovers. One should discuss strategy undetected in a room without echoing pillars, windows, or secret hiding places inside the walls; or else in a palace tower or forest.

The circle of counselors has twelve members according to Manu, sixteen according to Brihaspati, and twenty according to Ushanas. Others hold that there should be as many counselors as possible, yet one should interact with the counselors in a formal way, according to the rules, and strategize with a concentrated mind to enhance the success of a project. The king should deliberate about plans for action with each of them one by one, and, to advance his own interest, plumb their thoughts one by one. He should adhere to whatever a 50 wise, beneficial counselor—one experienced in action, and

५१ महापक्षो यथाशास्त्रं दृष्टकर्मा हितः सुधीः ।
यद्ब्रूयान्मतारूढस्तत्तत्साधु समाचरेत्॥

५२ नातीयात्कार्यकालं हि कृत्वा मन्त्रविनिश्चयम् ।
अतिक्रान्तं तु तं भूयो यथायोगं प्रकल्पयेत्॥

५३ न कार्यकालं मतिमानतिक्रामेत्कदाचन ।
कथंचिदेव भवति कार्ययोगः सुदुर्लभः॥

५४ सतां मार्गेण मतिमान्काले कर्म समाचरेत् ।
काले समाचरन्साधु रसवत्फलमश्रुते॥

५५ इति चेति च सम्पश्यन्काले देशे सहायवान् ।
विशुद्धपार्ष्णिः सद्वस्तु समाक्रामेन्न चापलात्॥१९

५६ अहिते हितबुद्धिरल्पधीरवमन्येत मतानि मन्त्रिणाम् ।
चपलः सहसैव सम्पतन्नरिखड्गाभिहतः प्रबुध्यते॥२०

५७ अविचार्य बलाबलं द्विषामहमित्येव समुद्धतोऽनयात् ।२१
चपलः स्वमतेन सम्पतन्निपत्याल्पमना न बुध्यते॥२२

५८ इति मन्त्रबलान्महीपतिर्महतो दुष्टभुजङ्गमानिव ।
विनयेन्नयमार्गमास्थितो वशमुद्योगसमन्वितो रिपून्॥

representing the majority opinion—says in accordance with *śāstra*. The king should make his opinion the foundation, and then put it into practice well. After deciding on a strategy, he must not let the appointed time for putting it into practice lapse. If somehow the appointed time does lapse, he should initiate another session of strategizing according to the rules.

An intelligent person never lets the time for work lapse, since if ever there is a lapse, it is very difficult to reinitiate an action. The intelligent man follows the path of good men and does work at the right time. When he does good work at the proper time, he tastes the sweet fruit of success. Making these kinds of observations—seizing the proper time, location, allies, and with his rear adversary in check—he should undertake a sound project and not act recklessly. 55

A king of weak intellect pursues something detrimental believing it to be beneficial and disdains the opinions of his counselors. Reckless, and suddenly springing into action, such a man wakes up only as he is being slain by his enemy's sword. 56

A reckless, small-minded king who fails to reflect on the relative strengths of the enemy—focusing only on himself in his arrogance, disregarding counsel, and attacking according to his own whim—does not wake until he is meeting his doom. 57

An enterprising king, however, who practices correct politics, will subdue his enemies by the power of strategy as set forth above, just as one subdues huge and vicious snakes by a magical incantation.[5] 58

दूतप्रचारप्रकरणम्

१ कृतमन्त्रः सुमन्त्रज्ञो मन्त्रिणां मन्त्रसम्मतम् ।१
यातव्याय प्रहिणुयाद्दूतं दूत्याभिमानिनम् ॥

२ प्रगल्भः स्मृतिमान्वाग्मी शस्त्रे शास्त्रे च निष्ठितः ।२
अभ्यस्तकर्मा नृपतेर्दूतो भवितुमर्हति ॥

३ निसृष्टार्थो मितार्थश्च तथा शासनवाहकः ।३
सामर्थ्यात्पादतो हीनो दूतस्तु त्रिविधः स्मृतः ॥

४ स भर्तुः शासनादच्छेद्वन्तव्यं ह्युत्तरोत्तरम् ।
स्ववाक्यपरवाक्यानामिति चेति च चिन्तयन् ॥४

५ अन्तपालांश्च कुर्वीत मित्राण्याटविकांस्तथा ।
जलस्थानानि मार्गांश्च विद्यात्स्वबलसिद्धये ॥

६ नाविज्ञातः पुरं शत्रोः प्रविशेन्न च संसदम् ।
कालमीक्षेत कार्यार्थमनुज्ञातश्च निष्पतेत् ॥

७ सारवत्तां च राष्ट्रस्य दुर्गं तद्दुर्गमेव च ।
छिद्रं च शत्रोर्जानीयात्कोशमित्रबलानि च ॥

८ उद्यतेष्वपि शस्त्रेषु यथोक्तं शासनं वदेत् ।
रागापरागौ जानीयाद्दृष्टिवक्रविचेष्टितैः ॥५

CHAPTER 13

An Emissary's Conduct

A king who fully grasps and has perfected his strategy should send an emissary—one whom his counselors endorse as skilled in strategy, and who is renowned for his skills as an emissary—to the enemy he plans to attack. The king's emissary should be learned in his craft, cultivated, intelligent, eloquent, and perfect both in scholarship and arms. The three types of emissaries in order of rank and ability are those with full authority to negotiate, those with limited authority to negotiate, and those who merely bear the king's command.

At the king's command the emissary should go to the enemy, considering the likely sequence of his own king's statements and the enemy king's responses. He should befriend the frontier-guards and forest people, and learn about the dry lands, wetlands, and roads of the enemy territory to advance his army's success.

The emissary should not enter the enemy's city or assembly unannounced. He should take his time to accomplish the task and depart only when granted permission. He should find out about the land's resources, as well as its fortifications and their defenses. He should learn about the enemy's weak points as well as his treasury, allies, and military forces. Even if weapons are raised against him, he should deliver his lord's message exactly. He should also discern the enemy's affection or disaffection from the character of his gaze as

5

९ सहेतानिष्टवचनं कामं क्रोधं च वर्जयेत् ।
नान्यैः शयीत संरक्षेद्द्वावं विद्यात्परस्य च ॥

१० रागापरागौ जानीयात्प्रकृतीनां च भर्तरि ।
कृत्यपक्षोपजापं च कुर्यादनभिलक्षितः ॥६

११ वध्यमानोऽपि न ब्रूयात्स्वस्वामिप्रकृतिच्युतिम् ।७
ब्रूयात्प्रश्रितया वाचा सर्वं वेद भवानिति ॥

१२ कुलेन नाम्ना द्रव्येण कर्मणा च गरीयसा ।८
कुर्याच्चतुर्विधं स्तोत्रं पक्षयोरुभयोरपि ॥

१३ विद्याशिल्पोपदेशेन संशिलष्योभयवेतनैः ।९
कृत्यपक्षं विजानीयात्तद्धर्तुश्च विचेष्टितम् ॥

१४ तीर्थाश्रमसुरस्थाने शास्त्रविज्ञानहेतुना ।१०
तपस्विव्यञ्जनोपेतैः स्वचारैः सह सम्पतेत् ॥११

१५ प्रतापं कुलमैश्वर्यं त्यागमुत्थानसौष्ठवम् ।
अक्षुद्रतां दक्षतां च भर्तुर्भेद्येषु कीर्तयेत् ॥

१६ भावमन्तर्गतं व्यक्तं सुप्तो मत्तश्च भाषते ।
तस्मादेकः स्वपेन्नित्यं स्त्रियः पानं च वर्जयेत् ॥

१७ काले व्रजति मेधावी न खिद्येतार्थसिद्धये ।१२
क्षिप्यमाणं च बुध्येत कालं नानाविलोभनैः ॥

well as the twitching of his mouth. He should put up with unpleasant words and refrain from eagerness and anger alike. He should not sleep near others.[1] He should conceal his own intentions and try to discover the enemy's. He should also learn about the subjects' affection or disaffection for their king. Undetected, he should coax the disaffected into dissension. 10

Even if he is about to be killed, he should divulge nothing about his master's weakness or the weakness of his state-elements. He should simply respond politely: "You sir already know everything." He should praise both sides on four counts: parentage, renown, wealth, and good works.

On the pretext of gaining instruction in various branches of learning and crafts, the emissary should gain the confidence of people employed by both sides. He should then figure out who else can be incited to change sides, and also learn from them about the activities of their lord. He should make contact with his own spies who, on the pretext of studying the *śāstras,* are living in the guise of ascetics at sacred bathing spots, hermitages, and temples. For the benefit of those who might be induced to change sides, he should glorify his lord's valor, lineage, prosperity, generosity, keenness of determination, decency, and dexterity in action. 15

Someone who is asleep or drunk will clearly express his inner feelings. Therefore the emissary should always sleep alone and avoid both women and alcohol. If he is smart he will move at the right time to accomplish his task so that he does not suffer in carrying it out. He should offer various material inducements to gather intelligence on how the enemy is passing his time. As he passes his days in the enemy

१८ एतेष्वहःसु गच्छत्सु तत्र नः पृथिवीपतेः ।
पश्यति व्यसनं किंचित्स्वयं वा कर्तुमीहते ॥

१९ स्वान्तःप्रकोपमथवा विनेतुं नीतिवित्तमः ।
सस्यादेः सङ्ग्रहं कर्तुं दुर्गे वा दुर्गसत्क्रियाम् ॥

२० स्वपक्षाभ्युदयाकाङ्क्षी देशकालावुदीक्षते ।
उत यात्रां स्वयं दातुं येनास्मान्न समीहते ॥

२१ यात्राकालक्रियार्थी वा तत्र चायं विलम्बते ।
काले विक्षिप्यमाणे तु तर्कयेदिति पण्डितः ॥

२२ कार्यकालविपत्तिं च व्यक्तां ज्ञात्वा विनिष्पतेत् ।१४
तिष्ठन्वार्ताविशेषार्थान्भर्त्रे सर्वान्निवेदयेत् ॥१५

२३ रिपोः शत्रुपरिच्छेदः सुहृद्बन्धुविभेदनम् ।
दुर्गकोशबलज्ञानं कृत्यपक्षोपसङ्ग्रहः ॥

२४ राष्ट्राटव्यन्तपालानामात्मसात्करणं तथा ।
युद्धापसारभूज्ञानं दूतकर्मेति कीर्तितम् ॥

२५ दूतेनैव नरेन्द्रस्तु कुर्यादरिविमर्शनम् ।१६
स्वपक्षे च विजानीयात्परदूतविचेष्टितम् ॥

territory, he should find out if the enemy is aware of calamities or vices besetting the king who employs him, or if the enemy intends to create some disaster or vice. Being politically astute he should find out if the enemy intends to try to suppress internal unrest, seize crops and other supplies from the populace, or fortify his fort.[2]

He should observe if, yearning for his own side's success, the enemy might be examining factors of time and place in order to launch a military expedition, in which the kingdom might be the target. If the enemy delays his attack, seeming to deliberately reject the opportune moment, then the wise emissary should reflect on the reason for delay, and whether it might not be a trick. When he discerns an evident danger, and urgency in the time for action, the emissary should quickly return to his own land, or else he can stay where he is, and—in either case—communicate the relevant facts in full detail to his lord. 20

The emissary's duties are to identify the enemy's enemies; to alienate the enemy's friends and kinsmen; to learn about the enemy's treasury, fortifications, and army; to collect information about those who can be incited to change sides; to win over the subjects, forest people, and frontier-guards; and finally, to understand the topography of the enemy territory for his lord's military advance. The lord of men should use his emissaries to conduct an inquiry into his enemy. And he must be aware of the enemy emissaries' activities against his own side. 25

चरविकल्पप्रकरणम्¹⁷

२६ तर्केङ्गितज्ञः स्मृतिमान्मृदुलघुपरिक्रमः ।
क्लेशायाससहो दक्षश्चारः स्यात्प्रतिपत्तिमान् ॥

२७ तपस्विलिङ्गिनो धूर्ताः शिल्पपण्योपजीविनः ।
चराश्चरेयुः परितः पिबन्तो जगतां मतम् ॥

२८ निर्गच्छेयुर्विशेयुश्च सर्ववार्ताविदोऽन्वहम् ।
चराः सकाशं नृपतेश्चक्षुर्दूरचरं हि ते ॥

२९ सूक्ष्मसूत्रप्रचारेण पश्येद्वैरिविचेष्टितम् ।
स्वपन्नपि हि जागर्ति चारचक्षुर्महीपतिः ॥

३० विवस्वानिव तेजोभिर्नभस्वानिव चेष्टितैः ।
राजा चारैर्जगत्कृत्स्नं व्याप्नुयाल्लोकसम्मतैः ॥

३१ चारचक्षुर्नरेन्द्रस्तु सम्पत्तेतेन भूयसा ।
अनेनासम्पतन्मार्गात्पतत्यन्धः समेऽपि हि ॥¹⁸

३२ सर्वसम्पत्समुदयं सर्वावस्थाविचेष्टितम् ।
चारेण द्विषतां विद्यात्तद्देशापार्थनादि च ॥

३३ प्रकाशश्चाप्रकाशश्च चरस्तु द्विविधः स्मृतः ।
अप्रकाशोऽयमुद्दिष्टः प्रकाशो दूत उच्यते ॥

३४ चरेण प्रचरेत्प्राज्ञः सूत्रेणर्त्विगिवाध्वरे ।¹⁹
दूते सन्धानमायत्तं चरे चर्या प्रतिष्ठिता ॥²⁰

166

Types of Spies

The spy should be adept at reasoning and reading gestures, have a retentive mind, and be both mild-mannered and swift-footed. He must be capable of enduring hardships and torments, as well as dexterous in action and resourceful. Spies should dress as ascetics, riff-raff, traders, or craftsmen, and wander around everywhere drinking in peoples' thoughts. The spies should go out and come back each day knowledgeable about all the goings-on, for they are the far-roaming eyes of the king. Through subtle, secret methods the spy should observe the enemy's activities. The lord of the earth who has spies for his eyes is ever awake, even when he sleeps.

Like the sun through its radiance, or the wind through its mobility, the king envelops the whole earth through his world-renowned spies. The lord of men with spies for his   30
eyes should spring into action drawing on their support. Should he fail to use spies, he will fall off the path, just as a blind man falls down even on even ground.

The king should learn through his spies about all the enemies' wealth and resources, their behavior in all situations, as well as their territories, wishes, and so on. There are two kinds of spies: secret and public. The secret one is what we are discussing now; the public one is what we discussed before: the emissary. The wise king should act by following his spies, as the Vedic priest acts in a sacrificial ritual by following the Vedic text. The emissary's responsibility is making alliances, while the spy is in charge of covert observation of enemy activities.

३५ संस्थानवत्यः संस्थाश्च कार्याः कार्यसमृद्धये ।
तिष्ठेयुर्यासु सञ्चाराः परचर्योपवेदिनः ॥

३६ वणिक्कृषीवलो लिङ्गी भिक्षुकोऽध्यापकस्तथा ।२१
संस्थाः स्युश्चारसंस्थित्यै दत्तदायाः सुखाशयाः ॥

३७ स्वपक्षे परपक्षे च यावान्कश्चिद्द्विवक्षितः ।२२
सर्वस्मिंस्तत्र सञ्चारास्तिष्ठेयुश्चित्तवेदिनः ॥

३८ तीक्ष्णः प्रव्रजितश्चैव सत्री रसद एव च ।२३
एते प्रधानं सञ्चाराः सर्वे नान्योन्यवेदिनः ॥

३९ स्वपक्षे परपक्षे वा यो न वेद चिकीर्षितम् ।
जाग्रत्स्वरिषु सुप्तोऽसौ न भूयः प्रतिबुध्यते ॥२४

४० कारणाकारणक्रुद्धान्बुध्येत स्वपरिग्रहे ।
पापानकारणक्रुद्धान्तूष्णींदण्डेन साधयेत् ॥

४१ ये तु कारणतः क्रुद्धास्तान्वशीकृत्य संविशेत् ।
शमयेद्दानमानाभ्यां छिद्रमण्वप्यरेर्मुखम् ॥२५

४२ कण्टकान्मुखभङ्गेन राज्यस्य प्रशमं नयेत् ।
उद्युक्तः सामदानाभ्यां छिद्रं च परिपूरयेत् ॥

४३ अणुनापि प्रविश्यारिश्छिद्रेण बलवत्तरम् ।
निःशेषं मज्जयेद्राज्यं पानपात्रमिवोदकम् ॥२६

Stations overseen by clandestine officers must be established to enhance operations, where the wandering spies, informed of enemy operations, can bring their information. The clandestine officers to whom the spies report should be merchants, farmers, ascetics, mendicants, or teachers. They should be well-paid and good people. Whenever there is a person of interest in either one's own realm or that of the enemy, spies should be stationed everywhere around him, reading people's thoughts. The principal types of spies include everything from ruthless killers, to agents dressed as mendicants, to agents adept at poisoning, and those dressed as Vedic priests. None of them should be aware of each other's identity. 35

If the king does not know peoples' designs in his own realm or in that of the enemy, he is sleeping while his enemies stay awake—and he never wakes up again. The king should learn who is angry in his retinue, whether for some good reason or for none. He should use covert assassination to deal with the wicked people who are angry for no good reason. On the other hand, he should try to win over those who are angry for some good reason. He should calm them down with gifts and honors, and then rest secure. Even a tiny point of weakness forms an entryway for the enemy. 40

He should neutralize the kingdom's thorn-like anti-state elements by crushing the ringleaders.[3] By vigorously applying both conciliation and donation, he should close all gaps. If there is even a tiny gap, the enemy will find a way in and sink even a greater power, just as a water pitcher with a hole sinks down when thrust into water.

Spies should impersonate idiots, the mute, blind, and

४४ जडमूकान्धबधिरच्छद्मानः षण्डकास्तथा ।
किरातवामनाः कुब्जास्तद्विधा ये च कारवः ॥

४५ भिक्षुक्यश्चारणा दास्यो मालाकाराः कलाविदः ।२७
अन्तःपुरगतां वार्तां निर्हरेयुरलक्षिताः ॥

४६ छत्रव्यजनभृङ्गारयानवाहनधारिणः ।
महामात्रबहिर्वार्तां विदुरन्ये च तद्विधाः ॥२८

४७ अन्नव्यञ्जनकर्तारः कल्पकाः स्नापकास्तथा२९ ।
प्रसाधका भोजकाश्च गात्रसंवाहका अपि ॥

४८ जलताम्बूलकुसुमगन्धभूषणदायकाः ।
कर्तव्या रसदा होते ये चान्येऽभ्याशवर्तिनः ॥

४९ संज्ञाभिर्लेच्छितैर्लेख्यैराकारैरिङ्गितैरपि ।३०
सञ्चारयेयुरव्यग्राश्चाराश्चर्या परस्परम् ॥

५० समापिबन्तो जगतां मतानि जलानि भूमेरिव सूर्यपादाः ।
अनेकशिल्पाध्ययनप्रवीणाश्चाराश्चरेयुर्बहुलिङ्गिरूपाः ॥

५१ येन प्रकारेण परानुपेयात्परापरज्ञः स्वसमृद्धिहेतोः ।
तमात्मनि स्वस्थमतिश्च तज्ज्ञैः प्रयुज्यमानं च परेण विद्यात् ॥

deaf, as well as eunuchs. They should come in the guise of Kirata dwarves, midgets, hunchbacks, and the like, as well as craftsmen, Buddhist nuns, minstrels, common prostitutes, flower-garland makers, and artists. They should go undetected into the women's inner quarters and bring back all the information they can. Others in the guise of royal-parasol holders and yak-tail fan-bearers, water-pot carriers, palanquin-bearers, horsemen and elephant-riders, as well as other similar types of people, should attend upon high officials and get to know about their public activities. Those who cook rice and curry, barbers, the servants who prepare the king's bath, valets, food servers, and masseurs, as well as those who provide water, betel, flowers, perfumes, and ornaments, can be made to administer poison; so too all others who work in close proximity to the king.

The spies should freely communicate with each other their secret observations of the above-mentioned people through signals, foreign languages, written codes, body language, and secret gestures.

These spies, skilled in many crafts and fields of study, should roam around in many guises, drinking up people's thoughts, as the sun's rays drink up the earth's waters.

Whatever tactic he employs to confront the enemy, in order to advance his prosperity, the king with focused mind—knowledgeable about both himself and the enemy—must in turn learn from his knowledgeable spies about how that same tactic is being used against him by the enemy.

चतुर्दशः सर्गः

उत्साहप्रशंसाप्रकरणम्

१   अन्वहं चरचर्याभिर्विफले दूतचेष्टिते ।
    यायाद्यथोक्तयानस्तु सूक्ष्मबुद्धिपुरःसरः ॥१

२   सूक्ष्मा सत्त्वप्रयत्नाभ्यां दृढं बुद्धिरधिष्ठिता ।२
    प्रसूते हि फलं श्रीमदरणीव हुताशनम् ॥

३   धातोश्चामीकरमिव सर्पिर्निर्मथनादिव ।
    बुद्धिप्रयत्नोपगताद्व्यवसायाद्ध्रुवं फलम् ॥

४   धीमानुत्साहसम्पन्नः व्यवसायसमन्वितः ।३
    भाजनं परमं श्रीणामपामिव महार्णवः ॥

५   नलिनीवाम्बुसम्पत्त्या बुद्ध्या श्रीः परिपाल्यते ।
    उत्थानाध्यवसायाभ्यां विस्तारमुपनीयते ॥

६   लक्ष्मीरुत्साहसम्पन्नाद्बुद्धिशुद्धं प्रसर्पतः ।
    नापैति कायाच्छायेव विस्तारं चोपगच्छति ॥

७   वीतव्यसनमश्रान्तं महोत्साहं महामतिम् ।
    प्रविशन्ति महालक्ष्म्यः सरित्पतिमिवापगाः ॥

८   सत्त्वबुद्ध्युपपन्नोऽपि व्यसनग्रस्तमानसः ।
    श्रीभिः षण्ड इव स्त्रीभिरलसः परिभूयते ॥

९   उत्थानेनैधयेत्सत्त्वमिन्धनेनेव पावकम् ।
    श्रियो हि सततोत्थायी दुर्बलोऽपि समश्नुते ॥

CHAPTER 14

The Value of Determination

Should he receive reports from his spies day after day that the emissaries' work is proving fruitless, a shrewd king will march against the enemy in the way already described.[1] A shrewd intellect firmly governed by courage and effort cannot but produce the fruit of royal power, just as kindling sticks produce fire. Mineral deposits yield gold, churning yields butter, and in the same way, resolve combined with intellect and effort yields certain fruit.

When a king is filled with fortitude and determination, and endowed with resolve, he becomes the supreme receptacle for royal majesty, like the ocean for water. Royal majesty is sustained by intellect, like a lotus plant by water, and flourishes when combined with determination and firm resolution. Fortune never forsakes a man endowed with determination, whose intellect is purified; it cleaves to him as his shadow cleaves to his body, and only increases. Great fortune pursues the man of great mind and vast determination, who is indefatigable and devoid of vices, just as rivers race to the ocean.

Even if he has courage and intellect, when his mind is corrupted by vices a king becomes as passive and impotent in the presence of royal powers as a eunuch in the presence of women. He should stimulate his own power, like a fire with kindling sticks. When he is ever active, even a weak man enjoys royal majesty.

१० भोक्तुं पुरुषकारेण दुष्टां स्त्रियमिव श्रियम् ।
    व्यवसायं सदैवेच्छेन्न हि क्लीबवदाचरेत् ॥

११ वशे श्रियं सदोत्साही सैंहीं वृत्तिं समाश्रितः ।⁴
    कचग्रहेण कुर्वीत दुर्वृत्तामिव योषितम् ॥

१२ किरीटमणिचित्रेषु मूर्धसु त्राणधारिषु ।
    नाकृत्वा विद्विषां पादं पुरुषो भद्रमश्नुते ॥

१३ प्रयत्नप्रेर्यमाणेन महता चित्तहस्तिना ।
    रूढवैरिद्रुमोत्खातमकृत्वेह कुतः सुखम् ॥

१४ हेलाकृष्टस्फुरत्तीक्ष्णखङ्गांशुपरिपिञ्जरैः ।
    श्रीमत्करिकराकारैराह्रियन्ते भुजैः श्रियः ॥

१५ उच्चैरुच्चैस्तरामिच्छन्पदान्यायच्छते महान् ।
    नीचो नीचैस्तरां याति निपातभयशङ्कया ॥

१६ प्रमाणाभ्यधिकस्यापि महत्सत्त्वमधिष्ठितः ।
    करोत्येव पदं मूर्ध्नि केसरी मत्तहस्तिनः ॥

१७ गतभीर्भीतिजननं भोगं भोगीव दर्शयेत् ।
    यथाबलं च कुर्वीत रिपोर्दण्डनिपातनम् ॥

174

Royal power is like a wayward woman, and to enjoy her with manly determination a king must always be decisive; he must never behave like a eunuch. With unceasing vigor, he must act like a lion and grab hold of royal fortune, like a wayward woman by the hair. A man never fares well unless he places his foot upon his enemies' heads, their helmets sparkling with crest jewels. What peace can there be for a king if he does not send out the great elephant of his mind to uproot the tall tree that is the enemy? He must drag away royal fortune by his arms powerful as elephant trunks, gilt with the rays of light pulsating from his sharp, glittering sword so casually unsheathed. 10

A great man steps higher and higher in his desire to ascend, while a lowly man stoops lower and lower in fear of falling to his doom. Because of his great power, the lion will place his paw on the head of an elephant, even though the latter is much larger in size. The king should be fearless, provoking his enemies' fear by displays of his power, as a serpent displays its hoods. He should inflict as much punishment as he can upon his enemy. 15

प्रकृतिकर्मप्रकरणम्

१८ प्रकृतिव्यसनं यत्स्यात्तत्प्रशाम्य समुत्पतेत् ।
अनयापनयाभ्यां तज्जायते दैवतोऽपि च ॥

१९ यस्मात्तद्ध्वस्यति श्रेयस्तस्माद्व्यसनमुच्यते ।
व्यसन्यधोधो व्रजति तस्मात्तत्परिवर्जयेत् ॥५

२० हुताशनो जलं व्याधिर्दुर्भिक्षो मरकस्तथा ।६
इति पञ्चविधं दैवं व्यसनं मानुषं परम् ॥

२१ दैवं पुरुषकारेण शान्त्या च प्रशमं नयेत् ।७
उत्थायित्वेन नीत्या च मानुषं कार्यतत्त्ववित् ॥८

२२ स्वाम्यादिमित्रपर्यन्तं प्राकृतं मण्डलं हि यत् ।
तस्य कर्म प्रवक्ष्यामि व्यसनं च यथाक्रमम् ॥

२३ मन्त्रो मन्त्रफलावाप्तिः कार्यानुष्ठानमायतिः ।
आयव्ययौ दण्डनीतिरमित्रप्रतिषेधनम् ॥

२४ व्यसनस्य प्रतीकारो राजराज्याभिरक्षणम् ।
इत्यमात्यस्य कर्मेदं हन्ति तद्व्यसनान्वितः ॥

२५ अमात्यैर्व्यसनोपेतैर्ह्रियमाणो हि भूपतिः ।
अशक्त एवोत्पतितुं छिन्नपक्ष इवाण्डजः ॥

२६ हिरण्यवस्त्रधान्यादि वाहनानि तथैव च ।९
तथान्ये द्रव्यनिचयाः प्रजातः सम्भवन्ति हि ॥

२७ वार्तां प्रजा साधयति वार्ता वै लोकसंश्रया ।
प्रजायां व्यसनस्थायां न किंचिदपि सिध्यति ॥

176

The State-Elements' Functioning

He should first suppress whatever vices and calamities there may be among his own state-elements, and then attack his enemy.[2] Vices and calamities come from lack of policy, faulty policy, or from destiny. The term "vice" ultimately means to throw away what is good.[3] A man consumed by vice only sinks down lower and lower; one must avoid it. Calamities coming from destiny are five: fire, flood, epidemic, famine, and plague. The other vices and calamities are human products. The king should suppress calamities of destiny by 20
human effort and apotropaic rites.[4] Understanding the true power of action, he should suppress human vices through action and sound policy.

I will now explain the mandala along with its constituent state-elements, from the ruler to the ally, also including their respective functions as well as their possible vices and calamities. The duties of the minister are strategy; consolidating the gains of strategy; carrying out projects; planning the future; monitoring income and expenditure; application of coercion; neutralizing enemies; counteracting vices and calamities; as well as protecting the king and his kingdom. A proclivity to vice on the part of the minister vitiates each of these projects. When a king is carried away by vice-prone ministers, he cannot rise up, as a bird cannot fly with its wings clipped. 25

Gold, grain, clothing, draft-animals, and other accumulated articles of value are the products that come from the people. The people produce the economy, and the economy is the refuge of the world. When the people are consumed by

२८ प्रजानामापदि त्राणं रक्षणं कोशदण्डयोः ।१०
पौराश्चैवोपकुर्वन्ति संश्रयायेह दुर्गिणाम् ॥

२९ तूष्णींयुद्धं जनत्राणं मित्रामित्रपरिग्रहः ।
सामन्ताटविकाबाधानिरोधो दुर्गसंश्रयात् ॥

३० स्वपक्षैः परपक्षैश्च दुर्गस्थः पूज्यते नृपः ।
एतद्धि दुर्गव्यसनात्सर्वमेव विपद्यते ॥११

३१ भृत्यानां भरणं दानं भूषणं वाहनक्रियाः ।
स्थैर्यं परोपजापश्च दुर्गसंस्कार एव च ॥

३२ सेतुबन्धो वणिक्कर्म प्रजामित्रपरिग्रहः ।
धर्मकामार्थसिद्धिश्च कोशादेतत्प्रवर्तते ॥

३३ कोशमूलो हि राजेति प्रवादः सार्वलौकिकः ।
एतत्सर्वं जहात्याशु कोशव्यसनवान्नृपः ॥

३४ क्षीणं बलं वर्धयति स्वतो गृह्णाति च प्रजाः ।
कोशवान्पृथिवीपालः पैरप्युपजीव्यते ॥

३५ मित्रामित्रहिरण्यानां भूमीनां च प्रसाधनम् ।
दूरकार्याशुकारित्वं लब्धस्य परिपालनम् ॥

३६ परचक्रविघातश्च स्वदण्डस्य परिग्रहः ।
दण्डादेतत्प्रभवति याति तद्व्यसने क्षयम् ॥

vices and calamities, nothing can be accomplished.

The fort protects the people in times of catastrophe, and it protects the treasury and military. The city-people provide aid to kings when they take refuge in his fortifications.[5] The fort provides the headquarters for secret warfare stratagems, and protection for the people; it is a place of welcome for friends and enemies, as well as a remedy for the perils of disaffected feudatories and forest people. His own people and enemies alike pay homage to a king who is ensconced in a fort. When the fort is compromised by vices and calamities, everything is destroyed.

30

All of the following come from the treasury: servants' maintenance; ceremonial donation; purchase of ornaments and animals for transport; maintaining the stability of the state; bribing enemies; renovating forts, building bridges, and subsidizing merchant ventures; providing favors to subjects and friends, as well as fulfilling the goals of dharma, pleasure, and power.

The saying "the treasury is the root of the king" is known far and wide. A king loses everything when his treasury is compromised. In possession of his treasury a king can replenish his army when it has been diminished, and satisfy the people by sharing the wealth. Even his enemies may come to depend upon him.

All the following come from the rod of coercion: winning over allies and enemies; gaining gold and lands; swiftly finishing projects in distant lands; protecting what has been acquired; ensuring the enemy army's destruction; and rein- 35 forcing one's own power of coercion.[6] All these things are likewise destroyed when the rod of coercion is compromised.

३७ अरयोऽपि हि मित्रत्वं यान्ति दण्डवतो ध्रुवम् ।
दण्डप्रायो हि नृपतिर्भुनत्त्याक्रम्य मेदिनीम् ॥

३८ संस्तम्भयति मित्राणि शत्रूनुत्सादयत्यपि ।
भूकोशदण्डैर्व्रजति प्राणैश्चाप्युपकारिताम् ॥

३९ तत्तत्करोति च बहिर्मित्रं स्नेहनिबन्धनम् ।¹²
तस्मिन्व्यसनमापन्ने मित्रकर्म न विद्यते ॥

४० उपकाराद्वतेऽप्याशु मित्रं श्रेयसि तिष्ठति ।
मित्रवान्साधयत्यर्थान्दुःसाध्यानप्यनादरात् ॥¹³

४१ अन्वीक्षणं च विद्यानां सद्वर्णाश्रमरक्षणम् ।
ग्रहणं शस्त्रशास्त्राणां युद्धमार्गोपशिक्षणम् ॥¹⁴

४२ व्यायामः शस्त्रविज्ञानं वर्मणां लक्षणानि च ।¹⁵
गजाश्वरथपृष्ठेषु यथावत्सम्प्रवर्तनम् ॥

४३ नियुद्धकौशलं माया परचित्तप्रवेशनम् ।¹⁶
धूर्तता शाठ्ययुक्तेषु सत्सु सद्वृत्तदर्शनम् ॥

४४ मन्त्रोद्योगोऽनुमन्त्रत्वं तद्रक्षा तात्स्थ्यमेव च ।
उपेक्षा साम दानं च भेदो दण्डश्च साधनम् ॥

४५ प्रशास्तृसूतसेनानीमन्त्यमात्यपुरोधसाम् ।¹⁷
सम्यक्प्रचारविज्ञानं दुष्टानां चावरोपणम् ॥¹⁸

४६ गतागतपरिज्ञानं दूतसम्प्रेषणानि च ।
प्रकृतिव्यसनापोहः क्रुद्धप्रशमनानि च ॥

Truly even enemies become allies for someone with the capacity to punish. The king is, in essence, coercion, and as such conquers and rules the earth. An enemy turned ally can reinforce the king's allies and annihilate his enemies. With land, treasure, and coercive power—even with his last life breath—he becomes a source of aid.

And thus an ally bound to him by pure affection, will do anything for him. However, when an ally succumbs to vice or calamity nothing can be expected of him. A friend is someone who, without incentive, immediately supports your interests. A man with friends can accomplish even difficult things without a thought.   40

The duties of a king are studying the sciences; safeguarding the pure castes and life stages; mastering both weapons and the *śāstras;* learning the ways of war and practicing fighting; knowing about weapons and the particulars of armor; studying the proper ways of mounting elephants, horses, and chariots; becoming adept at hand-to-hand combat; cultivating the power of illusion[7] and fully fathoming others' minds; employing trickery with those who deserve deception, while being faithful in one's vows to good men; strategizing and taking counsel in the company of one's counselors, while maintaining the secrecy and consistency of strategy; perfecting the practices of disregard, conciliation, donation, sowing dissension, and coercion; fully understanding the activities of his generals, charioteers, army-commanders, counselors, ministers, and household priests, as well as removing malicious people; keeping track of peoples' comings and goings   45
and the dispatching of emissaries; allaying the peoples' calamities and quelling their anger; obedience to gurus and

181

४७ गुरूणामनुवृत्तिश्च पूज्यानामनुपूजनम् ।
धर्मासनप्रतिष्ठानं राज्यकण्टकशोधनम् ॥

४८ भृताभृतपरिज्ञानं कृताकृतपरीक्षणम् ।
तुष्टातुष्टविचारश्च सर्वेषामनुजीविनाम् ॥

४९ मध्योदासीनचरितज्ञानं तत्सिद्धिप्रिपालनम् ।
प्रतिग्रहश्च मित्राणाममित्राणां च निग्रहः ॥

५० पुत्रदारादिगुप्तिश्च बन्धुवर्गपरिग्रहः ।
खनिद्वीपवनादीनां स्ववृत्तीनां प्रवर्तनम् ॥१९

५१ असतां च परिक्षेपः सतां च परिगूहनम् ।२०
अहिंसा सर्वभूतानामधर्माणां च वर्जनम् ॥

५२ अकार्यप्रतिषेधश्च कार्याणां च प्रवर्तनम् ।
प्रदानं च प्रदेयानामदेयानामसङ्ग्रहः ॥

५३ अदण्डनमदण्ड्यानां दण्ड्यानां चापि दण्डनम् ।
अग्राह्याग्रहणं चैव ग्राह्याणां ग्रहणं तथा ॥

५४ अर्थयुक्तस्य करणमनर्थस्य च वर्जनम् ।
न्यायतश्च करादानं स्वयं च प्रतिमोक्षणम् ॥

५५ समर्थनं प्रधानानां निरस्यानां निराकृतिः ।
वैषम्याणां प्रशमनं भृत्यानां चाविरोधनम् ॥

५६ अविज्ञातस्य विज्ञानं विज्ञातस्य च निश्चयः ।
आरम्भः कर्मणः शश्वदारब्धस्यान्तदर्शनम् ॥

५७ अलब्धलिप्सा न्यायेन लब्धस्य च विवर्धनम् ।
परिवृद्धस्य विधिवत्पात्रे सम्प्रतिपादनम् ॥

५८ अधर्मप्रतिषेधश्च न्यायमार्गेण वर्तनम् ।
उपकार्योपकारित्वमितिवृत्तं महीपतेः ॥

duly honoring those deserving of honor, establishing courts
of justice and annihilating the kingdom's anti-state elements;
being aware of the employees' remuneration or lack thereof;
assessing their performance or nonperformance of tasks as
well as their level of satisfaction with their remuneration;
being aware of the activities of the intermediate one and the
neutral one, as well as guarding alliances with them; receiving friends with hospitality and assailing enemies; arranging
for the protection of sons and wives, and receiving kinsmen
with hospitality; fostering economic activity, especially
developing mines, islands, and forest regions; rejecting bad   50
people and embracing the good; practicing nonviolence
toward all creatures and shunning the unrighteous; forbidding unrighteous deeds and practicing righteous ones;
giving to those deserving charity and withholding it from
the undeserving; refraining from punishing those who do
not deserve it and punishing those who do; not taking what
should not be taken and taking what should; doing what is
productive and not doing what is unproductive; taking taxes
justly and spontaneously offering remission; rewarding good
officials and removing the incompetent; alleviating calamities, and not obstructing servants; understanding what has   55
yet to be understood, and advancing to conclusions about
what has been understood; undertaking new actions and
always seeing these undertakings through to their comple-
tion; justly pursuing what has not yet been obtained, making
flourish what has been obtained, and finally, taking what has
been made to flourish and offering it in an honorable manner
to suitable recipients; prohibiting what is counter to dharma
and treading the path of justice; helping those who deserve

५९ एतत्सर्वममात्यादि राजा नयपुरःसरः ।
नयत्युन्नतिमुद्युक्तो व्यसनी क्षयमेव तु ॥

६० तस्मिन्धर्मार्थयोर्व्यग्रे तथैवास्वस्थचेतसि ।
सर्वमेतद्विशेषेण मन्त्री सन्नेतुमर्हति ॥

प्रकृतिव्यसनप्रकरणम्

६१ वाग्दण्डयोश्च पारुष्यमर्थदूषणमेव च ।
पानं स्त्री मृगया द्यूतं व्यसनानि महीपतेः ॥

६२ आलस्यं स्तब्धता दर्पः प्रमादो वैरकारिता ।
इति पूर्वोपदिष्टं च सचिवव्यसनं स्मृतम् ॥

६३ अतिवृष्टिरनावृष्टिर्मूषिकाः शलभादयः ।२१
असत्करश्च दण्डश्च परचक्राणि तस्कराः ॥

६४ राजानीकप्रियोत्सर्गो मारकव्याधिपीडनम् ।
पशूनां मरणं रोगो राष्ट्रव्यसनमुच्यते ॥२२

६५ विशीर्णयन्त्रप्राकारपरिखात्वमशस्त्रता ।२३
क्षीणघासेन्धनान्नत्वादुर्गव्यसनमुच्यते ॥२४

६६ व्ययीकृतः परिक्षिप्तो भक्षितोऽसञ्चितस्तथा ।
मुषितो दूरसंस्थश्च कोशव्यसनमुच्यते ॥

६७ उपरुद्धं परिक्षिप्तं विमानितममानितम् ।
अभृतं व्याधितं श्रान्तं दूरायातं नवागतम् ॥

६८ परिक्षीणं प्रतिहतं प्रहताग्रजवं तथा ।२५
आशानिर्वेदभूयिष्ठमनृतप्राप्तमेव च ॥२६

184

to be helped. All this is the king's duty.

A king who is determined and committed to sound politics brings the entire state apparatus—from the counselors on down—to prosperity, while a vice-ridden king leads it to ruin. If the king is too exclusively focused on dharma or matters of state, or if he is of unsound mind, then a counselor should take singular control over all these functions. 60

Vices and Calamities of the State-Elements

The vices of kings are severity in speech, severity in punishment, financial corruption, drinking, women, hunting, and gambling. The vices of counselors—which were enumerated above—are laziness, inertia, arrogance, rashness, and being prone to enmity.

The vices and calamities of the territory are excessive rains or drought; rats, locusts, and other pests; unjust taxes or punishments; invasion by enemy armies, bandits, and exactions by the king's army or friends; the afflictions of epidemic and plague; widespread death of animals; and disease.

The calamities of forts are the decay of machinery, ramparts, or moats, and shortages of weapons, fodder, kindling, or food. The calamities of the treasury are exces- 65 sive expenditure, wastage, misappropriation, lack of savings, theft, and being at an inaccessible distance.

The vices and calamities of the army are to be besieged, surrounded, dishonored, demoralized, unpaid, diseased, or exhausted; to have traveled too far; to consist entirely of new recruits; to be diminished in numbers; to be repelled or to have the front ranks killed off; to be filled with men

६९ कलत्रगर्भ्यतिक्षिप्तमन्तःशल्यं तथैव च ।
    भिन्नगर्भं ह्यपसृतमवमुक्तं तथैव च ॥

७० क्रुद्धमौलारिमित्रं च निविष्टं चापि विद्विषा ।२७
    दूष्ययुक्तं स्वविक्षिप्तं मित्रविक्षिप्तमेव च ॥

७१ विच्छिन्नवीवधासारं शून्यमूलं तथैव च ।
    अस्वामिसङ्गृतं चैव भिन्नकूटं तथैव च ॥

७२ दुष्पार्ष्णिग्राहमन्धं च बलव्यसनमुच्यते ।
    अत्र किंचिदसाध्यं तु किंचित्साध्यं तदुच्यते ॥

७३ उपरुद्धं तु युध्येत निर्गत्यान्यत ऊर्जितम् ।२८
    परिक्षिप्तं न निर्मार्गं सर्वतः परिवेष्टितम् ॥

७४ अमानितं हि युध्येत कृतमानार्थसङ्ग्रहम् ।
    न विमानितमत्यर्थं प्रदीप्तक्रोधपावकम् ॥

७५ युध्येताभृतमत्यर्थं तदात्वकृतवेतनम् ।
    न व्याधितमकर्मण्यं व्याधितं परिभूयते ॥

७६ परिश्रान्तं हि युध्येत विश्रान्तं सुविधानतः ।
    दूरायातं हतप्राणं न शस्त्रग्रहणे क्षमम् ॥

७७ नवागतं हि युध्येत तद्देश्यैर्मिश्रितं नयात् ।
    हतमुख्यप्रवीरं तु परिक्षीणं न युध्यते ॥

who have grown weary of hope; to run out of equipment; to become disorganized because of having women in the camp; to be impaled by the lance of enemy infiltrators; to suffer from dissension or to be scattered or disunited; to have one's native troops, troops defected from the enemy, or one's ally's troops become disgruntled; to be routed by the enemy; to be infected by traitors; have the forces disordered when defending one's territory, or to be scattered in the allies' territory; to have supply lines for allies and resources cut off, or have   70
one's base of support in the country removed; to be separated from the commander, or to be decapitated and without a general; to have a sinister rear adversary, or to be in a state of virtual blindness. Some of these vices and calamities can be remedied, while others cannot.

Once it extricates itself, a besieged force can fight vigorously from another side, but one that is completely surrounded and enclosed finds no way forward. An army that is demoralized can fight after it has received respect and wealth, while a dishonored army cannot fight—its anger becomes a fiercely blazing fire. An army that is unpaid can fight if it is immediately paid well, but a diseased, inactive army cannot: a diseased army meets defeat. An exhausted   75
army can fight if it rests in comfortable circumstances, but an army that has traveled too far, and thus spent its lifeblood, becomes incapable of even lifting weapons. An army can fight when new recruits are strategically mixed in with local soldiers. But the army cannot fight when its foremost warriors are wiped out, or when its numbers are too diminished.

When an army is defeated it can fight again when

७८ युध्यते हि प्रतिहतं प्रवीरैः सह सङ्गतम् ।
हताग्रवेगं शक्तं न प्रमाथितपुरःसरम् ॥२९

७९ आशानिर्वेदलब्धार्थं पूर्णाशित्वात्तु युध्यते ।३०
अभूमिष्ठं प्रसारे न निरुद्धेऽल्पतया भुवः ॥

८० युध्येतानृतसम्प्राप्तं यथार्हायुधवाहनम् ।३१
कलत्रगर्भि चोन्नीतकलत्रं समरक्षमम् ॥

८१ अनेकराज्यान्तरितमतिक्षिप्रं न युध्यते ।
अन्तर्गतामित्रशल्यमन्तःशल्यं हि न क्षमम् ॥

८२ अन्योन्यस्माद्विनिर्भिन्नं भिन्नगर्भं न युध्यते ।
तथैवापसृतं शक्तं नैकराज्यान्तरीकृतम् ॥

८२ अवमुक्तमपक्रान्तमुत्स्थ्यं तन्न क्षमं युधि ।
पितृपैतामहं मौलं तत्कुद्धं सान्त्वितं क्षमम् ॥

८४ मित्रं शत्रुभिरेकस्थं तदाक्रान्ततयाक्षमम् ।३२
शत्रोरुपनिविष्टं तत्सामर्थ्यान्न क्षमं युधि ॥३३

८५ दूष्ययुक्तं तदुद्धाराद्युध्येतोद्धृतकण्टकम् ।३४
प्रधानयोधसंगुप्तं दूष्ययुक्तं समुत्पतेत् ॥३५

८६ स्वविक्षिप्तं स्वविषये क्षिप्तमापद्युदाहृतम् ।
प्रकृष्टदेशकालत्वान्मित्रक्षिप्तमयौगिकम् ॥

reinforced with foremost warriors, but an army whose front ranks are routed and killed off is powerless and cannot fight. An army whose men are hopeless can indeed fight when those grown weary of hope have attained their aims, since their hope has been rewarded. And an army that is hemmed in on a narrow field with no room to maneuver cannot fight. An army that has run out of supplies can fight if it is given serviceable weapons and chariots. An army with women in the camp will be unfit for battle until the women are removed. An army separated by many kingdoms or made to travel too far cannot fight, nor can an army impaled by the lance of enemy infiltrators. An army suffering from internal dissension—with its members turning against each other— cannot fight, just as an army separated by even one kingdom, finding itself scattered, has no power to fight.

An abandoned army or an army whose commander has fled is not fit for battle. When the native soldiers of hereditary loyalty become disaffected, they can be made ready to fight by encouraging them. An army composed of allies, that is hemmed in under enemy attack, is not ready to fight. The same is true of an army camped close to enemy territory, because of the enemy's resulting advantage. An army infected by traitors can fight when the traitors have been removed, and the thorny anti-state element has thus been extracted. An army infected by traitors, but protected by the foremost warriors, can rise up again and attack. A disordered army is an army cast into danger while defending its own territory. It can be made to fight, but if, on the other hand, it is disordered while fighting away from home in its allies' territory, it becomes ineffective, owing to the excessive

८७ धान्यादेर्विवधः प्राप्तिरासारस्तु सुहृद्बलम् ।
विच्छिन्नवीवधासारं बलं युद्धाय नेष्यते ॥

८८ पितृपैतामहं मौलं तेन शून्यं हि न क्षमम् ।
कृतजानपदारक्षं शून्यमूलं युधि क्षमम् ॥३६

८९ युध्यते शून्यमूलं हि यत्नान्मौलेन पालितम् ।
अस्वामिसङ्गृहीतं नैव स्वामिना यद्विनाकृतम् ॥

९० न युध्यते भिन्नकूटं भिन्नकूटमनायकम् ।
पश्चात्कोपातिसन्तप्तं दुष्पार्ष्णिग्राहमक्षमम् ॥

९१ अदेशिकं स्मृतं ह्यन्यं तन्मूढत्वात्क्रियाक्षमम् ।३७
बलव्यसनमित्यादि तत्समीक्ष्य समुत्पतेत् ॥

९२ दैवोपपीडितं ग्रस्तं मित्रं शत्रुबलेन च ।
कामक्रोधसमुत्थैश्च दोषैः सम्परिकीर्तितैः ॥

९३ नरेन्द्राद्याः प्रकृतयः सप्त याः परिकीर्तिताः ।
पूर्वं पूर्वं गुरुतरं तासां व्यसनमुच्यते ॥

९४ इत्यादि सर्वं प्रकृतेर्यथावद्बुध्येत राजा व्यसनं प्रयत्नात् ।
बुद्ध्या च शक्त्या व्यसनस्य कुर्यादकालहीनं व्यवरोपणं सः ॥

distance and time required to regroup.

Supply lines are for transporting grain and other provisions. Allied forces are one's friend's army. An army whose supply lines and allied forces are cut off is not fit for battle.

An army devoid of native troops of hereditary loyalty is incapacitated, but when the people of the countryside provide it succor, this same army that had lacked a base of support in the country can again become battle-ready. An army without native troops can fight when it is again carefully guarded by native troops, but an army separated from its commander cannot fight, since it has been deserted. A decapitated army cannot fight. To be decapitated means to be without a general. When the rear adversary is sinister, and the army is violently scorched with unrest from the rear, it simply cannot fight. An army in unfamiliar territory 90 is said to be blind, since the confusion this generates makes the army unable to act. One should launch a war only after examining one's army and the vices and calamities to which it is susceptible.

An ally is said to be afflicted by destiny when he is devoured by his enemies, or else devoured by those vices already fully enumerated: those arising from sensual desire and anger. The ruler, minister, realm, fortification, treasury, army, and ally are the seven state-elements, which have been enumerated in this order. It is said that vices and calamities affecting each element are in succession each more grievous than the next.

Thus the king should diligently learn about the vices and calamities of the state-elements, and applying his intellect and power, he should eradicate them without delay. 94

९५ प्रकृतिव्यसनानि भूतिकामः समुपेक्षेत न हि प्रमाददर्पात् ।३८
प्रकृतिव्यसनान्युपेक्षते यो नचिरात्तं रिपवः पराभवन्ति ॥३९

९६ इदमिदमिति सम्यक्क्रमेण योजनीयं
नियतमिति विचिन्त्य प्रापयेदीहमानः ।
सुनयपिहितरन्ध्रः प्राकृतो यस्य वर्गः
क्षितिपतिरुपभुङ्क्ते स त्रिवर्गं चिराय ॥

A ruler desirous of prosperity should not, in heedless pride, overlook vices and calamities affecting his state-elements. Enemies swiftly triumph over a king who overlooks the vices and calamities of his state-elements. 95

The king should always seek to employ his state-elements in their proper functions after due reflection on each and every aspect. A king will long enjoy the fruits of the three life goals—dharma, power, and pleasure—when every vulnerable point of his entire collection of state-elements has been patched up by sound policy. 96

पञ्चदशः सर्गः

सप्तव्यसनवर्गप्रकरणम्

१ अमात्याद्याः प्रकृतयो मित्रान्ता राज्यमुच्यते ।
अशेषराज्यव्यसनात्पार्थिवव्यसनं गुरु ॥

२ राजा त्वव्यसनी राज्यव्यसनापोहनक्षमः ।
न राजव्यसनापोहे समर्थं राज्यमूर्जितम् ॥

३ आत्मामात्यप्रजादुर्गकोशानां दण्डमित्रयोः ।
व्यसनेभ्यः समुन्नेता राजा यः स त्रिवर्गभाक् ॥

४ अशास्त्रचक्षुर्नृपतिरन्ध इत्यभिधीयते ।
वरमन्धो न चक्षुष्मान्मदादाक्षिप्तसत्पथः ॥

५ मन्त्रिभिर्मन्त्रकुशलैरन्धः पथि निवेश्यते ।१
चक्षुष्मांस्तु मदान्धः सन्नात्मानं हन्त्यशेषतः ॥

६ शास्त्रचक्षुर्नृपस्तस्मान्महामात्रमते स्थितः ।
धर्मार्थप्रतिघातीनि व्यसनानि परित्यजेत् ॥

७ वाग्दण्डयोश्च पारुष्यमर्थदूषणमेव च ।
स्मृतं व्यसनतत्त्वज्ञैः क्रोधजं व्यसनत्रयम् ॥

८ कामजं मृगया द्यूतं स्त्रियः पानं तथैव च ।
व्यसनं व्यसनार्थज्ञैश्चतुर्विधमुदाहृतम् ॥

CHAPTER 15

The Seven Vices

The kingdom is said to consist of a set of elements from the minister to the ally.[1] Of all the vices and calamities of the kingdom, those affecting the king are the most serious. A king free from vice can purge the kingdom of vice, but even a strong kingdom cannot purge the king of vice. Only the king who liberates himself, as well as the counselors, the people, the fortifications, the treasury, the coercive power, and the allies from vice can attain the three ends of man: dharma, power, and pleasure.

The king who does not have *śāstra* for eyes is said to be blind. But it is better to be blind than to see with a vision thwarted from the right path by passion. Counselors skilled in strategy can place a king who has gone blind back on the right path. A king who has eyes, and yet is still blinded by passion, destroys himself completely. Therefore a king with *śāstra* for eyes and adhering to the counsel of his chief counselors should reject the vices, which destroy dharma and power.

Those who understand the true nature of vices hold there to be three emanating from anger: severity in speech, severity in punishment, and financial malfeasance. In addition, they count four arising from sensual desire: hunting, gambling, women, and drink.

Severe speech is the most disturbing and damaging thing in the world. One should not speak in an unpleasant

5

९ वाक्पारुष्यं परं लोक उद्वेजनमनर्थकम् ।
न कुर्याद्द्विप्रियां वाचं प्रकुर्याज्जनमात्मसात् ॥२

१० अकस्मादेव यः कोपात्परुषं बहु भाषते ।३
तस्मादुद्विजते लोकः सस्फुलिङ्गादिवानलात् ॥

११ हृदये वागसिस्तीक्ष्णो मर्मच्छिन्निपतन्मुहुः ।
तेजस्विनं दीपयति स दीप्तो याति वैरिताम् ॥४

१२ नोद्वेजयेज्जगद्वाचा रूक्षया प्रियवाग्भवेत् ।
प्रायेण प्रियवाक्कर्मा कृपणोऽपि हि सेव्यते ॥५

१३ असिद्धसाधनं सद्धिः शासनं दण्ड उच्यते ।६
तं युक्त्यैव नयेद्दण्डं युक्तदण्डः प्रशस्यते ॥७

१४ उद्वेजयति भूतानि दण्डपारुष्यवान्नृपः ।
भूतान्युद्वेज्यमानानि द्विषतां यान्ति संश्रयम् ॥

१५ आश्रिताश्चैव लोकेन समृद्धिं यान्ति विद्विषः ।
समृद्धाश्च विनाशाय तस्मान्नोद्वेजयेत्प्रजाः ॥

१६ लोकानुग्रहकर्तारः प्रवर्धन्ते महीभुजः ।
लोकवृद्ध्या नरेन्द्राणां वृद्धिस्तत्संक्षये क्षयः ॥

१७ महत्स्वप्यपराधेषु दण्डं प्राणान्तिकं त्यजेत् ।
ऋते राज्यापहारात्तु युक्तदण्डः प्रशस्यते ॥८

१८ दूष्यस्य दूषणार्थं हि परित्यागो महीयसः ।
अर्थस्य नीतितत्त्वज्ञैरर्थदूषणमुच्यते ॥

१९ तदकस्मात्समाविष्टः कोपेनातिबलीयसा ।
नित्यमात्महिताकाङ्क्षी न कुर्यादर्थदूषणम् ॥

196

manner, but instead treat people as one's own. People are frightened of someone who, in anger, suddenly bursts out in severe speech, just as they fear a fire shooting sparks. The sharp sword of speech, lunging again and again, cuts to the quick. It inflames a hot-tempered man, and once inflamed, he will become an enemy. You should not terrify people with harsh words: your speech should be pleasing. People will offer service to even a miserly king if his words and deeds are pleasing.

The wise call the use of force to achieve an end otherwise unachieved "the rod of coercion." One should apply it justly to those who deserve it; a king whose punishment is just is praiseworthy. A king severe in his application of the rod terrifies people, and when terrified the people seek refuge with the enemy. The enemy thereby grows prosperous, and when the enemy prospers, the ruler is destroyed. Therefore the king should not terrify the people. Kings who gratify the people grow strong. The people's prosperity is the king's prosperity, and their destruction is his destruction. Even for great offenses the king should reject the death penalty; it should be applied only for an attempted coup d'état. In this way he is praised as a ruler whose punishment is just.

According to scholars of politics, financial malfeasance comprises the loss or expenditure of great wealth in order to implicate an enemy whom one intends to defame. A king with his own real interests in mind, even when suddenly seized by powerful rage, should not commit financial malfeasance.

The problems stemming from kings' hunting expeditions are being jolted by or pitched from the royal conveyance,

२० यानक्षोभो यानपातो यानाभिहरणं तथा ।९
    क्षुत्पिपासाश्रमायासशीतवातोष्णपीडनम् ॥

२१ अभियानस्य सम्पत्त्या यानव्यसनजं महत् ।
    दुःखं प्रतप्तसिकताकुशकण्टकभूमयः ॥

२२ वृक्षसङ्कटजा दोषा लताकण्टकपाटनम् ।१०
    शैलपातशिलाजालस्थाणुवल्मीकपीडनम् ॥

२३ प्रच्छन्नोपगतैः शैलसरिद्द्विपिनकुक्षिषु ।११
    वधबन्धपरिक्लेशः सामन्ताटविकादिभिः ॥१२

२४ स्वसैन्यैश्च स्वकुल्यैश्च परभिन्नैश्च मारणम् ।१३
    ऋक्षाजगरमातङ्गसिंहव्याघ्रभयादि च ॥

२५ दवाग्निधूमसंरोधो दिङ्मोहभ्रमणानि च ।
    इत्यादि पृथिवीन्द्राणां मृगयाव्यसनं स्मृतम् ॥

२६ जितश्रमत्वं व्यायाम आममेदःकफक्षयः ।
    चलस्थिरेषु लक्ष्येषु बाणसिद्धिरनुत्तमा ॥१४

२७ मृगयायां गुणानेतानन्ये प्राहुर्न तत्क्षमम् ।
    दोषाः प्राणहराः प्रायस्तस्मात्तत्परिवर्जयेत् ॥१५

२८ आमादयो हि जीर्यन्ति योग्ययैव दिवानिशम् ।
    चलेषु यन्त्रलक्ष्येषु बाणसिद्धिश्च जायते ॥१६

२९ अथ चेन्मृगयाक्रीडावाञ्छा तन्नगरान्तिके ।
    कारयेन्मृगयारण्यं क्रीडाहेतोर्मनोहरम् ॥

३० परिक्षिप्तं परिखया मृगाणामप्यगम्यया ।१७
    आयामपरिणाहाभ्यामर्धयोजनसम्मितम् ॥

as well as its verging off course; hunger, thirst, exhaustion, and exposure to cold wind or heat. Great suffering can come 20 about from a protracted journey: riding over scorching sands, rough grass or thorns; exposure to the danger of forest thickets, including lacerations from branches and thorns; falling boulders and rocky impasses, tree-stumps and anthills. Hidden assailants can also attack, lurking behind boulders, rivers, or in the nooks of forests, leading to the disasters of death or imprisonment by neighboring feuda-tories, forest people, and others. One can even be killed by one's own soldiers or family members turned traitor by the enemy. There is also the danger of bears, pythons, elephants, lions, tigers, and so on. There can be forest fires where you are overwhelmed by smoke, where you lose all sense of direc-tion, and wander aimlessly. 25

Some cite the virtues of hunting: building endurance; physical exercise that diminishes excess bile, fat, and phlegm; and developing superlative aim with arrows against still and moving targets. But this is not credible, since the calamities of hunting are fatal. Therefore one should avoid it. Bile and other problems can be diminished by exercising day and night. Perfect aim with arrows can be developed by practicing with mechanical targets.

But if a king still yearns for the sport of hunting, then a delightful game reserve should be built at the edge of the city for his sport. It should be surrounded by a forbidding moat, which even animals cannot traverse; and be four and a half miles in both length and breadth.[2] It should be next 30 to a river or mountain and have sufficient water and grass; and also be free of thorns, branches, shrubs, and poisonous

३१ गिरेरुपान्ते नद्या वा पर्याप्तजलशाद्वलम् ।
अकण्टकलतागुल्मं विषपादपवर्जितम् ॥

३२ पादपैः पुष्पफलदैः प्रज्ञातैश्चित्तहारिभिः ।
स्निग्धनीलघनच्छायैर्विरलैरुपशोभितम् ॥१८

३३ पांसुपूरितनिश्छिद्रश्वभ्रप्रदरकन्दरम् ।१९
दलितस्थाणुवल्मीकपाषाणसमभूतलम् ॥

३४ शोधितग्राहसलिलमगभीरजलाशयम् ।२०
नानापुष्पसमाकीर्णं नानाविहगसेवितम् ॥

३५ सुपात्यमृगसम्पूर्णं हस्तिनीकलभान्वितम् ।२१
भग्नदंष्ट्रनखव्यालं छिन्नशृङ्गविषाणि च ॥

३६ सुखसंसेव्यलतया पुष्पवल्लीपिनद्धया ।२२
वनराज्या परिक्षिप्तं परिखातटजातया ॥

३७ बहिर्दूरान्तराभोगनिर्वृक्षस्तम्भभूतलम् ।२३
अगम्यं रिपुसैन्यानां मनःप्रीतिविवर्धनम् ॥

३८ तद्वनेचरचित्तज्ञैः क्लेशायाससहैर्हृष्टैः ।
रक्षितं रक्षिभिः स्वाप्तैर्भूभुजामभिवृद्धये ॥

३९ तत्कर्माप्तो नरेन्द्रस्य जनो जितपरिश्रमः ।
क्रीडनायात्र विविधा मृगजातीः प्रवेशयेत् ॥

४० अन्यकार्याविरोधेन प्रातश्चङ्क्रमणक्षमः ।
क्रीडनाय विशेद्राजा तदाप्तैः सहितो मितैः ॥

४१ यदा च प्रविशेद्राजा क्रीडनार्थं तदा बहिः ।
सन्नद्धं यत्नतस्तिष्ठेत्सैन्यं दूरान्तगोचरम् ॥

४२ सद्द्विषे मृगयायाने गुणाः साधु प्रकीर्तिताः ।२४
क्रीडाप्रीतो नरपतिस्तांस्तत्र समवाप्नुयात् ॥२५

trees. It should be beautified somewhat sparsely by famil-
iar lovely trees, offering fruits and flowers, with shade that
is rich, dense, and dark. It should be on even ground, with
stones, anthills, and tree stumps removed; with all chasms,
crevices, and caverns completely filled in by sand. It should
have pools of water that are not deep, with various birds
flocking to them, completely rid of crocodiles, and strewn
with all kinds of flowers. It should be teeming with animals
that are easy to kill: she-elephants and their cubs, beasts of
prey whose fangs and claws have been blunted, and horned
animals whose horns have been cut off. It should have rows   35
of forest along the edges of the moat, with gentle branches
and flowering vines twining around. Outside there should be
an extensive borderland cleared of trees and stumps, filling
the heart with delight and also inaccessible to enemy armies.
Such a hunting ground enhances a king's prosperity when it
is guarded by trustworthy and steadfast guards, who know
the hearts of the local forest people, and who are capable of
enduring pain and exhaustion.

Servants trained in the task should tirelessly bring in various types of animals for the king's sport. When he is not
hampered by other work, and when he is fit for strenuous
movement, the king should enter the hunting ground for
his sport in the morning, guarded by a handful of well-
known and trustworthy guards. When the king enters   40
for his sport, soldiers should stand outside in dense formation, spanning the distant horizons. In such a place the
king can enjoy the sport and realize all the benefits of hunting expeditions, which the learned have clearly enumerated.
But there is one key rule: the king should never go astray

४३ विधिरेष समुद्दिष्टो मृगयाक्रीडने वरम् ।
न गच्छेदन्यथा राजा मृगयां मृगयुर्यथा ॥२६

४४ महतोऽपि क्षणान्नाशो धनस्य ह्रीविमुक्तता ।२७
निःसत्यता निष्ठुरता क्रोधो वाक्शस्त्रखण्डनम् ॥

४५ लोभो धर्मक्रियालोपः कर्मणामप्रवर्तनम् ।
सत्समागमविच्छित्तिरसद्धिः सह वर्तनम् ॥

४६ अर्थनाशक्रियावश्यं नित्यं वैरानुबन्धिता ।
सत्यप्यर्थे निराशात्वमसत्यपि च साशता ॥

४७ प्रतिक्षणं क्रोधहर्षौ सन्तापश्च प्रतिक्षणम् ।
प्रतिक्षणं च संक्लेशः साक्षिप्रश्नः प्रतिक्षणम् ॥

४८ स्नानादिगात्रसंस्कारपरिभोगेष्वनादरः ।
अव्यायामोऽङ्गदौर्बल्यं शास्त्रार्थप्रत्युपेक्षणम् ॥

४९ गूहनं मूत्रशकृतोः क्षुत्पिपासोपपीडनम् ।
इत्यादींस्तन्त्रकुशला द्यूतदोषान्प्रचक्षते ॥२८

५० पाण्डवो धर्मराजस्तु लोकपाल इवापरः ।
द्यूतेन ह्रासता दीव्यन्कलत्राद्यपहारितः ॥

५१ नलश्च राजा द्यूतेन हृते राज्ये महोदये ।
धर्मदारान्वने त्यक्त्वा परकर्मकरोऽभवत् ॥

५२ तुल्यो भुवीन्द्रतुल्यस्य यस्य नास्ति धनुर्धरः ।
स रुक्मी रुक्मशैलाभो द्यूतदोषाद्गतः क्षयम् ॥

५३ राजा काशिकरूशानां दन्तवक्रोऽपि मन्दधीः
तीव्राद्द्यूतकृताद्दोषाद्दन्तभङ्गमवाप्तवान् ॥

202

in his hunting, taking to it like a common huntsman.

The following are some of the many problems scholars of the discipline of politics have enumerated for gambling: sudden loss of even great wealth; shamelessness; breach of promises; cruelty, anger, and annihilating people with the weapon of words; greed; neglect of religious acts and all other undertakings; discontinued interaction with good people, and interaction instead with bad; certain loss of wealth, and ceaselessly fostering enmities; hopelessness about money one has, and hope for money one does not have; anger and   45
excitement at every moment, agony at every moment, discomfort at every moment, and quizzing witnesses about doubtful results at every moment; lack of concern for bathing or embellishing the body, or for the pleasures of leisure; lack of exercise, weakness of the limbs, and disregard for the content of the *śāstras;* retention of urine and feces, as well as suppression of hunger and thirst.

The son of Pandu, the wise dharma-king Yudhishthira— who was like one of the deities who guard the horizons— was made to lose his wife and everything through dishonest gambling.[3] Through gambling King Nala lost his illustrious   50
kingdom, then abandoned his lawfully wedded wife in the forest, and then he was reduced to servitude. Rukmin—who had the marvelous appearance of the silver-peaked Mount Meru, who was equal to Indra and unequalled on earth as an archer—met his destruction through the vice of gambling.[4] The dull-witted, crooked-toothed Dantavaktra, king of the Kashikarushas, gnashed his teeth until he actually ground them down because of severe addiction to gambling.[5]

From gambling comes misfortune; from gambling comes

५४ द्यूतादनर्थसंरम्भो द्यूतात्स्नेहक्षयो महान् ।
पक्षाणां चापि महतां द्यूताद्भेदः प्रवर्तते ॥

५५ इति केवलदोषं हि राजा द्यूतं विवर्जयेत् ।
समाह्वयं च मेधावी दर्पिणां विनिवारयेत् ॥

५६ कालातिपातः कार्याणां धर्मार्थपरिपीडनम् ।
नित्याभ्यन्तरवर्तित्वात्साधुप्रकृतिकोपनम् ॥

५७ रहस्यभेदस्तत्पश्चादकार्येषु प्रवर्तनम् ।२९
ईर्ष्यामर्षस्तथा क्रोधो विरोधः साहसानि च ॥३०

५८ इत्यादि च स्त्रीव्यसने यच्च पूर्वं प्रकीर्तितम् ।
तस्मात्स्त्रीव्यसनं राजा राज्यकामः परित्यजेत् ॥

५९ स्त्रीमुखालोकनतया व्यग्राणामल्पचेतसाम् ।
ईहितानीह गच्छन्ति यौवनेन सह क्षयम् ॥

६० वमनं विह्वलत्वं च संज्ञानाशो विवस्त्रता ।३१
बह्वबद्धप्रलापित्वमकस्माद्व्यसनं मुहुः ॥

६१ प्राणग्लानिः सुहृन्नाशः प्रज्ञाश्रुतमतिभ्रमः ।
सद्विर्वियोगोऽसद्भिश्च संयोगोऽनर्थसङ्गमः ॥३२

६२ स्खलनं वेपथुस्तन्द्रा नितान्तं स्त्रीनिषेवणम् ।३३
इत्यादि पानव्यसनमत्यन्तं सद्भिर्गर्हितम् ॥

६३ श्रुतशीलबलोपेताः पानदोषेण भूयसा ।
क्षयमक्षीणनामानो जग्मुरन्धकवृष्णयः ॥

६४ योगीश्वरस्तु भगवान्भार्गवो भृगुतुल्यधीः ।
शुक्रः पानमदात्तीव्रादुद्भुजे शिष्यमौरसम् ॥

204

the loss of affection; from gambling comes the disaffection of even one's closest allies. Since it is nothing but vice, the king should reject gambling. A prudent king should always reject prideful men's challenge to gamble.   55

The following are the problems that come from the vice of women, among those which have already been enumerated: procrastination in one's duties; damage to dharma and economic prosperity; alienation of all the kingdom's noble functionaries because of the king's always remaining indoors in the harem; divulging secrets and then engaging in wrongful actions; as well as jealousy, irritability, anger, fights, and rash deeds. Because of all this a king whose passion is the kingdom's welfare should shun the vice of women. Through gazing on a woman's face kings become distracted and lose their wits. All their hopes, and with them their youth, are soon destroyed.

These and others are the problems that come from the vice of drinking, which good men severely revile: vomiting, dizziness, and loss of consciousness; disheveled dress or nudity; excessive and incoherent speaking; sudden illness, diminished vitality, loss of friends, and derangement of   60 one's intellectual, scholarly, and mental faculties; separation from good people, union with bad people, and meeting with sudden calamities; stumbling, trembling, drowsiness, and incessant sexual activity.

The Andhakas and Vrishnis, who were gifted with learning, character, and power, were destroyed—however indestructible their fame—through intense addiction to drinking.[6] The lord of yoga, Shukra, scion of the Bhrigu clan—who was equal to Bhrigu himself in intellect—

६५   पानाक्षिप्तो हि पुरुषो यत्र तत्र प्रवर्तते ।³⁴
      यात्यसंव्यवहारित्वं यत्र तत्र प्रवर्तनात् ॥³⁵

६६   कामं स्त्रियो निषेवेत पानं वा साधु मात्रया ।
      न द्यूतमृगये विद्वानत्यन्तव्यसने हि ते ॥

६७   तदपनयविधिज्ञैः श्रेयसां विघ्नकारि
      व्यसनमिदमुदारं सम्यधेहोपदिष्टम् ।
      जनयति हि निषङ्गादेकधैवाशु नाशं
      किमु न भवति हन्ता यौगपद्योदयेन ॥

६८   पटयति परिभोगग्राहितामिन्द्रीयाणां
      श्रुतमपि विनिहन्ति श्रेष्ठतां प्रष्ठतां च ।³⁶
      चलयति हि विभूतिं भूयसीमप्यनीचैर्
      अपि विबुधमतीनां सम्यकोऽयं दुरन्तः ॥

६९   अरिगणा नियतं व्यसने स्थितान्परिभवन्ति भवन्ति च दुश्छिदः ।
      अपगतव्यसनास्तु बुधा रिपून्परिभवन्ति भवन्ति च दुश्छिदः ॥

cannibalized his own dearest student on account of intense intoxication.[7]

Wherever a drunken man goes he becomes an outcaste by indiscriminate behavior. A wise man can certainly enjoy women and drink in the right measure, but he will not engage in gambling or hunting, since both are irredeemable vices. 65

Those knowledgeable about the various kinds of misconduct have amply elaborated the seven vices, which hinder higher goals. Attachment to even one of these vices brings swift destruction. Imagine how they can kill you when all come at once! 67

These seven vices have a nefarious trajectory. They sharpen the senses' obsession with pleasure. They destroy learning, preeminence, and the power of leadership. They annihilate the prosperity—however abundant—even of men of god-like intellect. 68

Enemy hordes become indomitable and will inevitably defeat a king who is addicted to vice. But wise kings overcome their vices, defeat their enemies, and become themselves indomitable. 69

षोडशः सर्गः

यात्राभियोक्तृप्रदर्शनप्रकरणम्

१ नानाप्रकारैर्व्यसनैर्विमुक्तः शक्तित्रयेणाप्रतिमेन युक्तः ।१
परं दुरन्तव्यसनोपपन्नं यायान्नरेन्द्रो विजयाभिकाङ्क्षी ॥

२ प्रायेण सन्तो व्यसने रिपूणां यातव्यमित्येवमुपादिशन्ति ।
तत्रैष पक्षो व्यसनं ह्यनित्यं क्षमस्तु सन्नभ्युदितो हि यायात् ॥२

३ यदा क्षमस्तु प्रसभं निहन्तुं पराक्रमादूर्जितमप्यमित्रम् ।
तदा हि यायादहितानि कर्तुं परस्य वा पीडनकर्शनानि ॥

४ सम्पन्नसस्यं विषयं परस्य यायात्रमृद्रन्विजयाय राजा ।३
सस्योपघातेन परस्य वृत्तेश्छेदः स्वसैन्योपचयश्च साधु ॥

५ विशुद्धपृष्ठः पुरतो विचिन्वन्नभयप्रदेशान्परकर्मवेदी ।
स्ववीवधासारविशुद्धमार्गो विशोद्धरित्रीं द्विषतोऽप्रमत्तः ॥

CHAPTER 16

A Conqueror and His Expeditions

Free of all the varieties of vice and incomparably endowed with the three powers,[1] the lord of men, if he is desirous of conquest, should launch an expedition against an enemy who is incapacitated by vice or disaster.[2]   1

Wise men generally advise a king to attack when an enemy is engrossed in vice or calamity, but there is also an opinion that since vices and calamities are transient, whenever the king is fit and on the ascent, he should march against him.   2 When he is capable of suddenly and forcefully annihilating even a powerful enemy, he should advance against and bring misfortune to him, ravaging and tormenting his kingdom.   3

If the enemy has a territory rich in crops, the king should march to victory, pillaging the crops on his way. The enemy loses his livelihood when his crops are destroyed, while the conqueror's troops gain good sustenance.   4

When he has pacified all danger from the rear, the king should advance, watching out for dangerous areas, and staying cognizant of the enemy's movements. After securing the way for his supply lines and for the replenishment of his forces by allied troops, the king should remain vigilant as he enters the enemy's land.   5

The healthy, fearless, and wise king should advance on

६ समे प्रदेशे विषमे च भूमेर्निम्ने स्थले वा स्वमुखेन यायात् ।
अनातुरः सन्नभयो हि विद्वान्सन्नद्धसैन्यो विहितान्ततोयः ॥

७ ग्रीष्मे प्रभूताम्बुवनेन यायान्निर्वापणार्थं करिणां पथा तु ।
ऋतेऽम्भसो ग्रीष्मकृतात्प्रतापाद्भ्रवन्ति कुष्ठानि मतङ्गजानाम् ॥

८ स्वस्थक्रियाणामपि कुञ्जराणामूष्मा शरीरेषु हि जाज्वलीति ।
आयासयोगेन च सम्प्रवृद्धः प्रसह्य हन्ति द्विरदान्प्रतापः ॥

९ सर्वाणि सत्त्वानि खलूष्णकाले विनाम्बुना यान्ति परामवस्थाम् ।
अत्यर्थमुष्णप्रतितप्तकायाः प्रयान्ति सद्यः करिणोऽपिबन्तः ॥४

१० सुगन्धिदानस्रुतिशीकरेषु दन्ताभिघातस्फुटितोपलेषु ।५
गजेषु नीलाभ्रसमप्रभेषु राज्यं निबद्धं पृथिवीपतीनाम् ॥

११ संकल्पितः संयति दृष्टमार्गः स्वधिष्ठितो वीरतमेन पुंसा ।६
तुरङ्गमानामपि कल्पितानामेको गजः षष्टिशतानि हन्ति ॥

१२ जले स्थले च द्रुमसंकटे च समे ऽसमे साधु चले ऽचले च ।
प्राकारहर्म्याट्टविदारणे च जयो ध्रुवं नागवतां बलानाम् ॥७

१३ तस्माद्यतो भूरिजलस्तु पन्था यतोऽन्नपानोपचयो ऽविशङ्कः ।
ततो हि यायाज्जनयन्प्रतापं शनैः शनैर्विश्रमयन्बलानि ॥

210

smooth or rough ground—whether the terrain be flat or sloping—with his army in tight formation and with adequate supplies of food and water.   6

If he advances in the summertime, he should travel on a route through groves rich in water so the elephants can cool themselves. Without water, the war elephants will develop scaly lesions from the summer heat.   7

The summer heat brutally scorches even healthy elephants' bodies, and compounded by physical exertion, the heat can kill them suddenly.   8

In the hot season, lack of water brings all creatures to the brink of death. When elephants cannot drink water and their bodies are scorched all over by extreme heat, they suddenly die.   9

The tusks of war elephants can shatter stones; with their blue-gray bodies they are like storm clouds; how fragrant is the ichor that flows when they are in rut. The welfare of a kingdom depends on them.   10

Well-outfitted, placed in battle formation, and conducted by a most valiant driver, a single elephant can kill six thousand well-outfitted horses.   11

Whether moving or still, on wet land or dry, in forest thickets, on even or uneven ground; whether smashing apart ramparts, palaces, or towers—armies with elephants are assured of victory.   12

Thus, the king's route should be free of danger; with ample water, and an assortment of food and drink. As he advances wreaking havoc, he must from time to time allow his soldiers to rest.   13

Even if his forces are minuscule, he can generate great

१४ अभ्युन्नतानामणुरप्युदारं पश्चात्प्रकोपं जनयेदरीणाम् ।
    तं चाप्रमत्तः प्रसमीक्ष्य यायान्न नाशयेद्दृष्टमदृष्टहेतोः ॥

१५ पश्चात्प्रकोपः पुरतः फलं च पश्चात्प्रकोपस्तु तयोर्गरीयान् ।
    रन्ध्रं हि तद्विप्रकृता महत्त्वं नयन्ति तस्मात्प्रविधाय यायात् ॥

१६ पुरश्च पश्चाच्च यदा समर्थस्तदाभियायान्महते फलाय ।
    पुरः प्रसर्पन्नविशुद्धपृष्ठः प्राप्नोति तीव्रं खलु पार्ष्णिभेदम् ॥

१७ यास्यन्पुरोरक्ष्यमनेकवर्गमनेकमुख्यं च बलं विदध्यात् ।
    अनेकमुख्यस्य हि नैकमत्यमनेकमुख्यं द्विषतामभेद्यम् ॥८

१८ अवश्ययातव्यतयोद्यतः सन्पश्चात्प्रकोपाहितयानशङ्कः ।
    सेनापतिं वाप्यथवा कुमारं बलैकदेशेन पुरो निदध्यात् ॥

१९ आभ्यन्तराद्बाह्यकृताच्च कोपादभ्यन्तरस्त्वेव तयोर्गरीयान् ।९
    आदाय गच्छेदबहिःप्रचारान्बाह्यांश्च कृत्वा विहितार्थकल्यान् ॥

२० पुरोहितामात्यकुमारकुल्याः सेनाभिगोप्तार इमे प्रधानाः ।
    एषां हि सन्तोऽन्यतमप्रकोपमन्तःप्रकोपं समुपादिशन्ति ॥१०

disturbance to the mightiest enemies from the rear. By the same token, as he advances he should pay close attention to his own rear. He should not destroy what he has for the sake of what he has yet to acquire. 14

Disturbance from the rear is more serious than a promising prospect in front. Hostile forces can make a slight gap in the defenses turn into a huge disaster. Therefore one must advance with caution. 15

When the king is strong both in front and at the rear, he should march forward for a great reward. If he advances without securing the rear, he will suffer severe damage from behind. 16

When the king wishes to advance, he should secure the army's vanguard such that its multiple fronts each have their own command. For an army with multiple commanders is not directed by just one mind. And an army with multiple commands becomes impervious to the enemy.[3] 17

When the king must focus on attacking the enemy frontally, and yet there is danger to his advance from the rear, he should send the army's commander, or the prince, to the front, along with a detachment of the army.[4] 18

Internal problems within the ranks are worse than external problems from enemies, so the king should advance only when he has taken the right measures to remedy internal disturbances as well as external problems. 19

The main constituents of the king's force are the royal priests, counselors, princes, and military leaders. Experts teach that a disturbance arising among any of these people constitutes "internal disturbance." 20

"External disturbance" comes from the disturbance of

२१ राष्ट्रान्तपालाटविकाभिसीम्नां बाह्यप्रकोपोऽन्यतमप्रकोपः ।११
उत्पद्यमानो निपुणप्रचारैस्तं मन्त्रिभिः सम्युगपाददीत ॥१२

२२ सामादिभिः संशमयेत्प्रकोपं परस्परावग्रहभेदनैश्च ।
तथा च धीरः शमयेद्विकारं यथा भजेरन्न परान्प्रतप्ताः ॥

२३ मनुष्ययुग्यापचयः क्षयो हि हिरण्यधान्यापचयो व्ययस्तु ।
तस्मादिमां नैव विदग्धबुद्धिः क्षयव्ययायासकरीमुपेयात् ॥

२४ अवश्यनिष्पत्तिमहाफलाढ्यामदीर्घसूत्रां परिणामकल्याम् ।
कामं व्ययायासकरीमुपेयान्न त्वेव जातु क्षयदोषयुक्ताम् ॥

२५ वस्तुष्वशक्येषु समुद्यमश्च शक्येषु चाकालसमुद्यमश्च ।
शक्येषु मोहादसमुद्यमश्च त्रिधैव कार्यव्यसनं वदन्ति ॥

२६ कामोऽक्षमादक्षिणतानुकम्पा ह्रीः साध्वसं क्रौर्यमनार्यता च ।
दम्भोऽभिमानोऽप्यतिधार्मिकत्वं दैन्यं स्वयूथस्य विमाननं च ॥१३

२७ द्रोहो भयं शश्वदुपेक्षणं च शीतोष्णवर्षास्वसहिष्णुता च ।
एतानि काले समुपाहितानि कुर्वन्त्यवश्यं खलु सिद्धिविघ्नम् ॥

214

any of the following: government officials, border-guards, forest people, and foreigners. When it arises, the king can set it right by employing counselors with clever stratagems. 21

He should quell disturbance through conciliation, or else by fomenting internecine conflict and turning people against each other. The resolute king must quell disturbance such that the aggrieved parties do not take recourse to the enemy. 22

The loss of men and animals is referred to as "destruction," while the loss of gold and grain is called "depletion." A king whose intellect is refined should undertake no military expedition that will result in destruction, depletion, or hardship. 23

Yet a king may undertake an expedition involving depletion and hardship if it is certain to result in great gains, promising excellent rewards within a short timeframe. But he should never proceed with an expedition likely to result in destruction. 24

There are three kinds of vices that pertain to action: effort toward unattainable objects; lack of effort for attainable objects within a suitable timeframe; and lack of effort, owing to confusion, toward attainable objects. 25

The following vices, when they arise at critical moments, undoubtedly hinder one's projects: sensual desire, anger, ineptitude, excessive sympathy, shame, rashness, cruelty, ignobility, treachery, arrogance, excessive religiousness,[5] dejection, disrespecting one's own troops, rebellion, cowardice, constant negligence, and the inability to bear cold, heat, or rains. 26–27

The wise say that there are seven types of people on one's own side: one's own people, allies, people who have sought refuge, relatives, people recruited for the

२८ निजोऽथ मैत्रश्च समाश्रितश्च सम्बन्धजः कार्यसमुद्भवश्च ।
भृत्यो गृहीतो विविधोपचारैः पक्षं बुधाः सप्तविधं वदन्ति ॥

२९ सदानुसृत्या गुणकीर्तनेन निन्दासहत्वेन च रन्ध्रगुप्त्या ।
तदर्थशौचोद्यमसङ्कथाभिः पक्षोऽनुरागीति स वेदितव्यः ॥१४

३० कुलीनमार्यं श्रुतवद्विनीतं मानोन्नतं सभ्यमहार्यबुद्धिम् ।१५
कृतज्ञतोर्जमतिसत्त्वयुक्तं सद्वृत्तपक्षं खलु तं च विद्यात् ॥

३१ उद्योगमेधाधृतिसत्त्वसत्यत्यागानुरागस्थितिगौरवाणि ।
जितेन्द्रियत्वं प्रसहिष्णुता ह्रीः प्रागल्भ्यमित्यात्मगुणप्रवेकः ॥

३२ मन्त्रस्य शक्तिं सुनयप्रचारं स्वकोशदण्डौ प्रभुशक्तिमाहुः ।
उत्साहशक्तिं बलवद्विचेष्टां त्रिशक्तियुक्तो भवतीह जेता ॥

३३ शैघ्र्यं सुदाक्ष्यं व्यसनेष्वदैन्यमुत्साहसम्पत्स्वतिधीरता च ।
औत्पादिकी शास्त्रसमुद्भवा च सांसर्गिकी धीः परिणामिनी च ॥१६

३४ उत्साहसत्त्वाध्यवसायचेष्टा दार्ढ्यं च कर्मस्विह पौरुषं च ।
अरोगता कर्मफलोपपत्तिर्दैवानुकूल्यं च निराधिता च ॥

occasion, servants, and people won over through various gestures of hospitality. 28

The loyalty of the people on one's own side can be discerned through these characteristics: constant obedience; singing their lord's praises; not tolerating slander of their lord; hiding the lord's weak points; and extolling his wealth, virtue, and effort. 29

The good conduct of the people on one's own side can be discerned through these characteristics: noble descent, noble conduct, learning, honorable behavior, politeness, loyal-mindedness, gratitude, vigor, and mental power. 30

Their personal virtues are enumerated as: effort, intellect, fortitude, strength, truthfulness, generosity, devotion, stability, gravity, conquest of the senses, forbearance, sense of shame, and maturity. 31

The "power of strategy" is conduct informed by sound politics. The "power of lordship" is a treasury combined with coercive power. The "power of determination" is forceful activity. The king who has all three powers becomes a conqueror.[6] 32

The power of determination is defined by swiftness, great dexterity, lack of dejection amid calamities, and extreme fortitude. Strategic intellect has four varieties: inborn; coming from study of the *śāstras;* coming from social interaction; and evolving over time. 33

Human effort consists of determination, courage, resolution, being active, and holding firm in action. Good destiny is being free from disease, having successful outcomes from actions, and being free of mental disorder. 34

Using the resources of the treasury, and drawing upon his

३५ पक्षादिनानेन गृहीतकोशः पक्षादिहीनं रिपुमभ्युपेयात् ।
इति प्रसर्पन्नियतं समुद्रप्रक्षालितां तां लभते धरित्रीम् ॥

३६ कालो गजानां सजलाभ्रजालो यातुं तदन्यश्च तुरङ्गमाणाम् ।
नात्यर्थवर्षोष्णतुषारयुक्तः सम्पन्नसस्यस्त्विति कालसम्पत् ॥

३७ रात्रावुलूको विनिहन्ति काकान्काकोऽप्युलूकात्रजनीव्यपाये ।
इति स्म कालं समुदीक्ष्य यायात्काले फलन्तीह समीहितानि ॥

३८ श्वा नक्रमाकर्षति कूलसंस्थं श्वानं च नक्रः सलिलाभ्युपेतं ।
व्यायच्छमानो ध्रुवमभ्युपैति देशस्थितः कर्मफलोपभोगम् ॥

३९ समं तुरङ्गैर्विषमं च नागैस्तथा जलाढ्यं समहीधरं च ।
नावाब्वृतं पत्तिबलानुयातैर्यथाबलं च प्रसमीक्ष्य मिश्रम् ॥१७

४० मरुप्रगाढं पततीह तोये ग्रीष्मे त्वनूपोदककक्षदुर्गम् ।
मिश्रे च संवीक्ष्य यथासुखं च गच्छेन्नरेन्द्रो विजयाय देशम् ॥

४१ न चातितोयं न च तोयहीनं युक्तं च सम्यग्यवसेन्धनेन ।
उपेत्य मार्गं बहुतज्ज्ञयुक्तं सुखं प्रयाणै रिपुमभ्युपेयात् ॥१८

ranks, the conqueror should march against the enemy when the latter is cut off from his ranks. Operating in this fashion, he will surely obtain the entire earth with its borders washed by the oceans.   35

The time to advance with elephants is when the sky shows a dark web of rainclouds. The time to advance with cavalry is not during the monsoon, but when it is not too hot, rainy, or frosty, and when the crops have ripened. These are the propitious times.   36

At night the owl kills crows; during the day, the crow kills owls. Therefore one should advance after carefully considering the timing. Designs bring successful results according to time.   37

A dog can drag away a crocodile on a riverbank, but the crocodile drags away the dog in water. Therefore taking action situated on the right terrain assures fruitful results.   38

Flat ground is better for cavalry, while uneven ground, wetlands, and mountainous areas are better for elephants. Over land submerged in water, one should travel by boat, with the elephants followed by detachments of the army. On mixed terrain one should evaluate one's forces and proceed.   39

On desert terrain one should advance when it rains. In the hot season, one should attack an enemy fort on marshlands, wetlands, or grasslands. On mixed terrain, the king should examine the situation and proceed according to convenience in order to conquer a territory.   40

He should advance comfortably in chariots against the enemy—over land that is neither without water nor too marshy, and where there is plenty of fodder and fuel—accompanied by many guides knowledgeable about the terrain.   41

४२ स्ववीवधासारमुपेततोयं विश्वासिताक्रान्तजनं विशुद्धम् ।१९
तन्मात्रमेव द्विषतामुपेयाद्यस्मान्न कुर्यादपयानमार्तः ॥

४३ ये दूरयात्रां सहसा विशन्ति मूढा रिपूणामविचार्य भूमिम् ।
ते यान्ति तेषामचिरेण खड्गधारापरिष्वङ्गमयत्नसाध्यम् ॥

४४ मार्गे च दुर्गोपनिविष्टसैन्यो विधाय रक्षां विधिवद्विधिज्ञः ।
सन्नद्धपार्श्वस्थितवीरयोधः सेवेत साध्वीं निशि योगनिद्राम् ॥

४५ भ्रमत्तुरङ्गद्विरदेन्द्रहेषाघण्टास्वनापूरितकर्णरन्ध्रः ।
तदन्तरा तु प्रतिबोधवर्ती के जाग्रतीत्याहित आद्रियेत ॥

४६ ततः प्रबुद्धः शुचिरिष्टदेवः श्रीमद्विभूषोज्ज्वलितः प्रहृष्टः ।
सेव्येत मन्त्रिप्रवरैर्यथावत्पुरोहितामात्यसुहृद्गणैश्च ॥

४७ कर्तव्यतां तैः सह सम्प्रधार्य यानं समारुह्य विचित्रयानः ।
कुलोद्गतैः शस्त्रिभिरात्मकल्पैर्बहिर्निरीयात्परिवारितः सन् ॥२०

220

He should advance into the enemy's territory only so far as there are roads with access to water, supply lines, and allied troops; reassuring any disturbed populations, after ensuring that the area is free of enemy infiltrators. This way he will not be forced to retreat in anguish. 42

Men who, without thinking, hastily undertake a long march into the enemy's terrain soon find themselves in the all-too-eager embrace of enemy sword-blades. 43

Aware of the proper methods, he should put in place proper security on the road, with his soldiers guarding the fort. At night he should remain alert, only sleeping in good yogic sleep,[7] with heroic warriors gathered in tight formation at his side. 44

At night when the neighing of restless horses or the sound of the bells worn on mighty elephants' necks reaches his ears, he should wake up and, keenly alert, ask who is keeping guard at that moment. 45

Then when the king has woken, bathed, and worshiped the household deities, he should wear majestic, resplendent ornaments, and in an elated mood, grant audience in due order to his chief counselors, priests, ministers, and friends. 46

After discussing plans of action with these men, he should mount an ornamental chariot, and go out on tour, surrounded by armed guards of hereditary loyalty whom he trusts like himself. 47

The king should examine the exercises of the elephants, chariots, horses, and foot soldiers—in group formation as well as individually—and twice a day he should also examine how his favorite animals are being cared for, especially the elephants and horses. 48

४८ पश्येन्नृपो हस्तिरथाश्वचर्या सामूहिकं योधगणं पृथक्च ।
विवक्षितांश्च द्विरदान्द्विरह्वस्तुरङ्गमांश्चापि विधानयुक्तान् ॥

४९ सुखोपगम्यः स्मितपूर्वभाषी प्रियं वदेद्वृत्त्यधिकं च दद्यात् ।
प्रियेण दानेन च सङ्गृहीतास्त्यजन्ति भर्तर्यपि जीवितानि ॥

५० रथाश्वनौकुञ्जरयानयोग्यो नित्यक्रियः स्याद्धनुषि प्रगल्भः ।
सुमेधसां कर्मणि दुष्करेऽपि नित्यक्रिया कौशलमादधाति ॥

५१ सन्नद्धमुच्चैर्द्विपमास्थितः सन्सन्नद्धसैन्यानुगतः प्रकुर्वन् ।
सामन्तदूतेन हि साधुमन्त्रं प्रवीरयोधान्तरितेन यायात् ॥२१

५२ आलोकयेद्बुद्धिगुणोपपन्नैश्चरैश्च दूतैश्च परप्रचारम् ।२२
एतैर्वियुक्तो भवति क्षितीन्द्रो जनैरनेत्रैश्च समानधर्मा ॥

५३ विलोभयन्किंचिदपि प्रयच्छन्कुर्वीत मित्रं द्विषतो ऽन्तपालम् ।२३
राष्ट्रादभीक्ष्णं द्विषतः प्रपण्यैः पण्यं हितं नाडिकयाददीत ॥

५४ उपक्रमं वाञ्छितमाशु कुर्याद्दूतोपयानात्क्रियमाणसंधिः ।
स चेद्विसंधिः स तु तत्र चैकः कृतो भवत्यात्मसमुच्छ्रयश्च ॥२४

222

The king should be approachable. He should always smile before he speaks, speak kindly, and pay more than the expected salary. Those who are gratified by courtesy and gifts will give up even their lives for their lord. 49

The king should constantly perform chariot, horse, boat, and elephant exercises; and he should master archery. Constant exercise grants mastery to men of keen intellect, even in difficult tasks. 50

The king should mount a lofty, well-equipped elephant, and advance undisturbed; escorted by a well-equipped army, shielded by a detachment of heroic warriors, and putting forward good policy with his neighboring feudatories' emissaries. 51

He should scrutinize the enemy's maneuvers employing intellectually gifted spies and emissaries. Without such spies and emissaries, the lord of the earth is like a blind man. 52

He should entice and offer bribes to the enemy's frontier-guards, and thereby befriend them. By offering goods, the king should continually acquire the enemy kingdom's beneficial goods through a series of exchanges.[8] 53

If a military assault is desired, then it should be accomplished quickly, and the king should use his emissaries to immediately forge an alliance. If the enemy is unwilling to forge an alliance, he only isolates himself, and the king will flourish. 54

As he makes his way forward, he should use conciliation combined with gifts to win over the guards of the enemy fortifications, the forest people, and the frontier-guards. If he is ever trapped in enemy territory, these kinds of people can show him the way out. 55

५५ दौर्गान्पथिष्वाटविकान्तपालान्संश्लेषयेद्द्वानवतापि साम्ना ।
विरुद्धदेशेषु हि सन्निरोधे ते ह्यस्य मार्गोपदिशो भवन्ति ॥

५६ अकारणादेव हि कारणाद्वा य एति कश्चित्पुरुषोऽरिसेवी ।
निजश्च विश्लिष्ट उपेत्य शत्रुमायाति यस्तस्य गतिं प्रपश्येत् ॥२५

५७ आरिप्सुना मन्त्रबलान्वितेन प्रागेव कार्यो निपुणं विचारः ।
दोष्णां बलान्मन्त्रबलं गरीयः शक्रोऽसुरान्मन्त्रबलाद्द्विजिग्ये ॥

५८ मनीषया निर्मलया विलोकितं फलाय कर्मोद्यममास्थितः परम् ।
अकालहीनं नयवित्समाचरेत्फलं ह्यकाले नियतं व्युदस्यति ॥

५९ प्रभावितानां श्रुतशौर्यशालिनां
यथावदालोकितमार्गचारिणाम् ।२६
चिराय दैवी द्युतिरुन्नतात्मनां
भुजङ्गदीर्घेषु भुजेषु लम्बते ॥

६० समुदितनरसम्पद्भूरिसम्पन्नसस्ये
विगतसलिलपङ्के काल उद्युक्तवृत्तिः ।२७
कुसुमितसहकारश्रीज्वलत्कानने वा
नरपतिररिभूमिं साधु गच्छेज्जयाय ॥

६१ इति नरपतिराहितादरः परमभियोक्तुमनाः समुत्पतेत्
इति विधिविषयोपसेवनान्नियतमरातिरुपैति गोचरम् ॥

224

If one of the enemy's men defects and joins you—whether or not he has a good reason—you must observe his movements very carefully; the same of course holds for one of your own men who becomes estranged, goes to the enemy's side, and then returns.   56

When the king wants to engage the enemy, he should first of all undertake careful strategic reflection. The power of strategy is more significant than the power of arms. Indra defeated the demons purely by the power of strategy.   57

When the king undertakes an action against the enemy, it will be successful if he first reflects on it with a lucid intellect. If he understands policy, he will not miss the opportune moment. For an action undertaken at an improper moment forecloses any positive results.   58

Powerful men of exalted soul, endowed with both learning and heroism—those who follow the path of thoroughly thought-out action—will ever cradle divine luster in their arms, long as divine serpents.[9]   59

When the king has a wealth of manpower, he must mobilize it at the proper moment—either the autumn season of abundant ripe crops, when the muddy earth has dried from the rains, or else the spring, when the forests are radiant with the majesty of mango blossoms—and head to the enemy land for conquest.   60

The king should launch an attack only once he has dedicated his mind to the above subject matter, and when his heart deeply longs for a military expedition. Through careful study of these rules of warcraft, he will most certainly bring the enemy under his control.   61

स्कन्धावारनिवेशप्रकरणम्

१ यात्वा वैरिपुराभ्याशं भूभागे साधुसम्मते ।
   स्कन्धावारनिवेशज्ञः स्कन्धावारं निवेशयेत् ॥

२ चतुरश्रं चतुर्द्वारं नातिविस्तारसङ्कटम् ।
   साट्टप्रतोलीप्राकारं महाखातसमावृतम् ॥१

३ शृङ्गाटमर्धचन्द्रं वा मण्डलं दीर्घमेव वा ।
   भूमिप्रदेशसामर्थ्यादगारमुपकल्पयेत् ॥

४ विभक्तैश्च विविक्तैश्च पार्श्वैरन्वितमायतैः ।२
   गुप्तं कक्षपुटाकारं महामार्गसमावृतम् ॥

५ तस्य मध्ये मनोह्लादि महामौलबलावृतम् ।३
   अन्तः कोशगृहोपेतं कारयेद्राजमन्दिरम् ॥

६ मौलं भृतं श्रेणि सुहृद्द्विषदाटविकं बलम् ।
   राजहर्म्यं समावृत्य क्रमेण विनिवेशयेत् ॥

७ अन्तः स्ववर्गिणः क्रूरानलुब्धान्दृष्टकर्मणः ।
   पर्याप्तवेतनानाप्तान्मण्डलेन निवेशयेत् ॥

CHAPTER 17

Building a Military Encampment

The king should be knowledgeable about how to set up a military encampment. He should go to an area of land near the enemy's city, as agreed upon by the learned, and set up a military encampment. It should have four sides and four gates; and be neither too wide nor too narrow. It should have watchtowers, gatehouses, and ramparts surrounded by a huge moat.

The king should build barracks with high walls, separated from each other and carefully positioned. They should have secret chambers hidden in the shape of underarms, as well as large roads encircling them. The structures can be arranged in a triangle, in the shape of a crescent moon, or a circle or oval, depending on the features of the land. At the center, he should construct an enchanting royal palace, at the core of which lies the treasury house, which should be guarded all around by loyal native troops.   5

Next to the royal palace, he should place in order various camps for the native soldiers, the troops provided by the guilds, the ally-troops, the soldiers defected from the enemy, and the army of the forest people. Inside, along the perimeter, he should keep his own fierce guards, men who are free from greed, and who have demonstrated their prowess. They should be well-paid and wholly competent.

८ हस्तिनो लब्धनामानस्तुरङ्गाश्च मनोजवाः ।
गृहोपकण्ठे नृपतेर्वसेयुः स्वाप्तरक्षिताः ॥

९ यामवृत्त्या सुसन्नद्धं रात्रिन्दिवमुदायुधम् ।
अन्तर्वंशिकसैन्यं च तिष्ठेद्राजाभिगुप्तये ॥

१० युद्धयोग्यो महादन्ती सन्नद्धः साध्वधिष्ठितः ।
तिष्ठेन्नरपतिर्द्वारे वेगवांश्च तुरङ्गमः ॥

११ सैन्यैकदेशः सन्नद्धः सेनापतिपुरःसरः ।
प्रयत्तवान्परिपतेन्मण्डलेन बहिर्निशि ॥४

१२ परसैन्यप्रचारांश्च सत्त्वाढ्याः शीघ्रगामिनः ।
वाताश्विका विजानीयुर्दूरसीमान्तचारिणः ॥

१३ तोरणाबद्धमाल्येषु यन्त्रवत्सु पताकिषु ।
द्वारेषु परमां गुप्तिं कारयेदाप्तकारिभिः ॥

१४ निर्गच्छेत्प्रविशेच्चैव सर्व एवोपलक्षितः ।
तिष्ठेयुः परदूताश्च राजशासनगोचराः ॥

१५ वृथाकोलाहलाद्घ्रास्याद्द्यूतात्पानाच्च वारितः ।
सज्जोपकरणस्तिष्ठेत्सर्वकार्योन्मुखो जनः ॥५

१६ बहिः खातात्तु सैन्यानां मुक्त्वा सञ्चारमात्मनः ।६
परसैन्यविघातार्थं सर्वां भूमिं विनाशयेत् ॥

१७ क्वचित्कण्टकशाखाभिः क्वचिच्छूलैरयोमुखैः ।
दूषयेत्परितो भूमिं प्रच्छन्नैः प्रदरैरपि ॥

228

Elephants whose names are famous and horses as fast as thought should be kept next to the king's residence, and looked after by trustworthy attendants. For the king's protection, well-equipped soldiers, tied to him by familial bonds, should stand with weapons at the ready day and night, changing shifts at every watch of the day and night. A great war-elephant with massive tusks, well equipped and well attended, should stand accompanied by a swift horse at the king's palace gate. 10

A well-equipped detachment of the army, led by the army's commander, should attentively patrol the camp at night. To ascertain the enemy troop movements, well-equipped men on horses swift as the wind should travel to the distant border areas. The king should have trustworthy workers establish maximum security at the camp gates, with weapon-launching machines on the gateways, camouflaged by garlands and banners. Everyone who leaves or enters should be recorded, but the enemy envoys should be detained until orders from the king are received. The guards should be prevented from making unnecessary racket, laughing, gambling, or drinking. They should be equipped with all the instruments for their work, and be ready to discharge all their duties. 15

Leaving aside a space for his own troops to advance, the king should completely raze the land outside the moat for the easy destruction of any advancing enemy troops. He should litter the area with thorny shrubs and iron barbs, as well as camouflaged pits. On a ground within the camp, which has been cleared of trees, shrubs, stones, tree-stumps, anthills, and crevices, he should make fields for the army to exercise and conduct drills with their various weapons.

१८ निर्वृक्षक्षुपपाषाणस्थाणुवल्मीकनिदरे ।७
कारयेत्करणैश्चित्रैः सैन्यव्यायामभूमिकाः ॥८

१९ यस्मिन्देशे यथाकामं सैन्यव्यायामभूमयः ।
परस्य विपरीताश्च श्रुतो देशः स उत्तमः ॥

२० आत्मनश्च परेषां च तुल्या व्यायामभूमयः ।
यत्र मध्यम उद्दिष्टो देशः शास्त्रार्थचिन्तकैः ॥

२१ अरातिसैन्यव्यायामसुपर्याप्तमहीतलः ।
आत्मनो विपरीतश्च यः स देशोऽधमः स्मृतः ॥

२२ नित्यमुत्तममाकाङ्क्षेत्तदभावे तु मध्यमम् ।
अधमं बन्धनागारं नोपसेवेत सिद्धये ॥

निमित्तज्ञानप्रकरणम्

२३ आक्रान्त इव केनापि रोगानीकैरभिद्रुतः ।
अकस्माद्द्रवदुद्वेगो रजोनीहारसंवृतः ॥

२४ विधूम्रैः परुषैर्वातैरकस्माच्च पतद्ध्वजः ।९
परस्परभवद्रोहो नतथातूर्यनिस्वनः ॥

२५ उत्प्रेक्षितभयत्रासो निर्घातोल्काभिदूषितः ।१०
उद्भ्रमत्प्रज्वलच्छस्त्रो विदक्षिणशिवारुतः ॥११

A field, favorable for the desired exercise and movement of one's own troops, and unfavorable for that of the enemy, is known as the "best land." Masters of *śāstra* call a field "middling" where one's own troops and those of the enemy find equal opportunity for exercise and movement.   20

A field with vast areas for the enemy army to exercise and maneuver, and none for one's own army, is known as the "worst land." One should always seek the best land, and failing that, a middling one. In the pursuit of success one can never resort to the worst kind of land. It is a virtual prison.

Knowing Omens

A military encampment is not commendable if it displays the following aberrant signs: when the camp is suddenly overcome by some mysterious force; when it is assaulted by battalions of disease; when for no reason there is sudden disquiet among the people inside; when there is a sudden shower of dust or mist; when harsh winds filled with smoke begin to blow, and the banners suddenly fall down on their own; when there is sudden outbreak of mutual animosity among the people, and no one blows the royal trumpets as before; when there is a sudden outbreak of groundless fear and terror, sudden thunderclaps or falling meteors, and swordblades blaze fire and fall out of their sheaths; when jackals howl from the left; when flocks of crows and vultures   25 fill the area with their sinister cackles; when the area is terrifyingly incandescent and drenched by downpours of blood;

२६ मण्डलैः काकगृध्राणामाकीर्णो रूक्षवाशिभिः ।
    मुहुरत्युग्रतादीप्तः संसिक्तो रक्तवृष्टिभिः ॥

२७ परीतराजनक्षत्रः क्रूरैरौत्पातिकैर्ग्रहैः ।
    सूर्यदृष्टकबन्धादिरकस्मान्मूढवाहनः ॥

२८ अकस्मान्मत्तमातङ्गः सुंशुष्यद्दानशीकरः ।
    इत्यादिविकृतोपेतः स्कन्धावारो न शस्यते ॥

२९ प्रहृष्टनरनारीकः प्रशस्तस्वनदुन्दुभिः ।
    गम्भीरहेषितहयः पूजितद्विपबृंहितः ॥१२

३० पुण्याहब्रह्मघोषाढ्यो नृत्तगीतसमाकुलः ।
    निरीतिको महोत्साह आकाङ्क्षितजनोदयः ॥

३१ विरजस्कोऽभिवृष्टश्च प्रादक्षिण्यस्थितग्रहः ।
    दिव्यान्तरिक्षैरुत्पातैः पार्थिवैश्च विवर्जितः ॥

३२ प्रशस्तकूजद्द्विहगः प्रदक्षिणशिवारुतः ।
    नीचैःप्रवृत्तानुलोममारुतः स्तुतमङ्गलः ॥

३३ हृष्टपुष्टजनः साधुः सुगन्धिज्ज्वलितानलः ।
    अमन्दमत्तमातङ्ग आसाराभ्युदयान्वितः ॥१३

३४ इत्यादिलक्षणोपेतः स्कन्धावारः प्रशस्यते ।
    शस्ते तस्मिन्दिषे भङ्गोऽशस्ते ज्ञेयो विपर्ययः ॥

३५ सिद्ध्यसिद्धी निमित्तानि यतः शंसन्ति कर्मणाम् ।
    विद्यादात्महिताकाङ्क्षी तस्मादेतानि तत्त्वतः ॥

when the royal asterism is enclosed by cruel and ominous planets; when headless corpses appear in the sun, and the horses are suddenly dumbstruck; when a rutting elephant's flow of ichor dries up all of a sudden.

An encampment with the following signs is commendable: where the men and women are happy, and the auspicious sound of drums is heard; where the horses' neighing is deep throated, and ceremonial elephants' roars resound; where the Brahmans' Vedic recitation is heard everywhere with the incantation "auspicious day"; where the sounds of song and dance are heard in every quarter; where there is no distress, great determination is on display, and the anticipated success of the people is at hand; where there is no dust, ample rain, and the planets are favorably positioned; where there are no celestial, atmospheric, or terrestrial calamities; where birds are chirping auspiciously and jackals howl from the right; where a gentle breeze blows in an auspicious direction, carrying the sounds of praises and incantations; where good people are happy and well nourished, and where fragrant fires burn; where the elephants are in full rut, and where there is a favorable monsoon.

When the camp is commendable in this way, the enemy's defeat is at hand. When it is in the opposite state, the opposite is at hand. Since omens betoken the success and failure of actions, it is in his best interests for a king to have expert knowledge of them. An action accompanied by auspicious omens, performed by a king who is pure to the core, will clearly culminate in the desired success. Whoever possesses a wealth of helpers, understanding, force, favorable destiny, effort, and resolution, shall meet with success.

३६ प्रशस्तेन निमित्तेन विशुद्धेनान्तरात्मना ।
व्यक्तमारभ्यमाणं हि सिद्धिं याति समीहितम् ॥

३७ सहायसम्पत्प्रज्ञानं सत्त्वं दैवानुकूलता ।
उद्योगोऽध्यवसायश्च यस्यैते तस्य सिद्धयः ॥

३८ तन्मूलत्वात्प्रजानां तु राजा स्कन्ध उदाहृतः ।
आवारोऽमात्यदण्डादिर्वृतिरावार उच्यते ॥

३९ भूतानां भूतिनिष्पत्तेरावारेण महीयसा ।
आवृतस्तु यतः स्कन्धः स्कन्धावारस्ततः स्मृतः ॥

४० समवस्कन्दघासाम्बुवीवधासारनिग्रहाः ।१४
एते प्रयत्नतो रक्ष्याः स्कन्धावारस्य मृत्यवः ॥

४१ इति प्रयत्नेन निवेशयेद्बलं शुभाशुभं चास्य तथोपलक्षयेत् ।
परस्य चैतन्निपुणं विलोकयेत्समारभेताशुभहीनदर्शने ॥

The king can be seen as the trunk of the tree; the subjects as the roots; the ministers, army, and so on as the canopy, since they offer cover. The trunk in the form of the king, cloaked by a great canopy in the form of the state apparatus, produces the people's prosperity, and the military encampment is therefore known as the "trunk and canopy."

One must carefully guard against destruction of the camp's armed forces, fodder, water supply, and access routes for supply lines and allies. When they are destroyed, the camp is dead.   40

Thus one should be mindful when encamping the army, and examine its good and bad characteristics. One should also keenly examine the enemy army's good and bad characteristics, and undertake actions only when no inauspicious omens are observed.   41

अष्टादशः सर्गः

उपायविकल्पप्रकरणम्

१ महाप्रज्ञानसम्पन्नः सहायैरुपबृंहितः ।१
उद्योगाध्यवसायाभ्यामुपायान्निक्षिपेत्परे ॥

२ चतुरङ्गं बलं मुक्त्वा कोशो मन्त्रश्च युध्यते ।
तत्साधुमन्त्रो मन्त्रेण कोशेन च जयेदरीन् ॥

३ साम दानं च भेदश्च दण्डश्चेति चतुष्टयम् ।
मायोपेक्षेन्द्रजालं च सप्तोपायाः प्रकीर्तिताः ॥

४ परस्परोपकाराणां दर्शनं गुणकीर्तनम् ।
सम्बन्धस्य समाख्यानमायतेः सम्प्रदर्शनम् ॥

५ वाचा पेशलया साधु तवाहमिति चार्पणम् ।
इति सामप्रभेदज्ञैः साम पञ्चविधं स्मृतम् ॥

६ यः सम्प्राप्तधनोत्सर्ग उत्तमाधममध्यमः ।
प्रतिदानं तथा तस्य गृहीतस्यानुमोदनम् ॥

७ द्रव्यदानमपूर्वं च स्वयंग्राहप्रवर्तनम् ।
देयस्य प्रतिमोक्षश्च दानं पञ्चविधं स्मृतम् ॥

८ स्नेहरागापनयनं सङ्घर्षोत्पादनं तथा ।
सन्तर्जनं च भेदज्ञैर्भेदस्तु त्रिविधः स्मृतः ॥

९ वधोऽर्थहरणं चैव परिक्लेशस्तथैव च ।
इति दण्डविभागज्ञैर्दण्डस्तु त्रिविधः स्मृतः ॥

१० प्रकाशश्चाप्रकाशश्च वधो द्विविध उच्यते ।२
प्रकाशदण्डं कुर्वीत लोकद्विष्टे तथा रिपौ ॥

236

CHAPTER 18

The Various Methods

When a king comes to be possessed of great wisdom and is fortified by allies, he is ready to begin using the seven methods against his enemy with effort and resolution.[1] War should be waged first by means of strategy and treasury, leaving aside the army with its four contingents. If his strategy is good a king can conquer his enemies merely using strategy and the treasury.[2]

The seven methods are: conciliation, donation, sowing dissension, and coercion, which make up the canonical four, while illusion, disregard, and magic, make seven.

Experts in the typology of conciliation consider it to be fivefold: display of mutual assistance; praise of virtues; declaration of kinship; disclosure of future plans; and expression of solidarity with endearing words such as "I am yours." Donation is also considered to be fivefold: distributing received wealth—whether of a superior, middling, or inferior type—and sanctioning the acceptance of such wealth; spontaneous gift; encouraging the taking of booty; and forgiving debts. Experts in the sowing of dissension hold it to be threefold: neutralizing affection and devotion, generating conflict, and threatening. Experts in the ways of coercion hold it also to be threefold: execution, seizure of wealth, and inflicting pain.

Execution is of two types: public and secret. One should publicly execute those who have become enemies of the

5

237

११ उद्वेज्यते हतैर्लोको यैर्ये स्युर्नृपवल्लभाः ।
बाधन्तेऽभ्यधिका ये तु तेषूपांशु प्रशस्यते ॥

१२ विषेणोपनिषद्योगैः शस्त्रेणोद्वर्तनेन वा ।
तथोपांशु नयेद्दण्डं यथान्यो न विभावयेत् ॥

१३ ब्राह्मणे जातिमात्रे ऽपि धार्मिके चान्त्यजे ऽपि वा ।
धर्मोन्निनीषया धीमान्न वधं दण्डमादिशेत् ॥

१४ उपेक्षया वा हन्तव्या येषूपांशु प्रशस्यते ।
उपेक्षां चापि निपुणः प्रत्यक्षं परिवर्जयेत् ॥

१५ प्रलिम्पन्निव चेतांसि दृष्ट्या साधु पिबन्निव ।³
स्रवन्निवामृतं साम प्रुयुञ्जीत प्रियं वचः ॥

१६ वागनुद्वेगजननी सामेति परिकीर्त्यते ।
सामाख्ये सूनृते सान्त्वे प्रिये स्तोत्रे च कीर्त्यते ॥

१७ आत्मनो विक्रयमिव कुर्वन्दद्यात्समीहितम् ।⁴
जलवत्पर्वताच्छत्रून्भिन्द्यादनुपलक्षितः ॥

१८ दण्डपाणिरिवाधृष्यो दण्डं दण्ड्येषु पातयेत् ।
प्रत्यक्षामपि चोपेक्षामप्रत्यक्षामिवाचरेत् ॥

१९ साम्नार्थसिद्धये विद्वान्यतेत यतमानसः ।
सामसिद्धिं प्रशंसन्ति सर्वतश्च विपश्चितः ॥

२० क्षीरोदो मथितः साम्ना फलायामरदानवैः ।
निजग्मिरे धार्तराष्ट्राः सामप्रद्वेषिणोऽचिरात् ॥

people, as well as external enemies. It is best to execute in   10
secret those favorites of the king who cruelly terrorize the
people; those, too, who are overly powerful and cause trou-
ble. When carrying out a secret killing, one should do it while
arousing no suspicions, by applying poison or sorcery, or else
using weapons or booby traps.

A wise king wishing to propagate dharma should never
order the death penalty for a Brahman—even if a Brahman
merely by birth—nor for an outcaste who practices dharma.[3]
It is a good idea to practice the method of disregard toward
people one plans to kill in secret; however, the disregard
should be tactfully applied and not draw attention to itself.

One should apply conciliation and speak pleasing words, as
if oozing nectar, touching people's hearts, and drinking them
up with kind glances. Conciliation is speech that causes no   15
agitation, speech that is kindhearted, reassuring, delightful,
and laudatory. One should give what the other desires, as if
offering oneself up for sale; but unperceived, one should split
the enemies apart, as drops of water gradually split apart
mountains.

The king must be as indomitable as the rod-bearing god
of death, grasp the rod of coercion, and let it fall on those
deserving punishment. Although he practices trickery
openly, it must remain covert. A wise man of controlled mind
should strive for political success through conciliation. The
learned always praise success that comes through conciliation. The gods and the demons churned the ocean of milk
and got great rewards by applying conciliation. Yet the sons
of Dhritarashtra were quickly slaughtered because they had
contempt for conciliation.   20

२१   दारुणं विग्रहं विद्वान्दानेन प्रशमं नयेत् ।
      इन्द्रोऽपचारे शुक्रस्य दानेन शममेयिवान् ॥

२२   अपराधेन दुहितुः कुपिते भृगुनन्दने ।
      वृषपर्वा च दानेन दानवेन्द्रो ऽभवत्सुखी ॥

२३   उपच्छन्द्यापि दातव्यं बलिने शान्तिमिच्छता ।५
      समूलमेव गान्धारिरप्रयच्छनतः क्षयम् ॥

२४   किञ्चित्प्रयच्छन्भूयस्या तृष्णया विप्रलोभयन् ।
      भिन्द्याच्चतुर्विधान्भेद्यान्प्रविश्योभयवेतनैः ॥

२५   अलब्धवेतनो लुब्धो मानी चाप्यवमानितः ।
      क्रुद्धश्च कोपितो ऽकस्मात्तथा भीतश्च भीषितः ॥६

२६   यथाभिलषितैः कामैर्भिन्द्यादेतांश्चतुर्विधान् ।
      परपक्षे स्वपक्षे च यथावत्प्रशमं नयेत् ॥

२७   भेदं कुर्वीत यत्नेन मन्त्र्यमात्यपुरोधसाम् ।
      तेषु भिन्नेषु भिन्नं हि युवराजे तथोर्जिते ॥

२८   अमात्यो युवराजश्च भुजावेतौ महीपतेः ।
      मन्त्री नेत्रं हि तद्विन्न एतस्मिन्नपि तद्वधः ॥

२९   सर्वावस्थं तु मेधावी तत्कुलीनं विकारयेत् ।
      विकृतस्तत्कुलीनस्तु स्वयोनिं ग्रसतेऽग्निवत् ॥

240

A wise man should calm a terrible conflict by donation. Indra calmed the gods' suffering at the hands of Shukra by donation.[4] When Shukra, son of Bhrigu, was infuriated because of Vrishaparvan's daughter's misdeed, the lord of demons, Vrishaparvan, found a happy resolution by gifting his own daughter.[5] Someone who wants peace must make gifts to a powerful rival, even if it means cajoling him into accepting them. Duryodhana, son of Gandhari, was completely annihilated because he failed to give.[6]

Using double agents, one should gain access to and sow dissension among the four types of people susceptible to it, by offering something and yet enticing their greed for more. The four types of people susceptible to dissension are: greedy people who have not been paid, honorable people who have been dishonored, angry people who have been angered for no reason, and fearful people who have been terrorized. One should sow dissension in these four types of people in the enemy camp by offering the objects of their desires. In your own camp, however, you must suppress dissension among those who are using the same technique. One should assiduously sow dissension among counselors, ministers, and priests. When you alienate these people, then even a mighty crown prince becomes alienated.

The minister and the crown prince are the two arms of the king. The counselor is the eye. When he is alienated from the king, it spells the king's death. A wise king will attempt to sow dissension among his enemy's kinsmen, since they are subject to all of life's vicissitudes. An alienated kinsman will burn up his own family, as fire consumes the very wood that is its source; and any man who lives inside the royal

241

३०　तत्कुलीनेन तुल्यस्तु पुमानभ्यन्तरोषितः ।
तस्मादेतौ परे भिन्द्याच्छमं चात्मनि सन्नयेत् ॥

३१　तत्रोपजापः कर्तव्यो यः कोपानुग्रहक्षमः ।
स कल्याणः शठो वेति परीक्ष्यः सूक्ष्मया धिया ॥

३२　कल्याणस्तु यथाशक्ति करोति सफलं वचः ।
शठः पक्षौ चलयति द्वावप्यर्थोपलिप्सया ॥

३३　पूर्वं सम्भाषितो ऽनीचः कालयापनमाश्रितः ।७
मिथ्याभिशस्तः श्रीकाम आहूयाप्रतिमानितः ॥८

३४　राजद्वेषी तत्कुलीनो द्विष्यते यश्च भूभुजा ।९
आहितव्यवहारश्च तथा कारनिवेशितः ॥१०

३५　रणप्रियः साहसिक आत्मसम्भावितस्तथा ।
विच्छिन्नधर्मकामार्थः क्रुद्धो मानी विमानितः ॥

३६　भीतः स्वदोषवित्रस्तः कृतवैरोऽतिसान्त्वितः ।
अतुल्येन सहासक्तस्तुल्यमानान्निराकृतः ॥

३७　अकारणनिरुद्धश्च कारणाच्च विशेषतः ।
अकारणात्परित्यक्तः पूजार्होऽप्रतिपूजितः ॥११

242

household is equivalent to a family member. Therefore one should sow dissension among these two groups within the enemy camp, and promote peaceful relations in one's own camp.

30

One should make overtures and try to turn anyone susceptible to either anger or enticement into an informer. The target individual may be loyal or cunning, so one must examine the situation with a subtle intellect. A loyal person will strive to the extent of his capacities to keep his word. The cunning person manipulates both sides out of greed for wealth.

The following types of people are prone to dissension: a noble man who has been promised a reward and then been made to wait indefinitely; someone falsely accused of a crime; someone seeking wealth; someone who has been summoned and then not properly honored; an enemy of the king; the king's kinsman; someone whom the king hates; someone with ambitious business interests; someone who has been imprisoned; someone addicted to war; a hotheaded person; a conceited person; someone who cannot satisfy the three goals of life, dharma, pleasure, and power; an angry person; an honorable person who has been dishonored; a coward; someone afraid of answering for his crimes; someone who was once consumed by enmity and then carefully appeased; someone made to work alongside those of lower rank; someone who has been rejected by those of equal rank; someone who has been obstructed for no reason; someone who has been severely obstructed for a good reason; someone deserted for no reason; someone deserving adoration who has not been properly adored; someone who has had

35

३८ हृतद्रव्यकलत्रश्च महाभोगाभिकाङ्क्षितः ।
     परिक्षीणो बहिर्बन्धुर्बहिर्द्रव्यो बहिष्कृतः ॥

३९ इति भेद्याः समाख्याता भिन्द्यादेतान्परे स्थितान् ।
     आगतान्पूजयेत्कामैर्निजांश्च प्रशमं नयेत् ॥

४० समतृष्णानुसन्धानमत्युग्रभयदर्शनम् ।१२
     प्रधानं दानमानं च भेदोपायाः प्रकीर्तिताः ॥

४१ भेदं कुर्वीत मतिमान्विगृहीतो बलीयसा ।
     शण्डामर्कौ सुरैर्भित्त्वा बलवन्तौ पराजितौ ॥

४२ दण्डेन हि समाहन्याद्विच्चारेः संहतं बलम् ।
     भिन्नं हि तत्काष्ठमिव घुणजग्धं विशीर्यते ॥१३

४३ उत्साहदेशकालैस्तु संयुक्तः सुसहायवान् ।
     युधिष्ठिर इवात्यर्थं दण्डेनास्तं नयेदरीन् ॥

४४ आत्मनः शक्तिमुद्वीक्ष्य दण्डमप्यधिके नयेत् ।
     एकाकी शक्तिसम्पन्नो रामः क्षत्रं पुरावधीत् ॥

४५ अलसं विक्रमश्रान्तं विहतोपायचेष्टितम् ।१४
     क्षयव्ययप्रवासैश्च सन्तप्तं विपरिद्रुतम् ॥१५

४६ भीरुं मूर्खं स्त्रियं बालं धार्मिकं दुर्जनं पशुम् ।
     मैत्रीप्रधानं कल्याणबुद्धिं सान्त्वेन साधयेत् ॥

his wealth or wife seized; someone who always yearns for more and more pleasures; someone who is destitute; someone whose kinsmen have been exiled or whose wealth has been expropriated; someone who has been banished. One should lure these types of people to dissension when they are on the enemy's side. When they have come over to your own side, you should lavish pleasures on them. And when your own people are in such a state, you must mollify them.

The methods of sowing dissension include pursuing a common interest or provoking extreme fear in order to draw someone to oneself. But the fundamental method is giving bribes and bestowing honors. When attacked by a more powerful enemy, a prudent king will sow dissension. When the gods were attacked by the mighty demons Shanda and Amarka, they sowed dissension in their ranks and thereby defeated them.[7] One should assail the enemy with violence, after weakening his unified army by sowing dissension. When dissension has been sown, the army will disintegrate, like a piece of wood devoured by insects. 40

If, however, a king is blessed with the advantages of determination, time, and place, as well as good allies, he should totally annihilate his enemies, as Yudhishthira did, through application of coercion. Based on an examination of his own powers, the king should apply extreme coercion to even a more powerful adversary. Rama Jamadagnya once slaughtered all Kshatriyas on his own, because he had the power.

Yet the king should win over the following types of people through conciliation: a lazy person; someone exhausted by combat; someone whose efforts and methods have all been thwarted; someone pained by loss, wastage, or banishment;

४७ लुब्धं क्षीणं च दानेन सत्कृत्य वशमानयेत् ।
अन्योन्यशङ्कया भिन्नान्दुष्टान्वै दण्डदर्शनात् ॥

४८ पुत्रान्भ्रातृंश्च बन्धूंश्च साम्नार्थेन च साधयेत् ।
एतैः कः सदृशो लोके दूरं विप्रकृतैरपि ॥१६

४९ सामैतेषु प्रयुञ्जीत दैवात्प्रस्खलितेष्वपि ।
दुष्करां यान्ति विकृतिमार्याः शीलनिबन्धनाः ॥१७

५० कुलं शीलं दया दानं धर्मः सत्यं कृतज्ञता ।
अलोभ इति येष्वेते तानार्यान्परिचक्षते ॥१८

५१ पौराञ्जानपदांश्चैव दण्डमुख्यांश्च दण्डवित् ।
साधयेद्दानभेदाभ्यां यथायोगेन चापरान् ॥

५२ अवरुद्धांस्तत्कुलीनान्सामन्तांश्च विचक्षणः ।१९
साधयेद्भेददण्डाभ्यां यथायोगेन चापरान् ॥

५३ देवताप्रतिमास्तम्भसुषिरान्तर्गता नराः ॥
पुमान्स्त्रीवस्त्रसंवीतो निशि चाद्भुतदर्शनम् ॥२०

५४ वेतालोल्कापिशाचानां देवानां च सरूपता ।२१
इत्यादिमाया विज्ञेया मानुषी मानुषेश्वरैः ॥

someone who has been routed in battle; a coward, a fool, a woman, a child, a religious mendicant, or a wretch; a destitute person who lives like an animal; someone who is a friend to all; or someone whose mind is completely devoted to human welfare.

The king should gain control of a greedy or destitute person by honoring him with gifts; and wicked people, by turning them against each other, as well as through displays of violence. He should win over sons, brothers, and kins- 45 men as far as possible with gifts and conciliation. For who in the world is equal to them in terms of the damage they can do, especially when estranged? If by some chance they are ever wayward in their conduct, the king should only apply conciliation. Noble men of good conduct can otherwise become deeply resentful. "Noble men" are defined as those possessed of noble birth, good conduct, compassion, charity, dharma, truthfulness, gratitude, and lack of greed. 50

A king who understands coercion, and who is discerning in the use of donation and dissension, should use donation and dissension to appease the people of the city and country, as well as the chiefs of the army, dealing with others however they deserve.[8] The discerning king should subdue those who have been banished, and also his wider network of kinsmen and feudatories, through sowing dissension and applying coercion; again, he may deal with others however they deserve.

Illusion, which men perform on kings' behalf, is understood as hiding men inside images of gods or inside hollow pillars; a man disguised as a woman; supernatural spectacles at nighttime; as well as taking on the form of

५५ कामतो रूपधारित्वं शस्त्रास्त्राश्माम्बुवर्षणम् ।
तमो ऽनिलो ऽचलो मेघा इति माया ह्यामानुषी ॥२२

५६ जघान कीचकं भीम आश्रितः स्त्रीसरूपताम् ।
चिरं प्रच्छन्नरूपोऽभूद्दिव्यया मायया नलः ॥

५७ अन्याये व्यसने युद्धे प्रवृत्तस्यानिवारणम् ।
इत्युपेक्षार्थकुशलैरुपेक्षा त्रिविधा स्मृता ॥

५८ अकार्ये सज्जमानस्तु विषयान्धीकृतेक्षणः ।
कीचकस्तु विराटेन हन्यतामित्युपेक्षितः ॥

५९ संरब्धो भीमसेनेन स्वार्थविच्छेदभीतया ।२३
हिडिम्बया निजो भ्राता हन्यतामित्युपेक्षितः ॥

६० मेघान्धकारवृष्ट्यद्रिपर्वताद्भुतदर्शनम् ।
दूरस्थानां च सैन्यानां दर्शनं ध्वजमालिनाम् ॥

६१ छिन्नपाटितभिन्नानां संसुतानां प्रदर्शनम् ।२४
इतीन्द्रजालं द्विषतां भीत्यर्थमुपकल्पयेत् ॥

६२ इत्युपायाः समाख्याता नाना नानार्थसाधकाः ।
साम तेषु हि कालज्ञो यथाकालं प्रयोजयेत् ॥२५

६३ सामभेदौ तु कर्तव्यौ दानमानपुरःसरौ ।
दानेन हि समायुक्तावेतावप्यर्थसिद्धये ॥

६४ दानरिक्तेन सर्वत्र साम्ना कृत्यं तृणेन वा ।२६
निर्दानं साम नायाति कलत्रेष्वपि संस्थितिम् ॥

corpse-spirits, floating torches, and ghouls. Superhuman illusion is shape-shifting; raining weapons; magical missiles, stones, or water; as well as conjuring darkness, wind, mountains, or clouds. Bhima killed Kichaka by dressing convincingly as a woman. Nala became invisible for a long time through divine illusion. 55

Experts in the matter consider disregard—which amounts to not opposing someone else's activity—to be of three types: relating to wrongdoing, relating to vice or disaster, and relating to war. When Kichaka was engaging in wrongful acts, his vision blinded by the objects of sensual enjoyment, Virata disregarded him in order to have him killed by Bhima. Hidimba also disregarded her own brother when he was being attacked by Bhima, in order to have him killed, because she feared that otherwise her own objectives might be compromised.[9]

One should use the following types of magic to terrify the enemy: displaying clouds, darkness, rain, fire, mountains, or other wonders; as well as distant armies, ringed with raised banners; and heaps of dead soldiers mangled, sliced apart, 60 with their limbs hacked off, and oozing blood.

Thus we have illustrated the king's various methods, which accomplish various purposes. A ruler knowledgeable about timing should first apply conciliation, as the occasion warrants. Conciliation and dissension should be applied after donation and paying respect. When conciliation and dissension are paired with donation, they accomplish the purpose at hand. Conciliation without donation is not even worth a blade of grass; conciliation without gifts does not even work with one's wives.

६५ इति ह्युपायान्त्रिपुणं नयज्ञो विनिक्षिपेच्छत्रुबले निजे च ।
निरभ्युपायो नियतं प्रपातं विचेष्टमानोऽन्ध इवाभ्युपैति ॥२७

६६ अवश्यमायान्ति वशं विपश्चितामुपायसंदंशबलेन सम्पदः ।२८
भवत्युदारं विधिवत्प्रयोजिते फलं हि राज्ञां क्वचिदर्थसिद्धये ॥

A king versed in politics should skillfully employ these methods on the enemy army as well as his own forces. If a man fails to use them, he will flounder about like a blind man and inevitably fall down. 64

Using these pincers, the seven methods, riches become powerless and come under the power of discerning kings. Properly applied, these methods afford kings abundant benefits, and sometimes even the fulfillment of their ultimate objectives. 65

सैन्यबलाबलप्रकरणम्

१ सामादीनामुपायानां त्रयाणां विफले नये ।
   विनयेन्नयसम्पन्नो दण्डं दण्ड्येषु दण्डवित् ॥

२ देवानभ्यर्च्य विप्रांश्च प्रशस्तप्रहतारकम् ।१
   षड्विधं तु बलं व्यूह्य द्विषतोऽभिमुखं व्रजेत् ॥

३ मौलं भृतं श्रेणि सुहृद्द्विषदाटविकं बलम् ।२
   पूर्वं पूर्वं गरीयस्तु बलानां व्यसनं तथा ॥

४ सत्कारादनुरागाच्च सहसङ्क्थनासनात् ।३
   नित्यं तद्भावभावित्वान्मौलं भृतबलादुरु ॥

५ सन्निकृष्टतया नित्यं क्षिप्रोत्थानतयापि च ।
   वृत्तेश्च स्वाम्यधीनत्वाद्धृतं श्रेणिबलादुरु ॥

६ तुल्यसङ्घर्षणामर्षात्सुखलाभात्तथैव च ।४
   बलाज्ज्ञानपदत्वाच्च मैत्राच्छ्रेणिबलं गुरु ॥

७ असंख्यदेशकालत्वादेकार्थोपगमात्तथा ।५
   बलान्मेदनयोगाच्च शत्रोर्मित्रबलं गुरु ॥६

CHAPTER 19

An Army's Strengths and Weaknesses

If the policy of the first three methods—conciliation, donation, and dissension—proves fruitless, then a king who is politically astute and who understands the ways of coercion should apply coercion against those who deserve it. After worshiping gods and Brahmans, upon an auspicious conjunction of the stars and planets, the king should draw up his army with its six troop-divisions, and advance against the enemy.

Each of the following six classes of troops is in order more important than the next: native troops, mercenary troops, troops from the guilds, ally troops, troops defecting from the enemy, and forest-people troops. The vices and calamities affecting them are also respectively more serious.

By virtue of honor, devotion, close interaction, and association, as well as their wants being the same as their ruler's, native troops are more important than mercenary ones. By virtue of their intimacy with the king, the swiftness of their endeavor, and their dependence on the lord for pay, mercenary troops are more important than those coming from the guilds. Since the latter share the struggle, fury, and success 5 of their lord—and have their origins in the same country— troops coming from the guilds are more important than the ally troops. Since the latter have a natural affection for the

८ प्रकृत्याधार्मिका लुब्धा अनार्याः सत्यभेदिनः।
तस्मादारण्यकतया तेभ्यः शत्रुबलं गुरु ॥

९ उभयं तद्विलोपार्थं कालापेक्षं व्यवस्थितम्।
विलोपे व्यसने चैव तत्रास्य विजयो ध्रुवः॥[7]

१० उपजापकृतात्तु स्याद्द्वयमस्मादि्द्विशेषतः।
परस्य चाप्युपजपेदुपजापाद्ध्रुवो जयः॥

११ स्फीतसारानुरक्तेन मौलेनोपचितः परः।
तत्तुल्येनैव यातव्यः क्षयव्ययसहिष्णुना॥

१२ प्रकृष्टेऽध्वनि काले वा गच्छेन्मौलैः सुमानितैः।[8]
मौलास्तु दीर्घकालत्वात्क्षयव्ययसहिष्णवः॥

१३ एषु वस्तुषु मेधावी भृतादीनि विवर्जयेत्।
दीर्घाध्वकालखिन्नेषु तेषु भेदभयं भवेत्॥

१४ बहुत्वादेव सैन्यानां दीर्घकालाच्च खेदतः।
नित्यप्रवासयानाभ्यां भेदोऽवश्यं हि जायते॥

१५ प्रभूतं मे भृतबलं मौलमल्पमसारवत्।
अरेरल्पं विरक्तं वा मौलं प्रायोऽल्पसारवत्॥

king and can be employed in countless places at countless times—because of a common interest with the king—ally troops are better than troops defecting from the enemy army. Forest troops are by nature unrighteous, greedy, ignoble, and they break promises. Therefore troops defecting from the enemy army are better than the wild forest people.

Both the troops defecting from the enemy and the forest troops are just waiting to plunder the enemy territory. When the enemy is subject to plunder and disaster, the king's victory is ensured. But the troops defecting from the enemy and the forest troops can both be seduced to dissension, and this leads to particular danger. If the king, by contrast, seduces the enemy's soldiers to dissension, victory is assured.   10

If the enemy is equipped with powerful and devoted native troops, only a king with an equal force should advance against him, and he must be ready to tolerate destruction and loss. With his well-respected native troops, he should advance via an excellent route at an opportune moment. Since the native troops have been with him for a long time, they can endure destruction and loss. For undertakings like this, a prudent king should avoid using mercenary and other such troops. Exhausted by travel and a protracted campaign, the danger of dissension can arise. Indeed, if the mercenary force is relatively large, and the campaign both protracted and exhausting, dissension is sure to arise from the hardship of being continually sent out to distant lands.[1] If the king thinks that his army of mercenary soldiers is strong and the native soldiers are few and weak—and also that the   15 enemy's native soldiers are few, disaffected, and weak—then he should wage a war of strategy with limited exertion. If

१६ प्रायो मन्त्रेण योद्धव्यमल्पायासेन चैव हि ।९
अल्पः कालस्तु देशो वाप्रभूतौ च क्षयव्ययौ ॥

१७ शान्तोपजापविश्वस्तमस्मत्सैन्यं परस्य वा ।
अल्पः प्रसारो हन्तव्य इत्युपेयाद्धृतैर्बलैः ॥१०

१८ स्फीतं श्रेणिबलं शक्यमाधातुं यानवस्तुनोः ।११
ह्रस्वौ प्रवासव्यायामाविति श्रेण्या समुत्पतेत् ॥

१९ प्रभूतं हि सुहृत्सैन्यं शक्यमाधातुमात्मनि ।
अल्पप्रवासो मन्त्राच्च भूयो व्यायामयोधनम् ॥१२

२० मित्रसाधारणे कार्ये मित्रायत्ते फलोदये ।
अनुग्राह्ये च पीड्ये च मित्रेणैव सह व्रजेत् ॥१३

२१ प्रभूतेनारिसैन्येन योधयेन्महतो रिपून् ।१४
श्वसूकरवधापेक्षी नयं चण्डालवन्नयेत् ॥१५

२२ अत्यूर्जितं कोपभयादभ्याशे तु रिपोर्बलम् ।१६
वासयेत्कर्शयेच्चैव दुर्गकण्टकमर्दनैः ॥

२३ नित्यमाटविकं सैन्यं दुर्गकण्टकशोधने ।
परदेशप्रवेशे च पुरस्कुर्वीत पण्डितः ॥

the campaign is one of short duration and limited travel, the loss and destruction involved are minimal. When his army is trustworthy—because the enemy's attempts at sowing dissension have been counteracted—he should advance with his mercenary soldiers against an enemy of limited means and kill him.

When the troops from the guilds are large and well-endowed with both chariots and supplies, the king can send them on expedition. And if the travel and exertion involved will be minor, he should attack the enemy with his guild troops. When he has capable ally troops, he can send them out on his own behalf. For them a war of exertion requires less time spent in travel than a war of strategy.

When the king shares an objective with his ally, and when success depends on the ally—when a friend needs help, and an enemy needs harm—he should advance with his ally. When fighting a powerful enemy army, the king can use his vast troops that have defected from the enemy. His political strategy should be like an untouchable hunter—who will eat either a dog or a pig—sending his hunting dog to kill a boar, and waiting to see which one ends up dead.[2] If the troops won over from the enemy grow too numerous in the king's immediate vicinity, in order to avert the danger of unrest, he should tire them out by sending them to maintain the fortifications and crush any thorns, so to speak, in the vicinity.[3]

A prudent king will always employ the forest people in maintaining the fortifications and removing any thorns in the vicinity. During a military expedition, he will send them first into the enemy territory. Each of the six classes of soldiers constitutes an army with four divisions: foot

२४ एतन्मौलादिषड्भेदं चतुरङ्गं बलं विदुः ।
षडङ्गं मन्त्रकोशाभ्यां पदात्यश्वरथद्विपैः ॥

२५ इति षड्विधमेतद्वि यथायोगं बलं बली ।
सुनिश्छिद्रं प्रतिव्यूह्य यायात्परबलं प्रति ॥

२६ योगमस्य विजानीयात्सर्वं मन्त्रादिना नृपः ।[१७]
कृताकृतं प्रचारं च साधु सेनापतेस्तथा ॥

सेनापतिप्रचारप्रकरणम्

२७ कुलोद्गतं जानपदं मन्त्रज्ञं मन्त्रिसम्मतम् ।[१८]
दण्डनीतेः प्रयोक्तारमध्येतारं च तत्त्वतः ॥[१९]

२८ सत्यसत्त्वक्षमास्थैर्यमाधुर्यार्यगुणान्वितम् ।
प्रभावोत्साहसम्पन्नमाजीव्यमनुजीविनाम् ॥

२९ मित्रवन्तमुदाराढ्यं बहुस्वजनबान्धवम् ।
व्यवहारिणमक्षुद्रं पौरप्रकृतिसम्मतम् ॥

३० नित्याकारणवैराणामकर्तारमनाविलम् ।
शुभानुबन्धिकर्माणमल्पामित्रं बहुश्रुतम् ॥[२०]

३१ अरोगं व्यायतं शूरं त्यागिनं कालवेदिनम् ।
कल्याणाकृतिसम्पन्नं सत्सम्भाव्यपराक्रमम् ॥

३२ गजाश्वरथचर्यासु शिक्षितं सुजितश्रमम् ।
खड्गयुद्धे नियुद्धे च शीघ्रचङ्क्रमणक्षमम् ॥

soldiers, cavalry, chariots, and elephant battalions—some scholars consider it to have two more divisions if you include the ministers and the treasury. After arraying his sixfold army in the correct proportion, and in such a way that it is impenetrable, the mighty king should advance against the enemy. He should assess each division's applicability in 25 terms of strategy and so forth. And he should fully examine the actions, inactions, and capabilities of the general.

A General's Conduct

The general should be of noble birth, of local origin, endowed with strategic skills, and someone in whom the ministers have full confidence. He should both practice and profess sound politics. He should have the virtues of truthfulness, might, tolerance, stability, gentility, and nobility. He should have power and determination, and support his dependents. He should have friends, be rich and liberal, with many relatives and kinsmen; he should be tactful, not base, and be accepted by the subjects and members of state. He should be untainted and always refrain from provoking meaningless hostilities. His deeds should have beneficial outcomes. He should have few enemies and much learning. He should be 30 healthy, exalted in stature, heroic, generous, and thoughtful about timing. He should have a handsome physique and uncommon valor; be schooled in the maneuvers of elephants, horses, and chariots; be immune to fatigue, and capable of swift maneuvering in both swordplay and hand-to-hand combat.

३३ युद्धभूमिविभागज्ञं सिंहवद्दृढविक्रमम् ।
अदीर्घसूत्रं निस्तन्द्रममर्षणमनुद्धतम् ॥

३४ हस्त्यश्वरथशस्त्राणां सम्यग्लक्षणवेदिनम् ॥
नरान्तरविवेकज्ञं कृतज्ञमनुकम्पकम् ॥२१

३५ वर्मकर्मसमायोगे कुशलं कुशलानुगम् ।२२
सर्वयुद्धक्रियोपेतं शक्तं तत्परिकर्मणि ॥

३६ स्वभावचित्तज्ञतया युक्तमश्वनृदन्तिनाम् ।
तन्त्राणां चापि वेत्तारं तद्विधानोपपादकम् ॥

३७ देशभाषास्वभावज्ञं लिपिज्ञं सुदृढस्मृतिम् ।
निशाप्रचारकुशलं शकुनज्ञाननिश्चितम् ॥२३

३८ उदयास्तमयज्ञं च नक्षत्राणां ग्रहैः सह ।
दिग्देशामार्गविज्ञानसम्पन्नं तज्ज्ञसेवितम् ॥२४

३९ क्षुत्पिपासाक्लमत्रासशीतवातोष्णवृष्टिभिः२५ ।
अनाहितभयक्लान्तिं तत्संविग्राभयप्रदम्२६ ॥

४० हन्तारं परसैन्यानां दुःसाध्याहितनिश्चयम् ।२७
हतानां च स्वसैन्यानां सम्यग्विष्टम्भनक्षमम् ॥२८

४१ अवस्कन्दाभिमन्तारं वेत्तारं सैन्यकर्मणाम् ।
परदूतप्रचारज्ञं महारम्भफलोपगम् ॥

४२ शश्वत्संसिद्धकर्माणं सिद्धकर्मनिषेवितम् ।
पराभवेष्वनिर्विण्णं श्रीमद्राजार्थतत्परम् ॥२९

He should know the divisions of the battlefield and have unwavering valor like a lion. He should not procrastinate or be lazy. He should be aggressive, yet not overblown. He should know exhaustively all aspects of elephants, horses, and chariots. He should know the distinctions of different types of men. He should have gratitude and compassion. He should be competent in assembling body armor and have skillful followers. He must be adept at all military maneuvers and capable of counteracting them as well. He should fathom 35 the natures and minds of horses, men, and elephants; know all their names; and make proper provisions for them. He must be fluent in local languages and lifeways, be literate, and possess a firm memory. He must be skilled at nocturnal maneuvers and at interpreting the omens of birds. He should study the rising and setting of constellations and planets. He should know various directions, routes, and lands, and be attended upon by men with expertise in these matters. He should not be disturbed or wearied by hunger, thirst, exhaustion, terror, cold, heat, wind, or rain, and he should comfort those who are disturbed by them. He must be able to slay enemy soldiers and confront difficult projects decisively. He must also fully restore his own troops when they are beaten down. He must protect against surprise attacks 40 and be aware of all the army's movements. He should keep track of the movements of spies and emissaries, and pursue great actions yielding great results. His actions must always yield complete success, and he should surround himself with men whose actions are successful. He should never be overwhelmed, even amidst defeat, and must always be focused on the majestic king's success.

४३ इत्यादिलक्षणोपेतं कुर्वीत ध्वजिनीपतिम् ।
ध्वजिनीं तु सदोद्युक्तः स गोपयेद्दिवानिशम् ॥३०

४४ नद्यद्रिवनदुर्गेषु यत्र यत्र भयं भवेत् ।
सेनापतिस्तत्र तत्र गच्छेद्व्यूहीकृतैर्बलैः ॥

प्रयाणव्यसनरक्षणप्रकरणम् ।

४५ नायकः पुरतो यायात्प्रवीरपुरुषावृतः ।
मध्ये कलत्रं स्वामी च कोशः फल्गु च यद्बलम् ॥३१

४६ पार्श्वयोरुभयोरश्वा अश्वानां पार्श्वयो रथाः ।
रथानां पार्श्वयोर्नागा नागानां चाटवीबलम् ॥

४७ पश्चात्सेनापतिः सर्वं पुरस्कृत्य कृती स्वयम् ।
यायात्सन्नद्धसैन्यौघः खिन्नानाश्वासयञ्छनैः ॥३२

४८ यायाद्व्यूहेन महता मकरेण पुरोभये ।
श्येनेनोद्धृतपक्षेण सूच्या वा वीरवक्रया ॥३३

४९ पश्चाद्द्वये तु शकटं पार्श्वयोर्वज्रसंज्ञितम् ।
सर्वतः सर्वतोभद्रं भये व्यूहं प्रकल्पयेत् ॥

Someone with these and other virtues should be chosen as general of the army, and such a person must be always engaged and guard the army day and night. Wherever there is danger—whether on a river, mountain, or within the fortification—the general should go there, surrounded by soldiers arrayed in battle formation.

Avoiding Disaster During a Military Expedition

A commander should advance first, surrounded by the foremost fighters.[4] The king with his wives, treasury, and common soldiers should go in the middle. There should   45
be cavalry on each flank and chariots flanking the cavalry. On the chariots' flanks, there should be elephants, and an army of forest people should flank the elephants. The army's accomplished general should go last, letting everyone else precede him; making sure all the waves of the army's formations stay firm, and gently encouraging the exhausted stragglers.

The army should advance into danger arrayed in the "crocodile" formation, or in the formation of the "spread-winged hawk," or else in the "needle" formation, with valiant warriors in the front. If there is danger to the rear, the army should be arrayed in the "cart" formation. If there is danger on the sides, it should be arrayed in the "lightning-bolt" formation. If there is danger on all sides, then the "blessed-on-all-sides" formation should be used.[5]

When the army is exhausted from a long march, wearied from hunger or thirst, and when traveling through hillside

५० कन्दरे शैलगहने निम्नगावनसङ्कटे ।
दीर्घाध्वनि परिश्रान्तं क्षुत्पिपासाहितक्लमम् ॥३४

५१ व्याधिदुर्भिक्षमरकपीडितं दस्युभिर्द्रुतम् ।३५
पङ्कपांसुजलच्छन्नं व्यस्तं पुञ्जीकृतं पथि ॥३६

५२ प्रसुप्तं भोजनव्यग्रमभूमिष्ठमसंस्थितम् ।
चोराग्निभयवित्रस्तं वृष्टिवातसमाकुलम् ॥

५३ एवमादिषु जातेषु व्यसनेष्वसमाकुलः ।
स्वसैन्यं साधु संरक्षेत्परसैन्यं च घातयेत् ॥

कूटयुद्धविकल्पप्रकरणम्

५४ विशिष्टो देशकालाभ्यां भिन्नारिप्रकृतिर्बली ।
कुर्यात्प्रकाशयुद्धं हि कूटयुद्धं विपर्यये ॥

५५ तेष्ववस्कन्दकालेषु परं हन्यात्समाकुलम् ।
अभूमिष्ठं स भूमिष्ठस्तद्भूमौ चोपजापतः ॥३७ ३८

५६ प्रकृतिप्रग्रहाकृष्टं पाशैर्वनचरादिभिः ।३९ ४०
हन्यात्प्रवीरपुरुषैर्भङ्गदानापकर्षणैः ॥

५७ पुरस्ताद्दर्शनं दत्त्वा तल्लक्षकृतनिश्चयः ।
हन्यात्पश्चात्प्रवीरेण बलेनोत्पीड्य वेगिना ॥

thickets and caves, over rivers, or through dense forests; when afflicted by sickness, famine, or plague; when chased 50 by bandits; when covered with mud, dust, or water; when scattered or forced to huddle together; when asleep, in the middle of a meal, on unfavorable terrain, disarrayed, terrorized by thieves or fire, pounded by rain or wind—in these and other circumstances of potential disaster, the general must remain unperturbed as he protects his own army and slaughters the enemy's.

The Ways of Underhanded Warfare

When the powerful king has the advantages of time and place and has alienated the enemy's state-elements, he should engage in open warfare. In other circumstances, he should engage in underhanded warfare.

At one of the vulnerable moments, he should launch a surprise attack, and slaughter the enemy army while it is disorganized.[6] He should be situated on favorable terrain in his own land, and then attack the enemy while the latter is on unfavorable terrain, simultaneously sowing dissension in the enemy's territory.   55

His foremost fighters should attack the enemy when the latter's state-elements have been trapped in the snare of forest troops and other soldiers; all the while sowing dissension, offering bribes, and harassing him. Showing himself in the ruse of a frontal attack—and keeping the enemy totally focused on this target—the general should attack forcefully and swiftly from the rear with his fore-

५८ पश्चाद्धा सङ्कुलीकृत्य हन्यात्सारेण पूर्वतः ।
आभ्यां पार्श्वावघातौ तु व्याख्यातौ कूटयोधने ॥

५९ पुरस्ताद्दिषमे देशे पश्चाद्धन्यात्तु वेगवान् ।
पुरः पश्चाच्च विषम एवमेव तु पार्श्वयोः ॥

६० प्रथमं योधयित्वा च दूष्यामित्राटवीबलैः ।
श्रान्तं सन्नं निराक्रन्दं हन्यादश्रान्तवाहनः ॥

६१ दूष्यामित्रबलैर्वापि भङ्गं दत्त्वा प्रयत्नवान् ।
जितमित्येव विश्वस्तं हन्यात्सत्रव्यपाश्रयः ॥४१

६२ स्कन्धावारपुरग्रामसस्यसार्थव्रजादिषु ।४२
विलोभ्य च परानीकमप्रमत्तो विनाशयेत् ॥

६३ फल्गुसैन्यप्रतिच्छन्नं कृत्वा वा सारवद्बलम् ।
मन्दयन्नं तद्विलोपे हन्यादुत्प्लुत्य सिंहवत् ॥४३

६४ मृगयासम्प्रसक्तं वा हन्याच्छत्रुमपाश्रयम् ।४४
अथवा गोग्रहाकृष्ट्या तल्लक्षं मार्गबन्धनात् ॥

६५ अवस्कन्दभयाद्रात्रौ प्रजागरकृतश्रमम् ।
दिवाप्रसुप्तं वा हन्यान्निद्राव्याकुलसैनिकम् ॥

६६ अहःसन्नाहतः श्रान्तमपराह्णे विनाशयेत् ।
निशि विस्रम्भसुप्तं वा तत्सौप्तिकविधानवित् ॥

most fighters. Or else he can draw the enemy's attention to the rear, and then attack with all his might in front. Similar methods of underhanded warfare also apply to the enemy's flanks.

If there is difficult terrain in front, he should swiftly attack the rear. If the rear terrain is difficult, he should attack in front, and similarly with the two flanks. The first assault should be carried out by conscripted convicts, troops defected from the enemy, and forest troops. Then when the enemy is exhausted, weakened, and helpless without the assistance of his rear supporter, the main force can advance and strike with energetic horses. Or else the general 60 can trick the enemy into thinking that his convict troops, troops defected from the enemy, and forest troops have been routed. Then when the enemy thinks confidently that he has won, the king should strike him from a hiding place.

Lulling the enemy army into a sense of safety in its camps, cities, villages, fields, and markets, he should single-mindedly destroy him. He should hide his powerful army behind a shield of common troops. Then when they have been routed and the enemy has relaxed his efforts, he should pounce like a lion and kill him.

If your enemy is addicted to hunting, you should kill him while he is exposed on the hunt, or by conducting a cattle raid to draw his attention, and then closing off his exit-route.[7] If the enemy has stayed awake all night in fear of a surprise attack, you should kill him while he is sleeping during the day, his army wracked with exhaustion. The soldiers who 65 are weary from wearing their armor in the morning should be killed off in the afternoon. Otherwise an expert in the

267

६७ सपादकोशावरणैर्नागैः कुर्यात्तु सौप्तिकम् ।
कुर्यादुग्रजवोपेतैर्नरैर्वा खड्गपाणिभिः ॥

६८ प्रतिसूर्यमहावातं हन्यात्सम्मिलितेक्षणम् ।
इत्येवं कूटयुद्धेन हन्याच्छत्रून्लघूत्थितः ॥

६९ नीहारतिमिराङ्गारश्वभ्राग्निवननिम्नगाः ।४५
वदन्ति सत्रमित्यादि सत्रं छद्म प्रकीर्तितम् ॥४६

७० साध्वप्रमत्तो व्यवसायवर्ती येन प्रकारेण परं निहन्यात् ।४७
चरैः समावेदिततत्प्रचारः शङ्केत तेनैव ततोऽप्रमत्तः ॥

७१ सुनियतमुपहन्यात्कूटयुद्धेन शत्रून्न
हि तिरयति धर्मं छद्मना शत्रुघातः ।४८
अचकितमवसुप्तं पाण्डवानामनीकं
निशि सुनिशितशस्त्रो द्रोणसूनुर्जघान ॥

268

technique of nocturnal raids should annihilate them at night while they are sleeping soundly. One should conduct a nocturnal raid by means of elephants—wearing leather foot-covers to prevent noise—and swordsmen furiously swift in their attack. One should kill the enemy while he has his eyes closed, when facing the sun, or blasted by the wind. Thus, by means of underhanded warfare, the nimble warrior should kill his enemies.

There are seven types of hideout, according to the kind of camouflage that is used: mist, darkness, coal, chasm, fire, forest, and river.[8] A hideout is defined as something camouflaged.

By whatever method he attacks the enemy, a conqueror must be resolute, vigilant, and kept informed by his spies of the enemy's movements. He should in turn fear the enemy's being informed of his own movements and attacking. This is why he must be vigilant.

70

One should decisively slaughter one's enemies through underhanded warfare. Surreptitious slaughter of one's enemies does not negate dharma. Drona's son slaughtered the Pandava army with very sharp blades at night while they were asleep and unaware.[9]

71

विंशः सर्गः

गजाश्वरथपत्तिकर्मप्रकरणम्

१ प्रयाणे पूर्वयायित्वं वनदुर्गप्रवेशनम्।१
अकृतानां च मार्गाणां तीर्थानां च प्रवर्तनम्॥

२ तोयावतारसन्तारावेकाङ्गविजयस्तथा।
अभिन्नानामनीकानां भेदनं भिन्नसङ्ग्रहः॥

३ बिभीषिकाभिघातश्च प्राकारद्वारभञ्जनम्।
कोशनीतिर्भयत्राणं हस्तिकर्म प्रचक्षते॥

४ चतुरङ्गस्य सैन्यस्य निषेधो बलरक्षणम्।
अभिन्नभेदनं भिन्नसन्धानं रथकर्म तत्॥

५ वनदिङ्गार्गविचयो वीवधासाररक्षणम्।
अनुयानापसरणे शीघ्रकार्योपपादनम्॥

६ दीनानुसरणं घातः कोटीनां जघनस्य च।
इत्यश्वकर्म पत्तेष्व सर्वदा शस्त्रधारणम्॥

७ शोधनं कूपतीर्थानां मार्गाणां शिबिरस्य च।
यवसादि च यत्किंचिद्विज्ञेयं विष्टिकर्म तत्॥२

८ जातिः सत्त्वं वयः स्थानं प्राणिता वर्ष्म वेगिता।३
तेजः शिल्पमुदग्रत्वं स्थैर्यं साधु विधेयता॥४

९ सुव्यञ्जनाचारतेति पत्तिकुञ्जरवाजिनाम्।
इति लक्षणमेतेन युक्तान्कर्मसु योजयेत्॥

CHAPTER 20

Elephants, Cavalry, Chariots, and Foot Soldiers

The functions of elephants are the following: leading a military expedition; breaking into forest fortifications; making roads or river crossings in rough terrain; wading through bodies of water and ferrying people across; achieving victory as a one-unit army; smashing apart the enemy's united forces, and herding together one's own dispersed forces; terrorizing and destroying the enemy army; smashing open ramparts and gates; guarding the treasury; and defending against danger from the enemy.

The function of the chariot is to block the enemy's four-limbed army, to protect one's own army, to break apart the enemy's united forces, and herd together one's own dispersed forces. The functions of the cavalry are scouting out routes through the forest; protecting supply lines and routes for allies; pursuing and thwarting the enemy; swiftly executing tasks; pursuing routed enemies; and attacking the front flanks and the rear. The function of the foot soldiers is to always bear arms. 5

The function of forced labor is to repair wells, river-crossings, roads, and camps; to gather grass for fodder, and any other tasks that need to be done.

For their various activities the king should only employ foot soldiers, elephants, and horses with the following traits: noble breeding, force, youth, vitality, robust physique,

पत्त्यश्वरथगजभूमिप्रकरणम्

१०   सस्थूलस्थाणुवल्मीकवृक्षगुल्मापकण्टका ।५
सापसारा पदातीनां भूर्नातिविषमा मता ॥

११   स्वल्पवृक्षोपला क्षिप्रप्रलङ्घनीयदरा स्थिरा ।६
निःशर्करा विपङ्का च सापसारा च वाजिभूः ॥

१२   निःस्थाणुसिकतापङ्का निर्वल्मीकोपला समा ।७
केदारव्रततिश्चभ्रवृक्षगुल्मविवर्जिता ॥

१३   निरुत्खाता निर्दरणा खुरचङ्क्रमणक्षमा ।८
स्थिरा चक्रसहा चैव रथभूमिः प्रकीर्तिता ॥९

१४   मर्दनीयतरुश्छेद्यव्रततिः पङ्कवर्जिता ।
सुगम्यशैलविषमा हस्तिभूरिति कीर्तिता ॥१०

१५   नागम्या नाम भूरेषां तेन नागाः स्मृता बुधैः ।
तस्मादेता भुवोऽत्यर्थं नागानां सम्प्रकीर्तिताः ॥११

१६   तुरगादीनि भिन्नानि प्रतिगृह्णाति यद्बलम् ।
प्रतिग्रह इति ख्यातः स तु कार्यो भरक्षमः ॥

१७   तेन शून्यस्तु यो व्यूहः स भिन्न इव लक्ष्यते ।
तस्माद्विद्वाञ्जयाकाङ्क्षी न युध्येताप्रतिग्रहः ॥

swiftness, vigor, training, stature, stability, extraordinary alacrity, as well as good overall character and behavior.

Terrain for Foot Soldiers, Cavalry, Chariots, and Elephants

Terrain is considered fit for foot soldiers if it is not too uneven, even if it has large tree-stumps, anthills, trees, and shrubs, so long as it has escape routes and thorns removed. A   10 tract of land fit for horses will have very few trees and boulders, as well as crevasses they can swiftly jump. It will have solid ground, no pebbles or mud, and also provide escape routes. A tract of land fit for chariots has no tree stumps, sand, mud, anthills, or stones; it will be level, and free of paddy fields, vines, chasms, trees, and thickets. It will be solid, have no open mines or crevasses, and will be suitable for chariot wheels and horses' hooves to move about freely. A tract of land suitable for elephants is free of mud, with trees that can be easily knocked aside, vines easily sliced away, and boulders easily stepped over. However scholars derive the word *nāga,* "elephant," from *nāgamya,* land that is "not unable to be traversed," because there is no terrain on which they cannot go. Therefore the terrain just mentioned is only particularly good for elephants.[1]   15

The section of the army that collects the broken ranks, such as those of the cavalry, is known as the "reserve troops," and it should be reinforced so that it is able to execute its task. A battle array lacking reserve troops is considered virtually broken. Therefore a knowledgeable king desiring victory should not fight without reserve troops. He should

१८ जयार्थी नृपतिस्तिष्ठेद्दूरं गत्वा प्रतिग्रहः ।
भिन्ने च प्रतिगृह्णीयान्न हि युध्येत तं विना ॥

दानकल्पनाप्रकरणम् ।

१९ गजेष्वारोपितः साधुः शीघ्रपातैरधिष्ठितः ।
यत्र राजा तत्र कोशः कोशाधीना हि राजता ॥

२० प्रत्यग्रे कर्मणि कृते श्लाघमानः कृतादरः ।
योधेभ्यस्तु ततो दद्यात्को हि दातुर्न युध्यते ॥

२१ दद्यात्प्रहृष्टो नियुतं भराणां राजघातिने ।१२
तदर्धं तत्सुतवधे सेनापतिवधे तथा ॥

२२ प्रवीराणां तु मुख्यस्य शतं शतगुणं वधे ।
तदर्धं कुञ्जरवधे प्रदेयं स्यन्दनस्य च ॥

२३ साहस्रोऽश्ववधः शत्यः पत्तिमुख्यवधः स्मृतः ।१३
शिरो विंशतिकं शेषं भोगद्वैगुण्यमेव च ॥१४

२४ युग्यं हेम च कुप्यं च यो यज्जयति तस्य तत् ।१५
दद्याद्वस्त्वनुरूपं वा हृष्टो योधान्प्रहर्षयेत् ॥१६

station himself far off, while the reserve troops advance to collect the broken ranks; and he should never fight without reserve troops.

Types of Giving

A well-stocked treasury should be mounted on the backs of elephants and guarded by swift horsemen. The king and the treasury should be made inseparable because kingship depends on the treasury. Warriors should be praised and honored for their outstanding acts, and the king should give wealth to them. Who will not fight on behalf of a generous benefactor?

The king should be pleased to give a hundred thousand coins to whoever kills the enemy king. He should give half as much to whoever kills the enemy king's son or his general. He should give ten thousand to the man who kills a chief of warriors, and half that to the man who kills an elephant- or chariot-driver. He should give a thousand to someone who kills a chief of the cavalry, and a hundred for killing a chief of foot soldiers. To those who kill chiefs of any of the other divisions he should give twenty. To those who kill anyone else, he should give double his salary. Soldiers can claim the animals, gold, and other metals they seize, or else when he pleases, he can give the fighters something of equivalent value. When the king is gratified he should gratify his warriors.

20

व्यूहविकल्पप्रकरणम्

२५ पञ्चारत्नि धनुस्तस्मिन्धन्विनं स्थापयेद्युधि ।
 त्रिगुणेऽश्वं गजरथौ योज्यौ पञ्चसु पञ्चसु ॥

२६ शमान्तरस्तु पुरुषस्तुरङ्गस्त्रिशमान्तरः ।
 कुञ्जरः स्यन्दनश्चैव स्मृतौ पञ्चशमान्तरौ ॥

२७ तथा वा खलु युध्येरन्पत्त्यश्वरथदन्तिनः ।
 यथा भवेन्न सम्बाधो व्यायामविनिवर्तने ॥

२८ असङ्करेण युध्येरन्सङ्करः सङ्कुलावहः ।
 महासङ्करयुद्धे च संश्रयेरन्महागजान् ॥१७

२९ अश्वस्य प्रतियोद्धारो भवेयुः पुरुषास्त्रयः ।
 इति कल्प्यास्तु पञ्चाश्वा विधेयाः कुञ्जरस्य च ॥

३० पादगोपाश्च तावन्तः पुरुषा दश पञ्च च ।
 विधानमिति नागस्य कथितं स्यन्दनस्य च ॥

३१ अनीकमिति विज्ञेयमिति कल्प्या नव द्विपाः ।
 अनीकस्य च रन्ध्रं च पञ्चचापं प्रचक्षते ॥

३२ इत्यनीकविधानेन स्थापयेद्व्यूहसम्पदः ।
 उरस्यकक्षपक्षांश्च तुल्यानेतान्प्रचक्षते ॥

३३ उरः कक्षो च पक्षौ च मध्यः पृष्ठः प्रतिग्रहः ।
 कोटी च व्यूहशास्त्रज्ञैः सप्ताङ्गो व्यूह इष्यते ॥

३४ उरस्यकक्षपक्षैस्तु व्यूहोऽयं सप्रतिग्रहः ।
 गुरोरेष च शुक्रस्य कक्षाभ्यां परिवर्जितः ॥

276

Types of Battle Arrays

The archers should be stationed at a distance of five cubits from each other, and the horses at three times that distance from them. Teams of one chariot and one elephant should be stationed in turn at a distance of twenty-five cubits from these squads. The foot soldiers should be stationed at a 25 distance of one yard from each other, while the horses should be stationed at a distance of three yards from each other. The elephants and chariots should be stationed at a distance of five yards from each other.

The foot soldiers, cavalry, chariots, and elephants should fight in such a way that they do not crowd each other while either advancing or retreating. The army should fight uncongested, since congestion brings disaster. In an extremely congested battle, they should rely on the great elephants.

There should be three foot soldiers to fight as front-guard for each horse, and five horsemen in front of each elephant. The proper arrangement is therefore: fifteen foot soldiers as supporting guards for each elephant and each chariot. A battalion requires nine elephants with a buffer zone of 30 twenty-five cubits from the next battalion. Through the varied configuration of battalions one should organize battle arrays.

They say there should be equal-sized components called "chest," "sides," and "wings." Scholars learned in the lore of battle arrays say a battle array has seven components: chest, sides, wings, middle, back, guard, and outer edges. Brihaspati holds that the array consists only of chest, sides, wings, and guard, while Shukra omits the two sides.

३५ अभेद्याः कुलजा मौला लब्धलक्षाः प्रहारिणः।
सेनाङ्गपतयः कार्या युद्धदृष्टप्रतिक्रियाः॥

३६ प्रवीरपुरुषैरेते तिष्ठेयुः परिवारिताः।
अभेदेनैव युध्येरन्नक्षेयुश्च परस्परम्॥

३७ फल्गु सैन्यस्य यत्किंचिन्मध्ये व्यूहस्य तद्ध्रुवेत्।
युद्धवस्तु च यत्किंचित्प्रायस्तज्जघने भवेत्॥

३८ युद्धार्थं युद्धकुशलं मुण्डानीकं प्रयोजयेत्।
युद्धं हि नायकप्राणं हन्येत तदनायकम्॥

३९ व्यूहोऽनुपृष्ठमचलः पत्त्यश्वरथदन्तिभिः।
तथाप्रतिहतो ज्ञेयो हस्त्यश्वरथपत्तिभिः॥

४० उरसि स्थापयेन्नागान्प्रचण्डान्कक्षयो रथान्।
हयांश्च पक्षयोर्व्यूहो मध्यभेदी प्रकीर्तितः॥

४१ मध्यदेशे हयानीकं रथानीकं तु कक्षयोः।
पक्षयोश्च गजानीकं व्यूहोऽन्तभिदयं स्मृतः॥

४२ रथस्थाने हयान्दद्यात्पदातींश्च हयाश्रये।१९
रथाभावे तु सर्वत्र नागानेव प्रकल्पयेत्॥

४३ विभज्य प्रक्षिपेद्व्यूहे रथपत्त्यश्वकुञ्जरान्।
यदि स्याद्दण्डबाहुल्यं स चावापः प्रकीर्तितः॥

४४ मण्डलोऽसंहतो भोगो दण्डश्चेति मनीषिभिः।
चत्वारः प्रकृतिव्यूहा भेदास्त्वेषां प्रकीर्तिताः॥

४५ तिर्यग्वृत्तिस्तु दण्डः स्याद्भोगोऽन्वावृत्तिरेव च।
मण्डलः सर्वतोवृत्तिः पृथग्वृत्तिरसंहतः॥

Men immune to dissension, of noble birth, of local origin, good marksmen, fierce attackers, and whose reactions have been battle-tested, should be made commanders of various sections of the army. The foremost warriors should surround these commanders in battle. They should fight united as a group and protect one another. The common soldiers should go in the middle of the array, while any mechanical weapons should generally be placed at the rear. During war one should employ a detachment of the army devoid of any special insignia and skilled in fighting to protect the commander. A war's life-breath is the commander. Without a commander, the army will be destroyed.

When foot soldiers, cavalry, chariots, and elephants are lined up one behind the other, this is known as the mountain array; when the order is reversed (elephants, chariots, cavalry, soldiers) this is the unobstructed array. When one places the fierce elephants at the chest, chariots on the sides, and cavalry on the wings, this is called the middle-splitting array. When one places the cavalry in the middle, the chariots on the sides, and the elephants on the wings, this is known as the edge-splitting array. One can also put the cavalry in the place of the chariots, and foot soldiers in the cavalry's place, but if there are no chariots, the shrewd commander will place elephants at the sides. One should divide the forces up and arrange them according to foot soldiers, cavalry, chariots, and elephants. If the forces are in excess then they can be considered potential reserves.

The four regular arrays are the circle, the decompressed, the cobra-hood, and the rod; wise men have identified several subdivisions among these. The rod array is horizontal, the

35

40

279

४६ प्रदरो दृढकोऽसह्यश्चापस्तत्कुक्षिरेव च ।१९
प्रतिष्ठः सुप्रतिष्ठश्च श्येनो विजयसञ्जयौ ॥

४७ विशालविजयः सूची स्थूणाकर्णश्च मूमुखः ।
झषास्यो वलयश्चैव दण्डभेदाः सुदुर्जयः ॥२०

४८ अतिक्रान्तः प्रतिक्रान्तः कक्षाभ्यां कक्षपक्षतः ।
अतिक्रान्तश्च पक्षाभ्यां त्रयोऽन्ये तु विपर्यये ॥

४९ पक्षोरस्यैरतिक्रान्तः प्रविष्टोऽन्यो विपर्यये ।
स्थूणापक्षो धनुःपक्षो द्विस्थूणो दण्ड ऊर्ध्वगः ॥

५० द्विगुणान्त्यस्त्यभिक्रान्तपक्षोऽन्योऽस्य विपर्यये ।
द्विचतुर्दण्ड इत्येते ज्ञेया लक्षणतः क्रमात् ॥

५१ गोमूत्रिकाहिसारी च शकटो मकरस्तथा ।
भोगभेदाः समाख्याातास्तथा परिपतन्तिकः ॥

५२ दण्डपक्षो युगोरस्यः शकटस्तद्विपर्यये ।
मकरो व्यवकीर्णश्च शेषः कुञ्जरवाजिभिः ॥२१

५३ मण्डलव्यूहभेदौ च सर्वतोभद्रदुर्जयौ ।
अष्टानीको द्वितीयस्तु प्रथमः सर्वतोमुखः ॥२२

५४ अर्धचन्द्रक उद्धानो वज्रो भेदास्त्वसंहते ।
तथा कर्कटशृङ्गी च काकपादी च गोधिका ॥२३

cobra-hood is curved, the circle goes in every direction, and the decompressed array is divided up.

There are many subdivisions of the rod array: the crevice,   45
the firmed up, the unbearable, the bow, the bow's belly, the foundation, the good foundation, the eagle, the victory, the complete victory, the vast victory, the needle, the pole-ear, the army-face, the fish-face, the armlet, and finally, the very indomitable.

The rod array can extend or retract just its sides, or else its sides and wings together, or else just its wings.[2] Finally we have the pole-wing (in which the pole array is formed at the wings), the bow-wing (in which the bow array is formed at the wings), the two-pole (a double pole formation also known as vast victory), and the upward-rod (a completely straight array, also known as the needle).[3] The wings can be doubled up, which gives the pole-ear; they can also be tripled, either advanced or retracted.[4] The rod formation can also be doubled or quadrupled.[5]   50

The hood arrays are the cow-urine-stream, the serpent-slither, the cart, the crocodile, and the pouncing. When the wings are arrayed as rods, with the chest doubled, this is the cart. The order can also be inverted, which yields the crocodile array, and the last of these, the pouncing, is either the cart or the crocodile reinforced by cavalry and elephants. Two kinds of circular array are: blessed-in-every-direction and indomitable: the first of these points in every direction, while the second has eight battalions with each section doubled-up. Variants of the decompressed array are: half-moon, fireplace, lightning-bolt, horned-crab, crow's foot, and lizard.

५५ त्रिचतुःपञ्चसैन्यानां ज्ञेया आकारभेदतः ।
इति व्यूहाः समाख्याता व्यूहभेदप्रयोक्तृभिः ॥

५६ एते सप्तदश प्रोक्ता दण्डव्यूहास्तु भेदतः ।
तथा व्यूहद्वयं चैव मण्डलस्य समासतः ॥

५७ असंहतास्तु षड्व्यूहा भोगव्यूहास्तु पञ्चधा ।
व्यूहज्ञैस्ते प्रयोज्याः स्युर्युद्धकाल उपस्थिते ॥

प्रकाशयुद्धप्रकरणम्

५८ पक्षादीनामथैकेन हत्वा शेषैः परिक्षिपेत् ।२४
उरसा वा समाहत्य कोटिभ्यां परिवेष्टयेत् ॥

५९ परकोटी समाक्रम्य पक्षाभ्यां सप्रतिग्रहः ।२५
कोटिभ्यां जघनं हन्यादुरसा च प्रपीडयेत् ॥

६० यतः फल्गु यतो भिन्नं यतो दूष्यैरधिष्ठितम् ।
ततो रिपुबलं हन्यादात्मनश्चोपबृंहयेत् ॥

६१ सारं द्विगुणसारेण फल्गु सारेण पीडयेत् ।
संहतं च गजानीकैः प्रचण्डैरपसारयेत् ॥

६२ दुर्जयान्करिणः सिंहवसासिक्तैर्मतङ्गजैः ।
आहन्यात्करिणीनां वा समूहैः साध्वधिष्ठितैः ॥

Authorities on the varieties of battle arrays have detailed them according to whether their forms have three, four, or five prongs. The rod array has seventeen varieties and the circle basically two. The decompressed has six varieties and the hood, five. Those who know arrays should use them when the moment of battle arrives. 55

Open Warfare

After attacking with one detachment of the army, the commander should then deploy the remaining forces, using his chest to strike hard, and then surrounding the enemy with his outer edges. Supported by his guard, he should advance on the enemy's outer edges with his wings, and then strike the enemy's rear with his outer edges, also assaulting with his chest.

He should hit the enemy's army wherever there are common soldiers, troops defecting from the enemy, and convict troops. Likewise he should swell his own forces in these areas. He should assault a strong enemy force with a force of double strength, and have his superior soldiers strike the common soldiers. He should use his fierce elephant battalions to scatter the enemy's consolidated forces. Finally he should attack indomitable elephants by means of elephants smeared with lion fat, or else with groupings of well-commanded she-elephants. 60

६३ सलोहजालैर्दृढबन्धदन्तैः सुकल्पितैरूर्जितपादरक्षैः ।
प्रवीरयोधैर्मददुर्निवारैर्हन्याद्द्विजेन्द्रैर्द्विषतामनीकम् ॥

६४ एकोऽपि वारणपतिर्द्विषतामनीकं
युक्तं निहन्ति मदसत्त्वगुणोपपन्नः ।२६
नागेषु हि क्षितिभृतां विजयो निबद्धस्
तस्माद्द्विजाधिकबलो नृपतिः सदा स्यात् ॥

With his elephants, unstoppable in their rut—their tusks firmly reinforced with webs of iron mesh armor, attended by robust, well-outfitted guards, and driven by the most valiant warriors—he should attack the enemy army.   63

One bull elephant, courageously rampaging, can slaughter an entire enemy battalion. A king's victory depends on elephants, and so he must always have abundant elephant forces.   64

This Ends *The Essence of Politics* by Kamandaki

ABBREVIATIONS

A   ed. of Ganapati Shastri (1912)
J   *Jayamaṅgalā* of Shankararya
AS   rev. ed. of Rajendralal Mitra (1982)
U   *Upādhyāyanirapekṣā*

NOTES TO THE TEXT

Sarga 1

१   वंश्यानाम्] वंशानाम् A
२   जलधौ] बलवत् A
३   तन्नाशोऽन्यत्] तदभावे AS
४   प्रयत्न] प्रवृत्ति AS
५   उप्रभयदाम्] उभयभयदाम् AS
६   सम्मोहात्] संलोभात् A
७   झनज्झनान्] झलज्झलान् A
८   विनयं] विनयी AS
९   समुद्धता] समुन्नता AS
१०   उपबृंहितो] उपसंहितो A
११   निधिम्] विधिम् AS

Sarga 2

१   योगक्षेमाय देहिनाम्] लोकसंस्थितिहेतवः A
२   अवस्थिताः] अवस्थिते AS
३   वार्तानुजीविनाम्] वार्ता तु जीवनम् A
४   नावृत्तेर्भयमृच्छति] न वृत्तेर्भयमृच्छति AS
५   धर्मदारेषु कल्येषु] धर्मो ऽयं गृहिणां काले AS
६   वाग्यमो] वाग्मनो AS
७   ध्यानयुक्तता] ध्याननित्यता AS
८   सर्व] स्वर्ग A
९   निराक्रन्दं] निरालम्भं AS

Sarga 3

१   धरणीपतिः] धरणीसमः A
२   सुजनैः] स्वजनैः AS
३   श्रुत] सतः AS
४   दीयते] नीयते A
५   सुजनाय] स्वजनाय AS
६   अशमात्मकैः] अनयात्मकैः AS
७   वन्द्यचरणाः] अनिन्द्यचरिताः AS
८   सद्भावेन॰ सम्भ्रमेण] स्वभावेन॰ सद्भावेन AS
९   चतुरश्रता] चरितानि च AS
१०   गर्वः] वर्गः AS

११ आयतालानितः] आनतो लालितः AS

Sarga 4

१ आशु परीक्षणम्] सुपरीक्षणम् AS
२ सुविग्रहः] स्ववग्रहः AS
३ श्लक्ष्णो] शक्तो AS
४ मितवाक्] स्मितवाक् AS
५ लोकयात्राविदि] लोकयात्राविधि AS
६ दाक्ष्यं] अदाक्ष्यं AS
७ पृथिवीपते:] शत्रुसङ्कटे AS
८ उद्धतस्य] उद्भूतस्य A
९ प्रवर्धते] प्रवर्तते A
१० विख्यातपौरुषो जन्यः] विख्यातपौरुषैर्जित्यः AS
११ अद्वैध्यं] अद्वेष्यं A
१२ कार्यार्थम्] मित्रार्थम् AS
१३ In the Trivandrum ed. (A), this verse is included in parentheses after verse 65, I read it here along with the Asiatic Society ed. (AS).
१४ वंशं] देशं A
१५ परा...ससाधनम्] परं...सुसाधनम् A
१६ अन्वितः] अर्चितः AS

Sarga 5

१ मन्त्री] मति AS
२ तत्क्रिश्यन्नपि] तदेव तस्य AS
३ रसोनभक्षास्तद्द्रन्धाः] रसो न भक्ष्यस्तद्द्रन्धः AS
४ भवत्यपेयः] भवत्यवश्यं A
५ अभिलक्ष्यं] अभिलष्यं AS
६ सिद्धैर्] सद्धिर् A
७ भर्तुर्न्वासने तिष्ठन्दृष्टिं] भर्तुरन्वासितो दृष्टिं मुहुः A
८ ब्रूयान्न किञ्चिदन्योन्यं] कुर्यात्किमयमित्यस्य AS
९ कासं] हासं A
१० भाषेत भाषितम्] भाषेण भाषितः AS
११ प्रबन्धं] प्रवृद्धं AS
१२ असभ्यं] असत्यं AS
१३ अर्थकारिणा] अनुकारिणा AS
१४ विद्विष्टिं च विनाशं] विद्विष्टमपि नाशं A
१५ तत्रोक्तं तद्वचो] तस्यैव तद्वच्च A
१६ आत्मशंसासु] आत्मसंसत्सु A

१७ हसत्य] वदत्य AS

१८ मन्त्राणि ब्रुवन्हासं प्रपद्यते] मर्माणि गुणैर्न बहुमन्यते A

१९ यत्नेनाराध्यमानो ऽपि] बलेन बोध्यमानो ऽपि AS

२० विरोधे कर्मधुर्याणां] विपत्सु धर्मधुर्याणां AS

२१ अल्पतोषस्य] अल्पदोषस्य A

२२ शुष्कं सर इव] शुष्कवृक्षमिव AS

२३ दुर्वृत्ते ऽप्यकुलीने ऽपि] दुर्वृत्ते वा सुवृत्ते वा A

२४ This verse is only found in the AS edition.

२५ This verse is only found in the AS edition. Orthography emended from को ऽनुवन्दते to को नु वन्दते.

२६ हि भर्तारं] अवमन्तारं AS

२७ यथारक्षेच्च निपुण॰ कण्टकि॰ तद्दस्द्रोग्यम्] सुसरंक्षेत निपुणः॰ कण्टक॰ दस्युभोग्यम् A

२८ पुष्पप्रदा यथा] पुष्पफलार्थिना AS

२९ अविश्वासी तथा च स्याद्यथा च व्यवहारवान्] विश्वासी च तथा च स्याद्यथा संव्यवहारवान् A

३० Only the Asiatic Society edition includes this verse labeled as an addition (क्रोड) by the commentary.

Sarga 6

१ संरक्षणं धर्मः] संशरणं धाम AS

२ धर्माय] पापिष्ठान् AS

३ प्रदूष्य वा प्रकाशं हि] अदृश्यं वा प्रकाशं वा AS

४ आसंज्ञिता] आसज्जिता A

Sarga 7

१ वर्जेत] बुध्येत A

२ सोदकत्वम्] मोदकत्वम् AS

३ तथा स्निग्धत्वमेव च] तथोष्मा स्निग्धमेचकःAS

४ क्रथने] क्रथनं A

५ स्याद्रसे] द्रवे च A

६ च दध्रो] सरन्ध्रा AS

७ तदन्तिके] वदन्ति के AS

८ वाग्भङ्गो] त्वग्भेदो AS

९ आवेशो] आवेगो AS

१० समाचरेत्] विवर्जयेत् AS

११ समुद्धूतामपरीक्षित] परिभ्रान्तां परीतानाप्त A

१२ ॰स्थितमाप्तसैन्यचक्रम्] ॰अन्तिकमाप्तसैन्यचक्रः A

१३ विवर्जयन्] विसर्जयेद् A

१४ वयोनुरूपं] वयोनुरूपैर् A

१५ सुवेग] सुवेष A
१६ करणेन] कारणेन AS
१७ आत्ययिकाद्रोगात्सर्वस्यैवातुरो] आत्ययिकात्कार्यात्सर्वत्रात्ययिको A
१८ वैरूप्यं] वैरन्त्य AS
१९ अहिवृत्तं] इति वृत्तं AS
२० प्रबाध्यते] प्रबुध्यते AS

Sarga 8

१ विजिगीषोर्गुणोदयः] विजिगीषुगुणाः स्मृताः AS
२ त्रस्यन्ति परे सिंहान्मृगा इव] ह्रस्यन्ति परान्सिंहा मृगानिव AS
३ प्रतापयुक्तो] प्रतापसिद्धौ AS
४ प्रभुः] परम् AS
५ तथारिमित्रमित्रं...स्थिताः] मित्रारिमित्रमित्रं...स्मृताः A
६ व्यस्तयोर्निग्रहे प्रभुः] समर्थो व्यस्तयोर्वधे AS
७ मण्डलाद्वहिर्] मण्डलत्वे हि चैतेषाम् AS
८ आहैव मन्त्र] आहैतत्तन्त्र A
९ महर्षयः] पुनर्मयः A
१० परे च नयवादिनः] अपरे परिवादिनः A
११ मण्डलशोधनप्रकरणम्] मण्डलचरितप्रकरणम् A
१२ संरञ्जनाद् (AS#52)] संवर्जनाद् A] संसर्जनाद् AS
१३ विजिगीषत्युदासीने] उदासीने विचलति A
१४ अरिः सम्पदा] अरिसम्पदा A
१५ कर्म च वित्तं च विजानाति] मर्म च वीर्यं च स A
१६ उपचयं] अपचयं AS
१७ वंशगतो...दुरवग्रहः] वशं गतो...दुरुपग्रहः A
१८ मध्य] सम A
१९ सानुशयं] संशयितं AS
२० पितान्यो] तथान्यो A

Sarga 9

१ बलिना विगृहीतः सन्] बलीयसाभियुक्तस्तु AS
२ From this point to the end of the sarga, the order of verses in the
  AS edition has been adopted.
३ ह्यप्रभावत्वात्] अन्यप्रमाणत्वात् A
४ को हि युध्यते] को ऽभियुज्यते A
५ आत्मसात्कृताः] स्वार्थसत्कृताः AS
६ सम्पत्तौ च विपत्तौ च] सम्पत्तेश्च च विपत्तेश्च AS
७ गजेन्द्रमपकर्षति] गजेन्द्रमपि कर्षति A
८ स सन्धितो] सुसंहितो A

९   संप्राप्योत्सादयेद्धि सः] स प्रायः सादयन्द्विषः A

१०   कदाचिदुपसर्पति] कदाचिदपि सर्पति A

११   संधितो] संहितो A

१२   सिंह इवोदग्रम्] सिंहमिवोदारम् A

१३   इह] इव A

१४   क्षते] क्षितौ AS

१५   आलभ्य] आलक्ष्य A

१६   प्रयत्नवान्] प्रतापवान् AS

१७   ऋच्छति] इच्छति AS

१८   अभियोक्तुः] अभियोक्तुं AS

१९   आत्मसंहितैः] अर्थसंहितैः A

२०   स्वपक्षे यात्यविश्वासम्] स्वपक्षे यस्य विश्वास AS

२१   अनिष्टम्...प्रधर्षयेत्] आतिष्ठन्...प्रसाधयेत् AS

२२   कलत्रमात्मा] आत्मा बलं वा AS

२३   युधि] इति A

२४   सन्धापयेत्] सन्तापयेत् AS

२५   सामन्तम्] सीमान्तम् AS

२६   सन्धानम्] सन्तापम् AS

२७   विनयेन॰ चेतरद्द्विधा] विजयन॰ चेति तद्द्विधाः AS

Sarga 10

१   ज्ञानस्य च बलस्य च] यानस्य च धनस्य च AS

२   ज्ञानापहार] यानापहार AS

३   जातस्यान्तं व्रजेद्दशी] जाते तत्र प्रियं वदेत्] AS

४   परेण स्तोभितो] दुष्टेन स्तम्भितो AS

५   akāle daivayuktena] akāladaivayuktena A

६   इमम्] अमुम् AS

७   मतिमन्तम्] धृतिमन्तम् AS

८   मनीषयान्वीक्षित] चरेक्षणैर्वीक्षित AS

Sarga 11

१   गणान्बलात्] गुणान्बली A

२   This verse is included and the numbering adjusted in accordance with the AS edition.

३   आविष्कृतं] अरिकृतं A

४   अवस्थानं] वास्थानं A

५   छित्त्वास्यासारवीवधान्] हत्वास्यासारवीवधौ A

६   विरज्यमानप्रकृतिं] विगृह्यमानः प्रकृतिं AS

७   व्यवस्थानं] समुत्थानं AS

८ उभयारिं हि वाञ्छन्तं] उभयारिर्हि वाञ्छेत AS

९ सर्वसम्पदा] तत्त्वधर्मणा AS

१० सन्निकृष्टमरिं तयोः] सन्निकृष्टतरस्तयोः A

११ तदोपसर्पन्] तदोपगच्छेत् AS

१२ भूमिसम्भवम्] भूतिसम्भवाम् A

१३ श्रियः] श्रितः AS

१४ वा काल उत्थितः] वृत्त्या बलं रिपुम्] AS

१५ I have emended the numbering of the verses from here to the end of the sarga.

१६ यस्मात्] तस्मात् AS

Sarga 12

१ विजयमश्नुते] भूतिं समश्नुते AS

२ अवधूयते] अवभूयते AS

३ पण्डितं वर्जयेदिह] मन्त्रिणं परिवर्जयेत् A

४ आकाशमास्वादयतः कुतस्तु कवलग्रहः] भवन्ति परितापिन्यो व्यक्तं कर्मविपत्तयः AS

५ अमलबुद्धिभिः] आसनबुद्धिभिः AS

६ शस्यते] दृश्यते A

७ उत्प्लुत्य] उत्पत्य A

८ पिण्डं महञ्ज्ञापि न] खण्डं स्कन्धं नैवापि]AS

९ संवृत्य] सद्वृत्त्या AS

१० कार्यद्वारेष्वनेकधा] कार्यद्वारेषु नैकधा A

११ तेन शीघ्रं] तेषु साधु A

१२ यत्र] यज्ञ A

१३ सहायोत्थान] सत्त्वायोत्थान AS

१४ पुरः] पुनः A

१५ आप्ताप्तसन्ततेर्मन्त्रं संरक्षेत्तत्परस्तु सन्] अप्राप्तसन्ततिर्मन्त्रं संरक्ष्येत परस्परम् AS

१६ निष्कुड्यान्तरसंश्रये] निर्भेद्धे ऽन्तरसंश्रये AS

१७ कार्यसिद्धिविवृद्धये] कार्यं बुद्धिविवृद्धये A

१८ एकैकेनापि कार्याणि] अकथ्यानि तु कार्याणि AS

१९ विशुद्धपार्ष्णिः सद्वस्तु] विशुद्धपार्श्वंसंसिद्धः A

२० अरिखड्गाभिहतः] अचिरं वै व्यसनी AS

२१ अनयात्] बलात् AS

२२ सम्पतत्रनिपत्य] सम्पतन्त्रिपत्य AS

Sarga 13

१ मन्त्रं] मन्त्रि A

२ शास्त्रे शास्त्रे च निश्चितः] शास्त्रे चास्त्रे च निश्चितः AS

३ शासनवाहकः] शासनहारकः A

४ स्ववाक्यपरवाक्यानाम्] स्वराष्ट्रपरराष्ट्राणाम् AS

५ दृष्टिवक्रविचेष्टितैः] प्रकृतीनां च भर्तरि AS

६ कृत्यपक्षोपजापं] कृत्यपक्षस्य चोपायं AS

७ वध्यमानोऽपि] पृच्छमानो ऽपि AS

८ कुलेन॰ गरीयसा] फलेन॰ महीयसा AS

९ उपदेशेन] अपदेशेन A

१० सुरस्थाने] आश्रयस्थाने AS

११ सम्पतेत्] संवसेत् AS

१२ अर्थसिद्धये] आत्मसिद्धये AS

१४ कार्यकालविपत्तिं च व्यक्तां]कार्यकालव्यपेतं च व्यक्तं A

१५ वार्ताविशेषार्थान्॰ सर्वान्] वार्ताविशेषार्थ॰ सर्व A

१६ कुर्यादरिविमर्शनम्] कुर्वीतारिविकर्षणम् AS

१७ चरविकल्पप्रकरणम्] दूतचरविकल्पप्रकरणम् A

१८ मार्गात्] मौढ्यात् AS

१९ प्राज्ञः] राजा AS

२० आयत्तं चरे चर्या] आयाते चरचर्या AS

२१ वणिक्] बालः AS

२२ विवक्षितः] व्यवस्थितः AS

२३ प्रव्रजितश्चैव] प्रव्रजिता चैव A

२४ जाग्रत्स्वरिषु सुप्तोऽसौ] जाग्रन्नपि सुषुप्तो ऽसौ AS

२५ छिद्रमण्वप्यरेर्मुखम्] छिद्रं च परिपूरयेत् (read as ४०क) AS

२६ मज्जयेत्॰ पानपात्रम्] मार्जयेत्॰ यानपात्रम् A

२७ मालाकाराः] नानाकार्य-AS

२८ महामात्र-] महामात्रा A

२९ कल्पकाः स्नापकास्तथा] तल्पका व्ययकास्तथा AS

३० म्लेच्छितैः] मूर्छितैः AS

Sarga 14

१ यानस्तु] लाभस्तु AS

२ दृढं] दृढा AS

३ व्यवसायसमन्वितः] प्रभुशक्त्या समन्वितः AS

४ सदोत्साही] सदोत्थायी A

५ व्यसन्यधो ऽधो] व्यसत्यधो वा A

६ मरकः] मरणम् A

७ च] वा A

८ च] वा A

९ वाहनानि] वाहनादि A

१० त्राणं] स्थानं AS

११ विपद्यते] न विद्यते AS

१२ तत्तत्करोति च बहिर्] ततः करोति सुबहु AS

१३ दुःसाध्यान्] दुःसाधान् A

१४ शस्त्र] शुद्ध AS

१५ शस्त्र] शास्त्र A

१६ प्रवेशनम्] प्रवेदनम् A

१७ प्रशास्तृसूतसेनानी] प्रशास्त्रध्यक्षसेनानां AS

१८ चावरोपणम्] चावरोधनम् AS

१९ खनिद्वीपवनादीनां] स्ववृद्धिपवनादिनां AS

२० परिक्षेपः] परिक्लेश AS

२१ मुषिकाः शलभादयः] शलभा मूषकाः शूकाः AS

२२ मरणं] व्यसनं A

२३ अशस्त्रता]अशास्त्रता A

२४ घास] वास AS

२५ प्रतिहतं] रहितायं AS

२६ आशानिर्वेदभूयिष्ठम्] आशानिर्वेद्यभूमिष्ठम् A

२७ अरिमित्र॰ निविष्टं] अविमिश्र॰ विशिष्टं AS

२८ अन्यतः] अत्यन्तम् AS

२९ हताग्रवेगं शक्तं] हताग्रजमनासक्तं AS

३० निर्वेद॰ पूर्णाशत्वन्न] निर्वेद्य॰ पूर्णाशत्वात्तु A

३१ अनृत॰ यथार्हं] आवृत॰ अपूर्व AS

३२ मित्रं] मिश्रं AS

३३ तत्सामर्थ्यान्न] चासामर्थ्यान्न AS

३४ तदुद्धारादु] न युध्येत AS

३५ समुत्पतेत्] समुन्नयेत् AS

३६ The two lines are in opposite order in the two editions. I have followed the AS order.

३७ ह्राम्यं तन्मूढत्वात्] युद्धं मूढत्वान्न AS

३८ व्यसनानि॰ समुपेक्षेत] व्यसनादि॰ स्वमुपेक्षेत A

३९ पराभवन्ति] पराजयन्ते A

Sarga 15

१ पथि निवेश्यते] सन्तार्यते नृपः AS

२ विप्रियां वाचं] प्रियया वाचा AS

३ परुषं] अभीक्ष्णं AS

४ तेजस्विनं दीपयति] तेन च्छिन्नो नरपतिः AS

५ प्रियवाक्कर्मा] प्रियकर्मा यो AS

६ सद्धिः] षड्धिः AS

७ तं युक्त्यैव नयेद्दण्डं] तद्युक्ते ऽपनये दण्डघे AS

८ युक्तदण्डः] तत्र दण्डः AS

९   यानपातो] यानवतो AS
१० दोषा॰ पाटनम्] देशा॰ पातनम् A
११ उपगतैः] उपहितैः A
१२ सामन्त] आसन्न A
१३ स्वकुल्यैश्च] स्वकल्पैश्च AS
१४ लक्ष्येषु] लक्षेषु A
१५ तत्परिवर्जयेत्] तद्व्यसनं महत् AS
१६ लक्ष्येषु] लक्षेषु A
१७ मृगाणामप्यगम्यया] दुर्गया मृगगम्यया A
१८ नील॰ विरल] शीत॰ विटप AS
१९ श्वभ्र] शुभ्र AS
२० अगभीरजलाशयम्] सम्भूतजलदाशयम् AS
२१ सुपात्यमृग] मृगसंघातAS
२२ पुष्पवल्लीपिनद्धया] पुष्पपर्णावनद्धया A
२३ स्तम्भ] सम AS
२४ ये गुणाः प्रकीर्तिताः] यो गुणः॰ प्रकीर्तितः A
२५ क्रीडाप्रीतो नरपतिस्तांस्तत्र समवाप्नुयात्] क्रीडाप्रीतिर्नरपतिस्तं तत्र स्वयमाप्नुयात् A
२६ मृगयां मृगयुः] मृगायायां मृगा AS
२७ महतोऽपि क्षणान्नाशो धनस्य ह्रीविमुक्तता] महता रक्षणेनापि धनस्य द्राग्विमुक्तता AS
२८ तन्नकुशला] तत्र निपुणा AS
२९ तत्पश्चाद्] तत्पक्षाद् A
३० विरोध [comm]] निरोध A
३१ वमनं] गमनं AS
३२ अनर्थ] अनर्थ्य A
३३ तन्द्रा] तन्द्री A
३४ यत्र तत्र] यत्र यत्र A
३५ यत्र तत्र प्रवर्तनात्] तत्रतत्राप्रवर्तनात् A
३६ पटयति] घटयति AS

Sarga 16

१   विमुक्तः] वियुक्तः A
२   तत्रैष पक्षो व्यसनं ह्यनित्यं] तत्रैव पक्षो व्यसने हि नित्यं AS
३   प्रमृद्नन्] प्रमृग्यं AS
४   अत्यर्थमुष्णाप्रतितप्तकायाः] अन्धत्वमुष्ण्प्रवितप्तकायाः AS
५   सुतिं] च्युत A
६   वीरतमेन] धीरतरेण AS
७   अट्ट] अद्रि AS
८   नैकमत्यमनेकमुख्यं] चैकमत्यमनैकमत्य AS] AS(comm) नैकमत्यमनैकमत्य sic.
९   कोपात्] दोषात् AS

१०   सन्तोऽन्यतम] मन्त्रोद्यत AS

११   अभिसीम्नां] आनतानां A

१२   उत्पद्यमानो निपुणप्रचारैः...मन्त्रिभिः] उत्पाद्यमानं निपुणं प्रचारैः...सत्रिभिः A

१३   अप्यति] अथ च A

१४   शौचो] शौर्यो AS

१५   मानोन्नतं सभ्यमहार्यबुद्धिम्] अलोलुपं सत्यमहार्यमन्यैः A

१६   औत्पादिकी] आत्यन्तिकी AS

१७   नावाब्वृतं emended (I must thank Dániel Balogh for suggesting this
        emendation) नावादितः पत्तिबलानुयातैः A] नागावृतं पक्षबलानुपेतैः AS

१८   तज्जयुक्तं] तक्षयुक्तः AS

१९   विश्वासिताक्रान्तजनं] विश्वासिभिः क्रान्तजलं AS

२०   आत्मकल्पैः] इष्टतुल्यैः AS

२१   साधुमन्त्रं] साधुमन्त्रः AS

२२   दूतैश्च] दान्तैश्च AS

२३   ऽन्तपालम्] न पानम् AS

२४   स तु...चैकः] न हि...भेदः AS

२५   उपेत्य शत्रुम्] उपेतशस्त्रो AS

२६   आलोकित] आलोचित A

२७   उद्युक्तवृत्तिः] उद्धृतवृत्तिः A

Sarga 17

१   साट्टप्रतोलीप्राकारं महाखातसमावृतम् A] महाप्रतोलीप्राकारं महापरिखयावृतम् AS

२   पार्श्वैः] शृङ्गैः AS

३   महा] महन् A

४   प्रयत्नवान्] प्रपन्नवान् AS

५   सर्वकार्योन्मुखो] सर्वः कार्योन्मुखो A

६   तु सैन्यानां॰ आत्मनः] स्वसिज्ञानं॰ आयतम् AS

७   निद्रैरे] निर्द्रवैः AS

८   भूमिकाः] अन्वहं AS

९   विधूम्रैः॰ ध्वजः] विधूत॰ रजाः AS

१०   अभिदूषितः] विभूषितः AS

११   उद्भ्रमत्प्रज्वलच्छस्त्रो] उद्धूमः प्रज्वलच्छत्रो AS

१२   पूजितद्विपबृंहितः(क in A)] पूरितद्विपबृंहितः A] शस्त्रबृंहितकुञ्जरः AS

१३   अमन्दमत्तमातङ्गः] अमद्यमाद्यन्मातङ्गः AS

१४   घास] वास AS

Sarga 18

१   सहायैः] सत्त्वदैव AS

२   वधो॰ उच्यते] पूर्वो॰ इष्यते AS

३ प्रलिम्पन्॰ दृष्ट्वा] प्रविशन्॰ दृष्ट्वा AS

४ विक्रयम्] विषयम् AS

५ उपच्छन्द्य] उपगम्य AS

६ भीतश्च भीषितः] अतीतो ऽवभाषितः AS

७ पूर्वं सम्भाषितोऽनीचः] पूर्वसेनापतिर्नीचः AS

८ आहूय] आद्रूयAS

९ द्विष्यते] दूष्यते AS

१० व्यवहारश्च...कार] व्यवसायश्च...कर AS

११ परित्यक्तः] परित्रस्तः AS

१२ अत्युग्र] समन्यु AS

१३ घुणजग्धं] तृणदग्धं AS

१४ विहतं] विहित AS

१५ सन्तप्तं] श्रमेण A

१६ विप्रकृतैः] रिपुकृतैः AS

१७ आर्याः शीलनिबन्धनाः] स्पर्धाशीलनिबन्धनात् AS

१८ अलोभ॰ तानार्यान्परिचक्षते] अद्रोह॰ आर्यास्तान्प्रचक्षते] AS

१९ अवरुद्धांस्तत्कुलीनान्सामन्तांश्च विचक्षणः] अपराद्धांस्तु सुस्निग्धान्स्नेहोत्त्या मानदानतः AS

२० दर्शनम्] दर्शनः A

२१ देवानां] शिलानां A

२२ तमो ऽनिलो ऽचलो] तमोनिलीनता चैव AS

२३ संरब्धो] ससज्जं AS

२४ संस्रुतानां] संस्कृतानां AS

२५ कालज्ञो यथाकालं] सामज्ञो यथाकामं AS

२६ तृणेन] भृशेन AS

२७ प्रपातं] प्रयाणं AS

२८ सन्दंशबलेन] सन्दर्शबलेन AS

Sarga 19

१ ग्रहतारकम्] ग्रहतारकाः A

२ The AS ed. reads भृतम् throughout for भृतम्

३ सहसङ्कथनासनात्] सह संकटनाशनात् AS

४ सुखलाभात्] सिद्धलाभात् /सिद्धिलाभात् AS

५ असंख्येदेशकालत्वाद्] संख्यातदेशकालत्वाद् AS

६ मेदनयोगात् A]अमतयोग्यात् AS

७ विलोपे व्यसने (emended)] विलोपेऽव्यसने A] विलोपव्यसने AS

८ सुमानितैः] समावृतैः AS

९ चैव हि] वै जयः AS

१० उपेयात्] उपेक्ष्या AS

११ यानवस्तुनोः] पानवस्तुनि AS
१२ भूयो व्यायामयोधनम्] मन्त्रेणेति सुहृद्बलैः AS
१३ पीड्ये च] पाण्डित्ये AS
१४ योधयेत्] प्रेषयेत् AS
१५ नयं चण्डालवत्] नयं वावचनं AS
१६ अत्यूर्जितं...अभ्याशे तु] अविचित्तं...अभ्यासेन AS
१७ मन्त्र] यन्त्र A
१८ मन्त्रिसम्मतम्] मन्त्रसम्मितम् AS
१९ तत्त्वतः] यत्रतः AS
२० शुभ] श्रुत AS
२१ नरान्तर॰ अनुकम्पकम्] चरस्थिर॰ अनुकल्पकम् AS
२२ वर्मकर्मसमायोगे] धर्मकर्मसमायोगं AS
२३ शकुन] कुशल AS
२४ तज्ज्ञसेवितम्] तन्निषेवितम् AS
२५ वृष्टिभिः] वृत्तिभिः AS
२६ क्रान्तिं॰ तत्संविग्राभय] ग्लानिं॰ सत्पुंसामभय AS
२७ हन्तारं] भेत्तारं AS
२८ हतानां॰ क्षमम्] भयानां॰ लक्षणम् AS
२९ पराभवेषु॰ राज] परापरेषु॰ राज्य AS
३० स गोपायेद् A] संगोपयेद् AS
३१ च यद्बलम्] महद्बलधनम् AS
३२ सन्नद्ध] सम्बद्ध AS
३३ वीरवक्रया] धीरचक्रया AS
३४ आहित] हिम AS
३५ मरक AS] मरण A
३६ छत्रं] क्षित्रं AS
३७ स भूमिष्ठः] हि भूमिष्ठं A
३८ उपजापतः] उपजायते AS
३९ आकृष्ट] आह्रष्ट AS
४० पाशैः] स्पशैः AS
४१ सत्र A (restored from commentary)] सत्त्व restored from A's *mūla*] शत्रुम् AS
४२ सस्यसार्थे] आस्यमानं AS
४३ मन्दयलं] मर्दयन्तं AS
४४ अपाश्रयम्] व्यपाश्रयः AS
४५ नीहारतिमिराङ्गारश्वभ्राग्नि॰] नीहारस्तिमिरं गावः श्वभ्राद्रि॰ AS
४६ छद्म] सत्र AS
४७ साध्वप्रमत्तो॰ येन प्रकारेण] साधुप्रवृत्तो॰ यानप्रकारेण AS
४८ तिरयति धर्मं छद्मना] निरयति धर्मछद्मना AS

Sarga 20

१ पूर्वयायित्वं] पूर्वजापितं AS

२ विष्टिकर्म तत्] विश्वकर्मवत् AS

३ जातिः सत्त्वं॰ प्राणिता वर्ष्म वेगिता] जातिस्थानं॰ प्राणिनां मर्मवेगिता AS

४ शिल्पमुदग्रत्वं] शीघ्रगत्वं AS

५ सस्थूलस्थाणु] सस्थूणछिन्न AS

६ क्षिप्रलङ्घनीयदरा] अछिद्रालतिका विदरा AS

७ समा] आसना AS

८ निरुत्खाता] निरुद्धाना AS

९ स्थिरा चक्रसहा चैव] सर्वप्रचारयोग्या च AS

१० सुगम्य] उर्वरा AS

११ Beginning with this verse, I include three of the six verses that are found in parentheses in the Trivandrum edition and in brackets in the Asiatic Society edition, which are not commented on by either J or A. I have eliminated verses preceding and following verse fourteen which appear disconnected and repetitive. I have excluded a verbatim quote from the अर्थशास्त्र. The numbering has been adjusted.

१२ राजघातिने] राजघातने A

१३ साहस्रो ऽश्ववधः] सहस्रं च चापिवधे AS

१४ शिरो] गवां AS

१५ युग्यं] गुण्यं AS

१६ प्रहर्षयेत्] नराधिपः AS

१७ महागजान्] महाकुलान् AS

१८ रथस्थाने हयान्दद्यात्पदातींश्च हयाश्रये] उरसि स्थापयेन्नागान्प्रचण्डान्क्षयो रथान् AS

१९ चापस्तत्कुक्षिरेव च] चापो वै तद्विप्रर्ययः AS

२० झषास्यः] सुखराव्यः AS

२१ वाजिभिः] राजिभिः AS

२२ अष्टानीको] गजानीको AS

२३ कर्कट] कुक्कुट AS

२४ अथैकेन] अनीकेन AS

२५ सप्रतिग्रहः] अप्रतिग्रहः AS

२६ युक्तम्] व्यक्तम् AS

NOTES TO THE TRANSLATION

Chapter 1: Conquering the Senses

1 The "rod" (*daṇḍa*), which the king wields, refers both literally and figuratively to the royal power of legitimate violence in a comprehensive sense, encompassing everything from acts of war to criminal justice. See Introduction. The god of death, Yama, also wields a rod.

2 Vishnugupta was the legendary minister of Chandragupta Maurya, the traditional author of the founding text of the discipline, the *Arthaśāstra*. He is also known by the epithet Kautilya, "the crooked/crafty one," and later also by the name Chanakya.

3 The emphasis on sorcery is significant, since Kamandaki's signature technical innovation is to add three new political methods (*upāya*), two of which are "illusion" (*māyā*) and "magic" (*indrajāla*); the other one also relates to trickery or managing perceptions: "disregard" (*upekṣā*).

4 An empire that ruled from Magadha in the fourth and perhaps fifth centuries B.C.E., which the Mauryan Empire deposed.

5 Karttikeya (a.k.a. Skanda) is one of the sons of Parvati and Shiva, born to kill the evil demon Taraka.

6 This is one of the three fundamental "powers" (*śakti*; here: *mantraśakti*) that the king employs. The other two are "lordship" (*prabhuśakti*) and "determination" (*utsāhaśakti*). See Introduction.

7 Chandragupta Maurya, founder of the Mauryan Empire (c. 324–297 B.C.E.).

8 There is a pun here: the people, *prajā*, would consider him a lord of people, *prajāpati*. Prajapati is also the name of a god, sometimes conceived to be identical with the creator god Brahma.

9 *Dharma*, "righteousness order/law"; *artha*, "power/prosperity/ political economy"; *kāma*, "pleasure/domestic pleasure."

10 The commentary tells the story that Vaijavana was a legendary king devoted to righteousness, who thereby ruled the earth for a long time and attained heaven, despite his ancestors having made a deal with a demon to avoid death by compromising dharma. Nahusha was exactly the opposite: he had attained the position of Indra, but because of lust for the latter's wife,

turned into a snake and entered hell in bodily form.

11 This is one of the most general terms for both the disciplines and texts of systematic thought in early South Asia; it is often used as a term for systematic thought/science itself, as opposed to verbal art (*kāvya*). The term immediately calls to mind early works on dharma (law and sacred custom), but includes political science and all the other branches of science and philosophy.

12 The logical school's (Nyaya) understanding is that perception of succession requires a succession of perceptions, which in turn requires an organ, the mind (*manas*), to process them. If all knowledge were simultaneous, this organ would be superfluous. This is parallel to the understanding of the need for the self (*ātman*) as unifying substratum.

13 This discussion of the mind as by nature sequential in its knowledge and apprehension, along with the basic understanding of the self and its conjunction with the mind articulated here, are drawn from classical Nyaya philosophy.

14 This discussion of the "inner instrument," as well as the enumeration of the various senses, is of course not unique to this tradition and was quintessentially spelled out by the early Samkhya school.

15 The knowledge-oriented senses (*jñānendriya,* or here, *buddh-īndriya*) are the first five senses referred to at 1.33, ears, skin, eyes, tongue, and nose, as opposed to the action-oriented senses (*karmendriya*), which are the five faculties referred to immediately after: anus, genitals, hands, feet, and faculty of speech. This classification is most well-known from the Samkhya school of philosophy.

16 Literally, subtract the mind or produce a state of "mindlessness" (*nirmanaskatā*).

17 Pandu, progenitor of the heroes of the *Mahābhārata* epic was cursed to die during intercourse after a hunting accident in which he killed a sage-couple having sex in the forest, who had taken on the appearance of wild deer through the ascetic power of shape-shifting. They cursed him because it is forbidden to kill animals while they are mating, so that if he had followed the rules, the accident would never have happened (*Mbh.* 1.173). Nala, famed king of the Nishadha tribe, temporarily forsook his wife Damayanti after losing everything in a dice match (*Mbh.* 3.50ff.). In the "Book

of the Clubs" (*Mausalaparvan*) of the *Mahābhārata,* Krishna's clan, the Vrishnis, completely annihilate each other down to the last man, in a drunken brawl, after being cursed.

18   King Dandaka raped the sage Shukra's daughter Ara, and from him the Dandaka forest takes its name. Angry at his deed, Shukra burnt up Danda's land, leaving it a wasteland or jungle. The story is told in the last book of the *Vālmīki Rāmāyaṇa* (*Uttarakāṇḍa* chapters 70–72). The reference to Janamejaya is to the story of his anger at his father's death by snakebite, and ensuing sacrificial massacre of all snakes. The commentary says Aila appropriated everything from the four orders of society and was finally stoned to death. The demon Vatapi and his brother Ilvala used to kill Brahmans by feeding them meat, which was actually Ilvala himself shape-shifting. Once eaten he would pop out of their stomachs, thereby killing them. According to the commentary this made the demons excited, and the sage Agastya used their carefreeness to trick them and kill them both (*Vālmīki Rāmāyaṇa,* Book 3, chapter 10). Finally, the reference is to the famous story told in the *Rāmāyaṇa* of the demon-king Ravana's refusal to return Sita, the abducted wife of Rama, which leads to a war with the rakshasas and finally, Ravana's death. Dambhodbhava was a very proud warrior who defeated the three worlds. He longed for a worthy rival in battle. The sage Narada suggested he fight the sage Nara, who defeated him with a blade of grass.

19   Jamadagnya (a.k.a. Parashurama) is a legendary warrior-Brahman and avatar of Vishnu, who annihilated the entire Kshatriya community twenty-one times. Ambarisha is a famed king of the Ikshvaku lineage.

20   I have indicated variations of meter here and throughout by numbering the verses separately.

Chapter 2: Branches of Knowledge

1   The king is identified with *daṇḍa,* "the rod," a term that stands for legitimate violence in all its aspects, from war to criminal justice (see the Introduction), here rendered alternately as "rod," "coercion," and "rod of coercion." The term for "governance" here is *daṇḍanīti,* literally the "politics" or "leading/directing" of the rod. Finally the author glosses the term *nīti* in the sense of politics, which comes from the root √*nī,* "to direct/lead."

2   *Dharma, artha, kāma, mokṣa.*

3   That is, "and not 'finding'." There are two identical verbal roots √*vid* in Sanskrit, each with a separate conjugation (though prehistorically one and the same): one meaning "to know" and one meaning "to find." The author is addressing the possibility that someone could etymologize the former in terms of the latter, which he considers wrong.

4   Respectively *śruti* and *smṛti.*

5   The *trivarga:* dharma, power, and pleasure (*dharma, artha, kāma*).

6   *Mātsyanyāya:* the proverbial condition in which the big fish eats the small, a term for anarchy or the Hobbesian state of nature.

Chapter 3: Demarcating Good Conduct

1   Incantations, mantras, were believed to cure snakebite.

2   The term here is *āstikya,* which means, very literally, the state of believing that something "is" (*asti*), which makes one an *āstika,* and which entails believing in the tenets of Brahmanical thought, including the status of the Vedas, karma, gods, heaven, and so on. It is used in contrast to other ancient heterodox schools, such as Carvakas ("hedonist-materialists") and Buddhists, which reject the authority of the Vedas, and are often referred to as "nihilists" (*nāstika*) by Brahmanical thinkers.

3   The term here is *guru,* which has been left untranslated in other contexts where it clearly means teacher or preceptor. Here it seems to be used in a wider sense to encompass one's elders broadly conceived.

Chapter 4: The State-Elements

1   Compare *Raghuvaṃśa* 1.24: "From imparting discipline to the subjects, protecting them, and supporting them, he was their father; their (biological) fathers were merely occasions for their birth."

2   The commentary *J* reflects that one places something near "in order to examine the state" of a thing (*bhāvaparīkṣaṇārtham*).

3   There is a slightly abrupt transition here to a discussion of the next of the state-elements (*prakṛti*) under consideration, namely the "realm" (*rāṣṭra*).

4   Again a slightly abrupt transition to discussion of the next of the

state-elements (*prakṛti*), namely the "fortification," "fortified town," or "fort" (*durga*).

5 The next state-element in the series: the treasury (*kośa*).

Chapter 5: The Conduct of the King and His Retinue

1 A mythical tree that literally blossoms forth the objects of one's desire: *kalpavṛkṣa*. Wish-granting gems (*cintāmaṇi*) and wish-granting cows (*kāmadhenu*) are parallel; and like the tree, they are often deployed figuratively to express someone's extraordinary generosity.

2 The transition to the discussion of displeased masters could not be more abrupt and is only really flagged in verse 47 below.

Chapter 6: Removing Anti-State Elements

1 The sages commit righteous violence by sacrificing animals in the Vedic ritual.

2 "Noble men" *ārya:* an old Vedic and Indo-Iranian term for those who perform the sacrifice, speak proper language, and uphold other customs; contrasted in the *Ṛg Veda* with terms meaning something like "slave" or "foreigner" *dāsa, dasyu*, etc. Later a term for higher-status members of Brahmanical society, i.e., "noble men who know Vedic lore."

3 That is, they falsely confess to the guards that they have been hired by the traitor to kill the king.

4 The term translated here as "thorny anti-state elements," *kaṇṭaka*, literally "thorn," is a technical one in Sanskrit statecraft, referring to, as Olivelle, Brick, and McClish define it, a "social miscreant, criminal, seditious person" (2015).

Chapter 7: Guarding Princes

1 The identification of the *bhṛṅgarāja* with the fork-tailed shrike is less than certain; so too in the following verses the identification of the *cakora* with the chukar partridge and the *krauñca* with the curlew.

2 Kiratas are the stock tribal figure of the mountains in Sanskrit literature (as the Nishadha forms the stock tribal figure of the forest), often represented as dwarves.

3 Both commentaries outline these legends in brief, but *J* provides the most information. Bhadrasena was a king of Kalinga (modern

Orissa) whose younger brother and wife were having an affair and contrived to kill him. The king of Karusha was killed in a conspiracy of one of his sons and the boy's mother, when he promised the kingdom to another son. The queen of Kashi distracted and poisoned her husband with honeyed rice as he was preparing to rape her. The king of Sauvira angered his queen through excessively harsh words, according to *U*, and she took her revenge by administering poison. Vairupya, king of Avanti, was killed by one of his wives who had been falsely accused by her co-wives and was facing some kind of disaster (*vipatti*). Jarushya king of Ayodhya was spending too much time with his other wives, and one of his queens murdered him in her jealousy. Viduratha spent too much money on prostitutes, and his wife Veni got her revenge with a dagger. Chapter 78 of Varahamihira's *Bṛhatsaṃhitā* briefly mentions the story of the king of Kashi and that of Viduratha. *Arthaśāstra* 1.20.16 likewise briefly mentions each of the same stories, while Kalhana's *Rājataraṅgiṇī* briefly mentions the story of Viduratha (8.1277).

Chapter 8: The Mandala's Center

1 Territory conceived as a circle orbited by other concentric circles. See Introduction.

2 The term used throughout is *vijigīṣu*, literally "one who wishes to conquer," which I translate as "expansionist king," and occasionally just "conqueror." All discussions of military strategy in the *Nītisāra* and *Arthaśāstra* alike are addressed to this ideal figure: the king who wishes to expand without limit, and thereby become a "wheel-turning emperor" (*cakravartin*), i.e., one who rules vast—if not all—territories. See Introduction.

3 "Rear adversary" *pārṣṇigrāha:* "ally who attacks the *vijigīṣu* [expansionist king] from the rear ... As the *pārṣṇigrāha* is the natural ally of the forward enemy ... he can be called upon to open a second front behind the attacking king, and thus force the king to fight on two fronts" (Olivelle, Brick, and McClish 2015: 250–251). "Rear supporter" *ākranda:* "the rescuer from an attack at the rear by the *pārṣṇigrāha*" (Olivelle, Brick, and McClish 2015: 74).

4 Branches: the allies and enemies respectively of the four main kings. Roots: expansionist king, enemy, intermediate one, and neutral one. Leaves: the seven state-elements (minister, kingdom,

fortification, treasury, rod of coercion, ally, and king) for each of the twelve kings of the mandala. Trunks: destiny and human will. (*J* says the edifice is based on both celestial action [i.e., destiny] and human action: *daive ca mānuṣe karmaṇi sthitam*). Flowers: the six chief tactics: alliance, war, advance, halt, duplicity, and taking refuge. Fruits: loss, maintenance, and enlargement of territory.

5 In Valmiki's *Rāmāyaṇa*, Vibhishana was the brother of Ravana, king of *rākṣasas*. He defected from his brother's camp, joined the side of Rama, and ultimately became postwar king of the *rākṣasas*. Valin was king of the monkeys. His brother Sugriva betrayed him and made a deal with Rama to assassinate him.

6 Trishiras was an ascetic with three heads. Indra feared his ascetic power (*tapas*) and decapitated him.

Chapter 9: Tactic One: Types of Alliances

1 Rama agreed to kill Sugriva's elder brother, the monkey king Valin, in exchange for the monkeys' help in locating his kidnapped wife (*Rāmāyaṇa, Kiṣkindhākāṇḍa*).

2 Presumably the name of this variety of alliance comes from the fact that his own man will not have to appear because the enemy will carry out the task entirely on his own.

3 The legendary warrior-Brahman Parashurama, "Axe-Rama," also known as Rama Jamadagnya, annihilated the Kshatriya caste twenty-one times to avenge his father's murder. He is considered one of Vishnu's primary avatars.

4 Also known as Parashurama (Axe-Rama); see note 3 above.

5 Indra, the king of the gods, killed the serpent demon Vritra in the *Ṛg Veda*. Some later versions of the story add that he tricked the demon with a nonaggression pact.

6 The exact interpretation of this verse is slightly tricky even if the overall sense is clear. The term *rājyālīḍha* "licked by the kingdom" is evocative but strange. It is taken by *U* simply as *rājyalakṣmyālaṅkṛta* "ornamented by royal majesty"; *J*, on the other hand, does not explain the expression itself, but sees the verse as an illustration of the fact that actions similar to those of Indra vis à vis Vritra can still be observed in present times (*tathādyatve 'py ayaṃ vyavahāro dṛśyate*). The point about the king's way of life being "totally different" is thus supported in the case of *J* by the implication that son can kill father and father son, and thus

everyone has to be careful and/or ruthless.

7 Sunda and Upasunda were two demons who fought over the nymph (*apsaras*) Tilottama and killed each other.

8 Diti was the mother of a class of demons, the *daityas*. Indra destroyed the child in her womb (who was destined to kill him in revenge for a previous attack on Diti's womb) when he found her sleeping in a vulnerable position.

Chapter 10: Tactic Two: Types of War

1 Note the double emphasis on "knowledge" in the mention both of "seizure of the means of knowledge" earlier in the list and here with "damage to knowledge." But it is far from clear what is meant by the key term here, *jñāna*. *J* notes the two discussions of learning and argues that "seizure" (*apahāra*) and "damage" (*vighāta*) are two distinct issues. He also states that the knowledge under consideration is directly political, i.e., that we are talking about preventing access to political science (of precisely the type we are reading here in the *Nītisāra*), without which formal learning a king will be "more immature" (*bāliśatara*). "Seizure" may refer very concretely to a library-archive (there are well-documented cases of kings seizing each other's libraries as war booty). About "damage," *J* asserts the text is referring to teachers (*ācārya*), access to whom one jealously (*īrṣyayā*) strives to prevent, just as Duryodhana jealously tried to interfere with Arjuna's martial arts training with the teacher Drona in the *Mahābhārata*.

2 The mandala is the geometrical model of interstate relations, with kingdoms represented as concentric circles (on which see Introduction and chapter 8). *U* glosses *maṇḍaladūṣaṇa* "subverting the mandala's stability" as "within the twelve-kingdom mandala, corrupting into hostility a kingdom which was not corrupted into hostility" (*maṇḍalasya dvādaśarājakasya madhye aduṣṭasyāpi dūṣaṇam duṣṭatvāpādanam*). This could mean something more on the side of appearance, i.e., making a friendly kingdom seem hostile, but it seems more likely to mean actually provoking hostilities (whether by generating false suspicions or otherwise). The arrangement of alliances and hostilities within the mandala interstate-system is obviously very delicate (on which, again, see chapter 8).

3 Twenty *casus belli* are here presented, followed by a discussion of

the means for preventing, stopping, or concluding some, but not all, of them. The discussion is brief, considering the weightiness of the topic.

4   The methods for stopping or preventing the various types of war are presented again briefly, and somewhat confusingly. Only some are clearly referenced, whereas some of the methods may have broader reach and address additional *casus belli*, however implicitly. This passage covers the first four causes listed earlier, and then skips to causes nine, eleven, and twelve. First, (1) usurpation of the kingdom; (2) abduction of women; (3) occupation of fortifications; and (4) occupation of territories. Next, (11) damage to one's economic interests; and (12) affront to moral order. Finally, (9) damage to one's territorial interests.

5   Here two causes are covered together, (5) seizure of the means of knowledge and (10) damage to knowledge.

6   These are countermeasures for wars launched (16) to remedy dishonor; and possibly also (15) subverting the mandala's stability.

7   Here we have clearly covered two causes: (17) because one's kinsmen have been killed; (20) because of vying for the same objective. Several others could be implicitly referenced in the discussion of "appropriation of wealth."

8   The phrasing is slightly indirect. *J* specifies that war arising among "prominent men" (*mahājana*) refers to war arising from (7) recklessness. This passage probably also covers (8) arrogance.

9   This passage clearly covers two causes: (17) because one's kinsmen have been killed; and (18) because of withdrawal of favor to people one has vowed to favor.

10 Here begins what seems to be a separate and complementary discussion of types of war and how to prevent, stop, or conclude them.

11 As noted in the Introduction, Kalidasa's *Raghuvaṃśa* (4.36) offers a parallel where the Suhma kingdom adopts "the way of the bamboo" (*vaitasīṃ vṛttim āśritya*) vis à vis the hero Raghu. On the way of the bamboo, also see *Arthaśāstra* 12.1.1.

12 For the sake of clarity I have inserted the implicit "which bends and does not break" and "which hisses and bites when provoked." The text says simply "way of the bamboo" (*vaitasavṛtti*) and "way of the snake" (*bhujaṅgavṛtti*).

13 The text returns repeatedly to three metaphors drawn from the

natural world: (1) the way of the snake (*bhujaṅgavṛtti*), which hisses and bites at the slightest provocation; (2) the way of the bamboo (*vaitasavṛtti*), which bends without breaking; and (3) the way of the lion (*siṃhavṛtti*), which ferociously attacks and devours the enemy at the opportune moment.

14 As noted in the Introduction, Bharavi's *Arjuna and the Hunter* or *Kirātārjunīya* (1.4) offers an especially vivid parallel, and a similar message is found at Valmiki's *Rāmāyaṇa* 3.31.9.

Chapter 11: Tactics Three, Four, Five, and Six: Advance, Halt, Duplicity, and Taking Refuge

1 Hanuman and the sun god, Surya, joined forces against the demon Rahu who causes eclipses. Hanuman, the monkey hero, was the son of the wind god. He broke his jaw after falling to the earth when leaping higher and higher in the sky, first toward the sun, then the bodiless demon Rahu (who swallows the moon and thus causes the lunar eclipse), and then finally toward Indra's elephant Airavata. Indra shot him down with his lightning bolt.

2 The significant detail from the story of Shalya is supplied for clarity.

3 Dhanamjaya is a name of Arjuna, one of the heroes of the *Mahābhārata* epic who fought off these two allied groups of demons on behalf of the gods. Hiranyapura was the grandiose city of the Kalakeya demons, while the Nivatakavacas were another demon group that joined the Kalakeyas in an attack on the gods. Both groups had received a boon that they could not be killed by gods, and thus Arjuna's support was requested because he was nominally human. Hiranyapura was the main target so Arjuna practiced "disregard" toward the Nivatakavacas in order to lay siege to it. The story of the demons' slaughter is told at *Mahābhārata* 3.170.

4 The name Ravana literally means "he who causes one to cry out." Ravana is here said to make his enemies scream and cry.

5 Krishna once stole the tree from Indra's celestial garden.

6 Because of his ineptitude Rukmin was not wanted by either side when the two factions drew up their forces in the *Mahābhārata*.

7 The crow's single eyeball moves undetected from one socket to the next. "The crow's eyeball" (*kākākṣin*) is a standard figurative way

of talking about one thing that does double duty. The back story is that a crow once pecked at Sita's breast, and to punish it, Rama destroyed one of its eyes, leaving a single eye that rolls between two sockets.

8   The underlying idea here seems to be that "independent duplicity" comes from within, i.e., is conditioned by survival and/or opportunism. In contrast "dependent duplicity" comes from without, i.e., is conditioned by the fact of being a career mercenary per se, where duplicity is an elementary exigency of collecting separate salaries from two antagonistic factions.

9   Eldest of the heroes in the *Mahābhārata* epic, he lost his kingdom in a rigged dice-match and later regained it through war.

Chapter 12: Types of Strategy

1   The six tactics (*guṇa*) are those which the preceding three chapters have discussed: (1) alliance (*sandhi*), chapter 9; (2) war (*vigraha*), chapter 10. Chapter 11 treats the remaining four: (3) advance (*yāna*); (4) halt (*āsana*); (5) duplicity (*dvaidhībhāva*); and (6) taking refuge (*saṃśraya*).

2   Here there is a pun on the word *mantra*, which can mean both "strategy" and "sacred incantation." The term translated as "evil spirit" is often synonymous with *rākṣasa*, the earth-dwelling demons who are depicted, especially in the *Rāmāyaṇa* of Valmiki, as defilers of sacrifices.

3   The *Atharva Veda* is the last of the four Vedas and is known especially as a work of magic spells and incantations.

4   The verse contains an implicit comparison between, on the one hand, the application of established political tactics against an unruly enemy, and the elephant trainer's use of honed techniques in taming a wild elephant.

5   There is a tradition of using magical *mantras* against both snakes and the effect of snakebite.

Chapter 13: An Emissary's Conduct

1   Since he might talk in his sleep and reveal his inner thoughts. See 12.46 and the discussion beginning with 13.16.

2   "Seize crops and other supplies": presumably to stockpile in preparation for war.

3   "Thorn-like anti-state elements": as noted in chapter 6, the term

here, *kaṇṭaka,* literally, "thorn," is a technical one in Sanskrit statecraft, referring to criminals, troublemakers, and anti-state actors.

Chapter 14: The Value of Determination

1 "Emissaries' work": to forge an alliance—see 13.34.

2 "Vices and calamities": the term *vyasana* encompasses a continuum from vice or moral disorder to the disorder of a disease or natural disaster. The two sides of the continuum are connected perhaps via the more or less explicit notion that "bad things happen to bad people." At times I translate as "vice," at times "calamity" or "disaster," and at times "vice and calamity."

3 Tracing the noun *vyasana* to the verbal prefix and root from which it is formed *vi* + √*as* (4P) "to throw/shoot," the author simply adds that the underlying metaphor is throwing away "the good" (*śreyas*).

4 Both commentaries specify the magical mantras of the *Atharva Veda.*

5 "City-people," *paura,* stands directly for the wealthy, influential citizens.

6 This may sound pleonastic: namely that coercion fosters itself. I take "reinforcing one's own power of coercion" (*svadaṇḍasya parigrahaḥ*) to mean that by winning in war, skirmishes, or in an arms race–type scenario, the coercive capability is (1) not damaged in a material sense, and (2) conversely in a broader projective sense, the coercive capability is magnified, akin to the way today's arms manufacturers' stock prices go up when the weapons are used somewhere (however unethically or illegally).

7 One of Kamandaki's signature methods. See chapter 18 for a detailed discussion.

Chapter 15: The Seven Vices

1 Namely: ruler, minister, realm, fortification, treasury, army, and ally.

2 A *yojana* is about nine miles. See Apte 1992.

3 The world-guardian deities (*lokapāla*), who guard the cardinal points, are Indra (East), Yama (South), Varuna (West), and Kubera (North).

4 Rukmin challenged the king Balabhadrarama to a game of

314

dice, since the latter had the reputation of being a bad player. Yet he lost everything, and when he failed to concede, Balabhadrarama killed him.

5   Dantavaktra, literally "tooth-face," was an incarnation of the demon Krodhavasha, who was king of the Karusha land.

6   The Andhakas and Vrishnis were groups within Krishna's clan, the Yadavas, who killed each other with makeshift maces in a drunken brawl after being cursed. This episode is the central episode of the *Mahābhārata's* sixteenth book, "The Book of the Clubs" (*Mausalaparvan*).

7   While drunk, Shukra the demons' priest was tricked into eating his favorite student, Kacha.

Chapter 16: A Conqueror and His Expeditions

1   The power of lordship (*prabhuśakti*), the power of strategy (*mantraśakti*), and the power of determination (*utsāhaśakti*). See Introduction.

2   This entire chapter is in the longer and slightly fancier *triṣṭubh* meter, in contrast to the modest *śloka* used throughout the bulk of every other chapter. It thus has a more lyrical feel, as do many passages describing battle and conquest throughout the work.

3   This verse is potentially one of the *Nītisāra's* most puzzling. The expression *naikamatyam* "not single-minded" or "not unanimous" sounds strange as a putative virtue, considering the overarching emphasis on the singularity of command and rule throughout the work. However, the basic idea of multiple fronts combined with multiple perspectives seems to shine through clearly enough. I must thank Whitney Cox for some ingenious suggestions regarding this verse's interpretation.

4   In other words, the main force should shift to focus on the problem area to the rear, while a subsidiary force guards the front.

5   *Atidhārmikatā*: "excessive righteousness"; "excessive devotion to dharma." *J* specifies that this is "concern for the other world" (*paralokāpekṣaṇam*), i.e., excessive concern for divine rewards and punishments.

6   In this and the following two verses, the discussion of virtues specific to members of the king's retinue segues into an interlude on broader virtue-prerequisites for successful conquest: the three royal powers (*śakti*), intellectual cultivation, as well as human

effort and destiny. Verse 35 returns to the conquest-expedition, which provides the immediate material context for these virtues.

7 The term *yoganidrā* (lit., "yoga-sleep") is widespread in modern yoga practice, but has a complex and somewhat obscure history, referring in its early usage to a sleep-inducing goddess as well as Vishnu's sleep in between cycles of creation-destruction. See Birch and Hargraves (2015) for a detailed discussion. It must refer here to some kind of meditative state distinct from ordinary sleep, and also distinct from the modern yoga-studio meaning, yet perhaps not utterly alien to the latter.

8 I translate *nāḍikayā*—a word that should mean something like "through a straw" (for drinking), "through a reed," or "through a stalk" (as of a lotus)—as "through a series of exchanges," though it is far from clear exactly what it means here. *U* understands it in the most straightforward manner as "like someone might take water through a lotus stalk-straw" (*yathā kaścit padmanālena jalam ādadīta*), while *J* glosses it as "through sequence of routes/passages/exchanges" (*sañcāraparamparayā*). I think the underlying metaphor of a stalk or straw is basically about a straight, uninterrupted line, i.e., a sequence, or "series," and thus follow *J* in the less obvious but more contextually comprehensible meaning.

9 Long arms hanging down to the knees are considered auspicious and often attributed to heroes in Sanskrit literature.

Chapter 18: The Various Methods

1 One commentary (*J*) identifies wisdom here with the virtues of the intellect enumerated at 4.21: "The virtues of the intellect are willingness to listen, learning, comprehension, retention, positive and negative reasoning, the understanding of things, as well as knowing the truth."

2 The author of commentary *J* seems to identify "good strategy" with the five components of success specified at 12.36: "Success is said to have five components: allies, methods, order of time and place, disaster-prevention, and successful conclusion."

3 "A Brahman merely by birth": by birth alone and not ritual observances, Vedic education, etc.

4 The reference here seems to be to Indra's donation, from the side of the gods to the side of the demons, which eventually led

to better relations between the two camps. The demons' priest Shukra accepted Kacha from the side of the gods as his disciple. The demons were infuriated and killed Kacha several times. Each time Shukra used his magical power of reviving the dead (*mṛtasaṃjīvanī*) to bring him back to life. Eventually Kacha passed on the knowledge of the revivification-magic to the gods, and so the gift economy seems to have worked both ways. See Mani 1975.

5 Devayani was pushed into a well by Vrishaparvan's daughter Sharmistha. Vrishaparvan later punished her by making her Devayani's servant.

6 In the *Mahābhārata,* the Kauravas refused to grant any land to their cousins the Pandavas, at which point war became inevitable.

7 One commentary (*U*) tells that Shanda and Amarka were sons of sages and students of Shukra who became masters of the esoteric and magical methods of war taught by him. They threatened to unseat Indra, Vedic king of gods. The gods gave them a share of the sacrifice, which alienated them from their teacher, and they were subsequently defeated. *J* says that they were brothers of Sunda and Upasunda, and the gods turned them against each other by employing the nymph (*apsaras*) Tilottama.

8 "Understands coercion" *daṇḍavit: J* understands this especially in terms of the king potentially being on the receiving end of coercion from his generals, since they have the power of coercion (*daṇḍa*) themselves and can use it against him. Thus the other methods should be used.

9 All examples from the *Mahābhārata.* The heroes' common wife Draupadi was being sexually harassed by King Virata's brother Kichaka while they were living incognito in his palace. Draupadi set up a rendezvous with Kichaka; Bhima showed up dressed as a woman, and then killed him in secret. Hidimba was a female *rākṣasa* with whom Bhima later had a child. Her brother was incensed at her romance with Bhima and threatened to kill her, at which point Bhima killed him.

Chapter 19: An Army's Strengths and Weaknesses

1 Presumably being in larger numbers would give the soldiers more possibility of a successful mutiny, and thus a larger force in this context would be more prone to dissension.

2 The reference is to an outcaste (*cāṇḍāla*) engaging in the extremely

low-status occupation of hunting, but doing it effectively. Cf. *Bhaṭṭikāvya* 12.33 where there is a reference to the "dog and boar" method.

3 "Thorns" (*kaṇṭaka*) seems literally intended here, i.e., the physical task of keeping up the grounds around the fortification, but it should be noted that this same term is more often used figuratively for political obstacles in general so that whether or not intended as a *double entendre,* the latter resonance cannot but present itself to the reader's mind.

4 "Commander" *nāyaka:* Olivelle, Brick, and McClish (2015) define as "mid-level military commander who commands 1,000 military *aṅga*s (e.g., 1 chariot, five horses, and 30 infantrymen according to AŚ 10.59–11)."

5 See chapter 20 for a detailed and technical discussion of the "battle array" (*vyūha*).

6 The vulnerable moments are mentioned in verses 19.50–53.

7 One commentary (*J*) glosses the subject as "the expansionist king" (*vijigīṣu*). I translate with an indefinite subject, since the general was just being discussed, and to one degree or another, the passage evokes an inclusive, complex agency encompassing both the general and the king.

8 Or alternatively, following the AS reading, "coal" and "fire" are replaced with "cows" and "mountain." Presumably the coal would be smeared on the hideout to camouflage it.

9 The Kaurava general Drona's son, Ashvatthaman, slaughtered large numbers of sleeping warriors in the Pandava camp during a nocturnal raid in revenge for his father's death in battle (itself accomplished by devious, underhanded tactics). The story is recounted in the tenth book of the *Mahābhārata: The Nocturnal Raid* (*Sauptikaparvan*).

Chapter 20: Elephants, Cavalry, Chariots, and Foot Soldiers

1 Beginning with this verse, I include three of the six verses that are found in parentheses in the Trivandrum edition and in brackets in the Asiatic Society edition, which are not commented on by either *J* or A. I have eliminated these types of verses preceding and following verse 14, which appear disconnected and repetitive, and have also excluded a verbatim quote from the *Arthaśāstra.* The numbering has been adjusted.

2   The commentaries specify that these variations are the crevice (only sides extended), firmed up (only chest extended), and the unbearable (only wings extended); their counter variations are the bow (sides retracted, everything else extended), the bow's belly (chest retracted, everything else extended), and the foundation (wings retracted, everything else extended). The wings and chest can be extended or retracted together, which yields the good foundation (wings extended, sides midway, and chest retracted) and its counter: the eagle (chest extended, wings retracted).

3   Here for the sake of clarity material from the commentary is included in parentheses.

4   Which gives the fish-face and army-face arrays, respectively.

5   Which yields the armlet and the very indomitable arrays, respectively.

BIBLIOGRAPHY

Editions and Translations

Kamandakiya Nitisara or the Elements of Polity. 1896. Translated by Manmatha Natha Dutt. Calcutta: H. C. Dass.

The Nitisara of Kamandaka with the Commentary Jayamangala of Shankararya. 1912. Edited by Ganapati Shastri. Travancore: Trivandrum Sanskrit Series.

Kāmandakīyanītisāraḥ. 1958. Edited by Rajeshwar Shastri Dravid, Ganapathi Shastri Hebbar, et al. 2 vols. Pune: Ananda Ashram Sanskrit Series (*Ānandāśramasaṃskṛtagranthāvaliḥ*). [With both commentaries: *Jayamaṅgalā* and *Upādhyāyanirapekṣā*.]

The Nītisāra by Kāmandaki. 1982. Edited by Rajendralala Mitra. Revised and translated by Sisir Kumar Mitra. Kolkata: The Asiatic Society. [With the commentary *Upādhyāyanirapekṣā*.] 1st edition, 1849.

Il Nītisāra Di Kāmandaki. 1899–1904. Translated by Carlo Formichi. *Giornale della Società asiatica italiana* 12–17.

I Primi Principi Della Politica Secondo Kâmandaki. 1925. Translation, introduction, and notes by Carlo Formichi. Rome: Instituto Romano Editoriale. First version published serially in: *Giornale della Società Asiatica Italiano* 12–17, *parte seconda*, 1899–1904.

Other Sources

Ali, Daud. 2004. *Courtly Culture and Political Life in Early Medieval India.* Cambridge: Cambridge University Press.

———. 2007. "Violence, Courtly Manners, and Lineage Formation in Early Medieval India." *Social Scientist* 35, 9/10: 3–21.

Apte, Vaman Shivaram. 1992. *The Practical Sanskrit English Dictionary.* Rev. enl. ed. Kyoto: Rinsen.

Bharavi. 2016. *Arjuna and the Hunter.* Edited and translated by Indira Viswanathan Peterson. Murty Classical Library of India 8. Cambridge, Mass.: Harvard University Press.

Bhaṭṭi. 1934. *Bhaṭṭikāvya.* Edited by Vināyak Nārāyan Shāstrī Joshi and Vāsudev Lakṣmaṇ Śāstrī Paṇśikar. With Jayamaṅgalā. Bombay: Nirnaya-Sagara Press.

Birch, Jason, and Jaqueline Hargreaves. 2015. "Yoganidrā: An Under-standing of the History and Context." Luminescent Blogspot: https://www.theluminescent.org/2015/01/yoganidra.html.

Chattopadhyaya, Brajadulal. 1994. The Making of Early Medieval India. Delhi: Oxford University Press.

Corpus Inscriptionum Indicarum III: Inscriptions of the Early Gupta Kings and Their Successors. 1888. Edited by J. F. Fleet. Calcutta: Superintendent of Government Publishing.

Falk, Harry. 2009. "The Name of Vema Takhtu." In Exegisti Monu-menta: Festschrift in Honour of Nicholas Sims-Williams, ed. Werner Sundermann, Almut Hintze, and François de Blois. Wiesbaden: Verlag.

Fernquest, Jon. 2008. "The Pali Imaginaire of Pre-modern Burmese Warfare and History." Unpublished working paper.

Kalhaṇa. 2003. Rājataraṅgiṇī. Vol. 3. Edited by Aurel Stein. Delhi: Motilal Banarsidass.

Kālidāsa. 2003. Raghuvaṃśa. The Raghupañcikā of Vallabhadeva Being the Earliest Commentary on the Raghuvaṃśa of Kālidāsa. Edited by Dominic Goodall and Harunaga Isaacson. Groningen: Egbert Forstein.

Kautilya. 1969. The Kauṭilīya Arthaśāstra. 3 vols. Critical edition, translation, and notes by K. P. Kangle. Delhi: Motilal Banarsidass. Reprint, 2010.

——. 1992. The Arthashastra. Edited, rearranged, translated, and introduced by L. N. Rangarajan. Delhi: Penguin.

——. 2013. King, Governance, and Law in Ancient India: Kauṭilya's Arthaśāstra. Annotated translation by Patrick Olivelle. Oxford and New York: Oxford University Press.

Kozok, Uli. 2006. A Fourteenth-Century Malay Code of Laws: the Nītisārasamuccaya. Singapore: Institute of Southeast Asian Studies.

Kumar, Akash. 2017. "All the World on a Board." UC Santa Cruz, Cultural Studies Colloquium. Unpublished working paper.

Magha. 2017. The Killing of Shishupala. Edited and translated by Paul Dundas. Murty Classical Library of India 11. Cambridge, Mass.: Harvard University Press.

Mahābhārata. 1933–1959. Critically edited in 19 volumes. General editor, Vishnu Sitaram Sukthankar. Poona: Bhandarkar Oriental Research Institute.

Mani, Vettam. 1975. Purāṇic Encyclopaedia: A Comprehensive Dictionary with Special Reference to the Epic and Purāṇic Literature. Delhi: Motilal Banarsidass.

McClish, Mark. 2019. The History of the Arthaśāstra: Sovereignty and Sacred Law in Ancient India. Cambridge and New York: Cambridge University Press.

———. 2014. "The Dependence of Manu's Seventh Chapter on Kauṭilya's Arthaśāstra." Journal of the American Oriental Society 134, 2: 241–262.

McFate, Sean. 2019. The New Rules of War: Victory in an Age of Durable Disorder. New York: Harper Collins.

Olivelle, Patrick, David Brick, and Mark McClish, eds. 2015. A Sanskrit Dictionary of Law and Statecraft. Delhi: Primus.

Pollock, Sheldon. 1998. "The Cosmopolitan Vernacular." Journal of Asian Studies 57, 1: 6–37.

———. 2006. The Language of the Gods in the World of Men: Sanskrit, Culture, and Power in Premodern India. Berkeley: University of California Press.

Rāmāyaṇa. 1960–1975. The Vālmīki-Rāmāyaṇa. Critically edited in 7 volumes. General editors, Govindlal Hargovind Bhatt and Umakant Premanand Shah. Baroda: Oriental Institute.

Singh, Upinder. 2010. "Politics, Violence, and War in Kāmandaka's Nītisāra." Indian Economic and Social History Review 47, 1: 29–62.

Varāhamihira. Bṛhatsaṃhitā. 1981. Sanskrit text edited and translated by M. Ramakrishna Bhat. 2 pts. Delhi: Motilal Banarsidass.

Venkatasubbiah, A. 1965. "Some Sanskrit Stanzas in the Javanese Tantri Kamandaka." Bijdragen tot de Taal-, Land- en Volkenkunde 121, 3: 350–359.

Vidyasagara, Jibananda. 1875. Kāmandakīyanītisāraṭīkā. Calcutta: Sarasvatiyantre.

INDEX

Agastya, 305n18
Aila, 13, 305n18
Airavata, 312n1
Amarka, 245, 317n7
Ambarisha, 13, 305n19
Andhakas, 205, 315n6
Ara, 305n18
Arjuna, 310n1; Dhanamjaya, 141, 312n3
Arthaśāstra of Kautilya, vii, xiii, xxvinn2–3, xxviin15, xxxin7, 303n2, 308n3, 311n11, 318n4; audience of, ix; *Kāmandakīya Nītisāra* and, vii–viii, xi, xiv, 3, 308n2, 318n8, 318n1; lost or discovered, viii, xxvin3, xxx; quotations from, 318n1
Ashvatthaman, 269, 318n9
Atharva Veda, 21, 45, 153, 313n3, 314n4
Avanti, 308n3
Ayodhya, 308n3

Bahudanti, 133
Balabhadrarama, 314–315n4
Bhadrasena, 91, 307n3
Bharadvaja, 123
Bharavi, xiv, xxviin13, 312n14
Bhaṭṭikāvya, xiv, 317n2
Bhima, 249, 317n9
Bhrigu, 205, 241
Brahma, 143, 303n8
Brahmanism, xxvin2
Brahmans, vii, xiii, xxvin2, 23, 133, 151, 233, 239, 305n18, 306n2,

316n3; gods and, 117, 119, 253
Bṛhatsaṃhitā, 308n3
Brihaspati, 19, 73, 95, 99, 123, 147, 149, 157, 277
Buddhists, 171, 306n2
Burma, xxvin1

Carvakas, 306n2
Chanakya, vii. *See also* Arthaśāstra; Kautilya
Chandragupta Maurya, vii, 3, 303n2, 303n7

Damayanti, 304n17
Dambhodbhava, 13, 305n18
Dandaka, King, 13, 305n18
Dantavaktra, 203, 315n5
Devayani, 317n5
Dhanamjaya. See Arjuna
Dhritarashtra, 239
Diti, 125, 310n8
Draupadi, 317n9
Drona, xxiv, 269, 310n1, 318n9
Duryodhana, 141, 241, 310n1

Essence of Politics. See Kāmandakīya Nītisāra

Gandhari, 241
Ganges, 57
Gupta dynasty or empire, vii, xiii, xvii–xviii, xxvi

Hanuman, 139, 312n1
Hidimba, 249, 317n9

ABOUT THE BOOK

Murty Classical Library of India volumes are designed by Rathna Ramanathan and Guglielmo Rossi. Informed by the history of the Indic book and drawing inspiration from polyphonic classical music, the series design is based on the idea of "unity in diversity," celebrating the individuality of each language while bringing them together within a cohesive visual identity.

The Sanskrit text of this book is set in the Murty Sanskrit typeface, commissioned by Harvard University Press and designed by John Hudson and Fiona Ross. The proportions and styling of the characters are in keeping with the typographic tradition established by the renowned Nirnaya Sagar Press, with a deliberate reduction of the typically high degree of stroke modulation. The result is a robust, modern typeface that includes Sanskrit-specific type forms and conjuncts.

The English text is set in Antwerp, designed by Henrik Kubel from A2-TYPE and chosen for its versatility and balance with the Indic typography. The design is a free-spirited amalgamation and interpretation of the archives of type at the Museum Plantin-Moretus in Antwerp.

All the fonts commissioned for the Murty Classical Library of India will be made available, free of charge, for non-commercial use. For more information about the typography and design of the series, please visit *http://www.hup.harvard.edu/mcli*.

Printed on acid-free paper by Maple Press, York, Pennsylvania.